M000195370

IDENTITY REBOOT

*Reimaging Data Privacy
for the 21ˢᵗ Century*

ARWEN SMIT

First published by MINTBIT LTD

Text Copyright © Arwen Smit 2020

The moral right of the author has been asserted

A CIP catalogue record of this book
is available from the British Library

Links provided to third party websites are provided by the
publisher in good faith and for information only.
MintBit Ltd disclaims any responsibility for the materials
contained in any third-party website referenced in this work.

While the author has made every effort to provide accurate
references and quotations, the author assumes no liability for
any future changes or errors.
Correction requests for future reprints can be submitted via
www.identityreboot.com

eBook ISBN: 978-1-9163144-0-5
Soft cover ISBN: 978-1-9163144-1-2

For Rolf, always

This book is greatly in debt to many intellectual giants who have shared their ideas and visions with the public throughout the centuries. This is an open invitation to build upon the ideas proposed inside, and it is my hope you will use them as tools to build a better world.

"In order to change an existing imagined order, we must first believe in an alternative imagined order."
— Yuval Noah Harari
Sapiens: A Brief History of Humankind

TABLE OF CONTENTS

I

CHAOS

Is human behaviour being devalued to an **optimisation game**?

If **privacy** is dying, who should **mourn**?

In a **world of AI**, what power do **individuals** still hold?

1. Optimisation Games

"Technology is capable of doing great things. But it does not want to do great things. It does not want anything. That part takes all of us."
- Tim Cook, CEO Apple[i]

You are no longer the only authority on you. Whether we like it or not, human identities are becoming increasingly digital. A quick search for Lebanese food. A "like" for the latest podcast. Browsing books on Amazon. Listening to lounge music on Spotify. Killing the boredom of the daily commute by playing a quick game on your phone. Every online action compounds our "digital footprint". And recently, we have started to realise that this footprint is leaving a rather big mark. If a digital footprint is logged behaviour, "attention footprint" defines what we pay attention to. The latest data shows that on average human attention breaks every 40 seconds.[ii] If you examine your own life, how would you answer the following question: *Are you in control?*

Controversies such as the Cambridge Analytica scandal and the explosion of dis-information surrounding the US 2016 presidential election and Brexit globally sounded the alarm. A list of familiar villains captures the headlines. Yet Cambridge Analytica is not the problem. Neither is the US 2016 presidential election. Neither is Brexit. These events are symptoms of a larger, more integrated, and much scarier societal development and will go down in history books as catalysts for change, symbolising all which had been simmering underneath the surface. As venture capitalist Benedict Evans put it; *"They did not prise open a locked window at the back of the building – they knocked on the front door and walked in. They did things that you were supposed to be able to do but combined them in an order and with malign intent that had not really been anticipated."*[iii]

The tally of *"what had not really been anticipated"* currently stands at influenced elections as described in the investigative Mueller report, dis-information proliferating across social media, damaging "deep fakes" (detailed faked videos), commercial campaigns targeting deeply held values, filter bubbles strengthening online division and tribalism, online surveillance and behavioural manipulation. The red thread running through this toxic turbulence is data. Waking up to the abuse of the underlying infrastructure goes hand in hand with waking up to all uses of that infrastructure. And this realisation will ultimately lead to an examination of our own humanity in the digital age.

From Descartes to Kant, philosophers long speculated humanity to be defined by human capability for reason. The capability to make up one's mind across a spectrum of alternatives and choose to act accordingly. This book argues that in the 21st century data privacy precedes human capability for reason, which in turn precedes the spectrum of human choices and actions. This book argues that human behaviour has become an optimisation problem, and that us humans are providing the data that is being optimised for. Whether it involves companies maximising profits or governments sculpting the perfect citizen, identity and data reside at the very heart of the "optimisation equation".

The decay of privacy happened so fast one would expect public outrage, but we have not seen this so far. Why is that? Do people not care about data privacy? One reason is convenience. We carry tracking devices at all times, only we do not call them tracking devices – we call them smartphones.[iv] Devices equipped with an accelerometer (motion sensing), gyroscope (orientation), magnetometer (magnetic fields), GPS (location), barometer (air pressure), proximity sensor (infrared LED and light detector), ambient light sensor (measuring light), microphone (audio) and touch functionalities (pressure). Most people are willing to sacrifice a little privacy in exchange for a lot of convenience and doing away with our toys is terribly inconvenient. It feels strange, unusual, even upsetting not to be connected. The new optimisation games do not feel like the dystopian warnings from George Orwell novels. Free to over-use, our Pavlov-like compulsion is quite entertaining actually. Look at this funny cat video. Like. Share. Forget. We do not look beyond the screen.

Another reason why privacy has taken a backseat is that the enormous promise of connecting the world has been blinding. So overwhelmingly awesome that it was almost rude to even consider the drawbacks, most notably the degradation of human privacy and autonomy.

Yet, the uncomfortable truth is that lack of privacy is engineered into our systems. I invite you to pause on that. Lack of data privacy is consciously engineered because there is a business case as well as a political case to do so. Today, if you are online, chances are somebody is using your information. The challenge does not stop at data collection at unprecedented scale but extends to what happens when it has been collected.

Knowing (newsfeeds, algorithmic curation and ampli-fication), interacting (messaging, payments), moving (geolocation, facial recognition) and even loving (dating apps) are all becoming areas of life open to control. Preferences of and predictions on human be-haviour are valuable commodities in this day and age, with the explicit goal to better control those preferences and predictions in the future.[v] Technically, preferences are not the end-product, but future behaviour is. This book will write the blueprint for a world where this does not have to be the case.

The Dragon & The Eagle

The moment the concept of privacy comes up in conversation, fingers in the West firmly point towards China. Those fingers waggle at the incredulous trade-off between privacy and reputation, before further accusing China of using the concept of reputation – branded the "social credit system" – as an excuse to gain further surveillance capabilities to keep the world's largest population in check. With the social credit system Big Brother well and truly landed in Beijing. Privacy is dead, so they say. Poor Chinese citizens.

This is true of course, but here is the full picture: the West is confidently marching along that very same road. In the West privacy died a slow death too, albeit by different hands. Where Beijing propagates the trade-off between privacy and reputation, technology visionaries in Silicon Valley preach a trade-off between privacy and personalisation. The end result is eerily similar.

When it comes to privacy, the power of the Chinese government strangely resembles US tech behemoths. For one, the Chinese government has the power to unilaterally mandate access to, or removal of, messages, as do companies like Google and Facebook. Reportedly Facebook CEO Mark Zuckerberg personally made a call on removing genocide-inducing messages in Myanmar from Facebook Messenger.[vi] Just as the Chinese government decides what information is censored and which companies compete, executives at Amazon, Google and Facebook have the power to set content moderation policies and to adjust the algorithms underpinning how billions access their daily information diet. Facebook decreed: right-wing commentator Alex Jones is bad; cat videos are good. Breastfeeding is bad; political news is good.[vii] The decision is based on a combination of ethics and profit optimisation, but remains a conscious decision nonetheless. After a meeting between the Facebook CEO and French President Macron, both proudly announced that Facebook will facilitate French judges with identifying data of suspects of hate speech.[viii] In the 21st century, privacy of individuals is a variable negotiated between companies and governments.

The same "what" is not bound to the same "why". Where the Chinese are working hard on their social credit scores to successfully navigate society (and to avoid punishment), the West exchanges its data for cute puppy videos. The dragon and the eagle. Sticks and carrots. Punishment and puppies. Different route, same destination.

An Incomplete Puzzle

Human behaviour is being devalued to an optimisation problem, and we are providing the data that is being optimised for. We, the people. We, the world. This is a systemic, pervasive issue. Two optimisation games have dominated the beginning of the 21st century: *Power* and *Profit*.

The players in the Power game are governments. Governments play the optimisation game to sculpt the perfect citizen. The current identity structure nods to the managerial intent of society. Authority in society is increasingly expressed algorithmically. In parallel, there has been a breakdown of institutional power. The combination of the two explains why governments flock to these new tools to assert authority, demanding backdoors in popular systems in light of national security, as well as introducing infrastructure of their own. As we will see, playing the power optimisation game is not exclusive to the East nor West, but in fact a global phenomenon. The incredulous reaction of politicians to the tech industry – shaming Facebook is the *cri du jour* – would almost make you forget that governments are playing the same game.

The second optimisation game is Profit. Players in the profit game are technology giants increasingly tying data with services and services with data. This data is then transformed to yield behavioural analytics and consumer insights for internal use (services) as well as external use (advertisers and partners). For both, the best way to maximise profits is to make behaviour more predictable. For example, guaranteeing 200,000 "views" comes at a cost to those 200,000 doing the viewing. These people might or might not have the desire to see this particular content and might or might not be positively affected. There is a trade-off between certainty of success and the cost of guaranteeing that certainty. Should it be possible to assign a dollar value to human behaviour?

As we debate such questions, corporate power lives at unprecedented heights. Nearly 40 percent of the world's population interacts on Facebook, almost 50 percent of cloud services are hosted by Amazon, and around 90 percent of the global search traffic flows through Google.[ix] If we believe that individuals are more than a means to an end, more than preferences and behavioural output, it becomes palpable that instant gratification and minimalistic design mask long-term structural deficiencies.

Meanwhile, in the background, balance steadily rotates towards the few over the many, centralising control. What is more, assuming the interest of these aggregators are aligned with their subjects in perpetuity is a big assumption to make. Data has been abstracted to such an extent that we have forgotten big data is living people. In this brave new world, individual actions can be sculpted – to buy and to obey – to fit the agenda of those controlling the data.

Today's digital breadcrumbs cover any interaction between man and machine as well as machine and machine. The linkability across datapoints is staggering. When given an anonymised credit card dataset of 1.1 million people, MIT researchers just needed four additional data points to exclusively identify over 90 percent of the people in the dataset. This was back in 2015.[x] People think they have a level of privacy that they do not have. An individual data profile has become a lot like a digital fingerprint. This digital fingerprint is not related to your body, but behaviour. In effect, digital information environments are a second order interpretation of that same behaviour. The content you consume and the information you interact with are carefully analysed for conscious and unconscious preferences. With every online interaction, this profile is refined further. Refined until the desired optimisation goal is achieved, may that be advertisements, purchases or engagement, after which it becomes a loop. This is the invisible hand of algorithms. These are optimisation games.

This new perspective gives rise to a whole host of deeply uncomfortable questions. What does it mean to obey a nudge you have not created? Are we self-directed individuals responsible for our own choices, or beings shaped and constrained by the labels and roles society gives us? The comparison with George Orwell's dystopian Big Brother is tempting. Indeed, this is a popular response to controversies such as Cambridge Analytica. The competing camp wonders what the big deal is – it is just data science after all. What few people realise is that George Orwell's famous novel is actually widely misunderstood. The true warning was not a society where you are watched at all times, but one where you could be. The main character narrates: *"You had to live – did live, from habit that became instinct – in the assumption that every sound you made was overheard, and, except in darkness, every moment scrutinised."*[xi] One is the watcher and the other feels being watched. The difference between the two is whether the tools in question are applied to an agenda that is, or is not, yours.

Technology ethics examines what technology is capable of doing and ponders potential consequences. With this in mind it is worth stressing that today's ethical blindness was wilfully imposed. The greater the appeal of micro-targeting to advertisers, the greater the incentive to platforms to span a wider and wider net, until all niche audiences can be confidently made available, from high net worth gay black men between 20 and 40 to middle-aged sub-urban swing voters in the American Midwest. Yet instead of holiday pictures for seemingly innocent likes and clicks, dis-information was pushed along the same channels for malicious manipulation. Politicians have long crafted messages to grow and strengthen their base, only now rival governments can deploy the same tools to detract from it.

When "tools" are misused, who is at fault? The platform enabling the misuse, as Facebook in the Cambridge Analytica scandal? The actor consciously misusing the platform, Cambridge Analytica? The entity hiring Cambridge Analytica to act out the activity in question, without verifying the conditions of that activity? The individual neglecting to oversee the wider implications of their privacy settings; perhaps you? Who should we be angry at? Is the crime lack of curiosity, wilful blindness or malicious manipulation? As anger is frustration with the status quo, should our anger not be re-channelled into efforts changing the underlying mechanisms facilitating this misuse? No matter who fingers point to, we still have not gotten it right.

The root of today's realities is the same unstoppable force that has transformed society beyond recognition over the past fifty years: the Internet. The design of the Internet came with a fundamental flaw: it was never built with an identity layer. More specifically, as the Internet focused on enabling the sharing of information by everyone with anyone, curiously little time has been spent on identification mechanism on either end. A great part of the chaos today is related to a multitude of players, with wide-ranging agendas, trying to fill this gap.

No single explanation can explain all of reality and all its nuances, and this attempt is redacted to focus on identity as a principle of interaction. Going deeper than just a name or an address, identity is a collection of claims of who you are and who you have been. The combination of those claims is something that allows you to do things. To go to university, you need a valid secondary school diploma, and to go to secondary school you need a valid primary school diploma. In the US, nationality, residence status and age are verified to determine the right to vote. In most countries, opening a bank account requires a valid proof-of-address and proof-of-ID. Babies receive an ID from the day they are born. From that day onwards, we spend our lives building attestations about ourselves to navigate society. To signal who we are and to get what we want. In other words, identity is nothing less than the foundation of rights in society.

To measure rights, *Identity Proxies* are being used. Are you allowed to cross country borders? Nationality will be one of the first variables taken into account. Are you entitled to receive child support? You will need to prove that you meet government requirements. Are you old enough to drive? Prove it. As inseparable from us as our shadow, identity is an ever-present reference to the degree of freedom we have within the constraints of those rights. Yet the concept of "identity" as we know it today is incomplete.

To match the new realities for the 21st century this book argues three puzzle pieces are missing: *Data Autonomy*, *Data Equity* and *Data Privacy*. Interdependent, these three themes intertwine throughout the book. The first puzzle piece, Data Autonomy, is made up of three parts. *"Autonomy of Being"*, for a person must be in control of his or her identity, granting access at discretion. *"Autonomy of Thought"*, for a person must be in control of their information environment in order to make up their mind. And third, completing autonomy, *"Autonomy of Reason"*, for it is paramount to understand what role algorithms play in the great hacking of thoughts and feelings and the resulting human autonomy crisis. The second puzzle piece is Data Equity, in that incentives shape our reality and should work for all stakeholders. And finally, Data Privacy, because personal information in the wrong hands could have far reaching consequences. Together, these three puzzle pieces lay the foundation for a unifying *Identity Meta-System*.[xii] Data autonomy, equity and privacy have eroded over time, arguably to a critical point. Rebooting identity could not be more pressing.

The Dark Side of the Moon

"There will always be a version of Facebook that is free. It is our mission to help connect everyone around the

world and to bring the world closer together. In order to do that we believe we need to offer a service that everyone can afford, and we are committed to do that". Amidst the Cambridge Analytica fallout, Mark Zuckerberg was called to Washington to answer a few questions. Over the course of two days, live streamed of course, senators tried their best to unearth the mystics of Facebook's business model. In response to Zuckerberg's statement, one senator countered: *"If so, how do you sustain a business model in which users do not pay for your service?"* *"Senator, we run ads,"* Zuckerberg responded, audibly barely containing an incredulous chuckle faced with such stupidity. *"I see,"* the senator replied. *"That's great."*[xiii] The phrase was soon emblazoned on T-shirts in Menlo Park. In another courtroom, a few months later, one of Facebook's lawyers provided the following argument during a Cambridge Analytica related class-action lawsuit: *"There is no invasion of privacy at all, because there is no privacy."*[xiv]

The patronising attitude of Silicon Valley to those who dare doubt its underlying mechanisms basks in scorn, belittling anyone who tries. The default response has been: if they do not support it, this simply means they do not get it. The "it" in question being to move fast and break things to satisfy shareholder returns whilst "making the world more open and connected." When publicising its second quarter earnings soon after the Senate hearing, Facebook lost $120 billion of its market capitalisation. The equivalent of two thirds of the 1929 stock market crash in today's dollars.[1] More than most companies are ever worth. Over subsequent months, however, the stock price gradually recovered.

---

[1] The 1929 stock market crash lost the equivalent of $396 billion today.

It seems the market cares, but not that much. The market cares, but not that long.

And yet, people are beginning to get fed up. Policy has gradually, but firmly, echoed these sentiments. Under the new EU General Data Protection Regulation (GDPR), every EU citizen is allowed to request all data a company has on them. One woman decided to ask the dating app Tinder.[xv] She received 800 pages, tracking over 1,700 Tinder messages. Tinder records which joke someone repeats to suitors. The percentage of white men, black men, or Asian men someone might have matched. How long one lingers on a photo. When humans have forgotten these tiny little details, Tinder's database remembers. The inevitable result is an imbalance of knowing. And, unfortunately, the subject is you. Taken together, all these seemingly trivial observations can be combined to profile inner human experiences. Are you lonely? Are you cheating? What are your sexual preferences? It is difficult for humans to care for things that are not visible. This is not naive, it is human. You cannot feel data.

We have strayed a long way from the original meaning of the word "data": "something given." Embracing the thinking that the only way for the Internet to be open was to be free, businesses had to create value elsewhere. The result is that the Internet is neither free, nor open.

The web would be a different place if the question was: *please allow us to share your information with fifty other companies to build detailed profiles about your life.* Rather, consent is coerced. Choosing not to use popular platforms such as Facebook, Google and Amazon is not a real choice to begin with; these platforms, running in the billions of users and worth many billions of dollars, are too omnipresent to avoid. What to do if we cannot unplug, even if we wanted to? At the same time, the only business model on offer is data exploitation for optimisation games. To maximise the value of data extraction, data is collected centrally, creating honey pots to which busy hacker bees flock in droves, creating further vulnerabilities. Data breaches run in the aggregated billions, from ignorant negligence at Equifax to wilful blindness at Facebook. Author and scholar Shoshana Zuboff pointedly asserts that the power to shape behaviour for others' profit or power is entirely self-authorising – it has no foundation in democratic or moral legitimacy.

Technology is like the moon; it has a bright and a dark side. The bright side is undeniable and bright; the dark side has been quietly swept under the carpet. This book will force it into the light. The need for transparency on what is truly going on underneath the surface swells with every scandal. The writing on the wall is that our current identity systems are fundamentally un-sustainable and unsuitable for the 21st century. If it will not bend, it will break.

A Path Forward

This is a story about what comes after. This book continues where others stopped; suggesting a way forward. This is a book for those who feel that the promise of the Internet has been compromised along the way. This is a book for politicians, business leaders and technologists who have country and career defining decisions to make. And this is also a book for those who love data and want to preserve the many benefits it can bring to the world. Building on research and interviews with technology experts and politicians from around the world, *Identity Reboot* aims to provide a blueprint for identity in the 21st century, offering insights into emerging technologies such as blockchain and artificial intelligence (AI), examining the role of citizens and governments, politics and business, weaving a path between what is and what could be. A Magna Carta for identity.

The consequences of the lack of foresight of Silicon Valley to fully comprehend its creation will haunt us for some time to come. This book aims to break down the challenges we face (*Part One, Chaos*), to provide a blueprint for a new identity meta-system (*Part Two, Reboot*), and to assess the infrastructure requirements needed to make it a reality (*Part Three, Change*). Should we change; how to change; could we change?

The remainder of Part One scrutinises the relationship between data ethics and the invisible hand of algorithms (Chapter 2: Our Invisible Asset), before investigating how data is captured, by whom and why (Chapter 3: House of Surveillance). The next chapter explores what the data gold rush has to do with artificial intelligence, critically examining motivations of both companies and governments (Chapter 4: Benevolent Gods), before concluding the section with the limitations of existing identity proxies, such as the passport, social login and reputation, and how these proxies reinforce the status quo (Chapter 5: Identity Proxies).

Deeper questions crave deeper answers. Part Two, Reboot, lays the foundation for an identity meta-system respecting data autonomy, equity and privacy. Opening with the notion that individuals can own their identity, introducing the *Five Laws of Identity* (Chapter 6: The Sovereign Individual). The second challenge of autonomy is today's digital information environment, rife with manipulation and censorship, which we will contrast with the human right to independent information of high integrity in the next chapter (Chapter 7: Information Wars). The final challenge of autonomy is that even perfect data ownership does not fully protect from faulty third-party assumptions, predictions and conclusions, warranting an examination of algorithms (Chapter 8: Algorithmic Truths). Autonomy of being, thought and reason.

One could rightly wonder; what is the point of owning data which should not exist in the first place? If data ownership were the sole solution, this would only further institutionalise and legitimise excessive data capture.[xvi] Yet, putting data on trial is not the solution either. For one, data is the lifeblood of AI and it is widely agreed that AI could realise many meaningful benefits for humankind. No, something else is needed entirely. The billion-dollar question is how to address profit games: how to extract value from data in a way which preserves autonomy, equity and privacy (Chapter 9: Liberating Data)? Part Two concludes with an exploration of how governments use data, weighing society defining decisions, such as the individual vs. the collective, freedom of speech vs. censorship and security vs. privacy, addressing power games and their geopolitical consequences (Chapter 10: The New Social Contract).

Finally, a house is only as strong as its foundation. This holds true for society also. After reimagining the society that we want to live in, the final section is dedicated to ensuring this foundation holds. This is the focal point of Part Three, *Change*. Evaluating the politics and economics of change, the penultimate chapter addresses political trade-offs as well as pressing business questions, such as what new business models could look like and who might become irrelevant (Chapter 11: Actors of Change). The last chapter imagines two worlds, one where we change course, and one where we continue marching down our current path (Chapter 12: Blue Pill, Red Pill).

Identity Reboot

In addition to the danger of slipping backwards, there is a cost of not going forwards. The public trust in the

Internet is eroding.[xvii] Losing human autonomy, equity and privacy comes at a cost. This book will argue that individual integrity is bigger than any individual. It is directly relevant to humanity as a whole. When individual autonomy, equity and privacy crumble, so do collective individual rights. As the rights of the individual crumble, so too will, eventually, democratic society. The opening quote of this chapter is from a speech by Apple CEO Tim Cook. In this same keynote he warned: *"We shouldn't sugar-coat the consequences. This is surveillance."* These words might sound radical and harsh, but as we will see they decidedly point towards an inconvenient truth. Traditionally laws are voluntary restrictions by society, but when the Internet's invisible laws are unilaterally imposed and universally condoned, it will redefine what it means to be human in the 21st century.

This book is called "Identity Reboot" for three reasons. Identity will be both online and offline, and rather than discarding the digital, we need to embrace the new-found online character. Secondly, data privacy is personal. Our decisions regarding data privacy directly influence our identity. Finally, because the status quo is deeply ingrained in our current society, changing course will require a hard reboot for which, like any reboot, we will need to be prepared.

This is a deeply personal book, for it involves all of us. From the US to China, these challenges are global challenges. Both profit and power games need individuals accepting the terms of the games to survive. People decide to use one product and service over the other. People decide to vote. Deciding how to move forward begins with an objective examination of where we are now, no matter how uncomfortable that examination may be. As the economist Adam Smith established, it is not companies that degrade our world; it is our appetites that they merely serve.[xviii] If we want something to change, we must want something else.

What do we want to become? What do we not want to become? This book argues that we should build the infrastructure for the society that we want. One of the most radical shifts of the 21st century will start at the individual level spiralling outwards. You are more powerful than you might think.

2. Our Invisible Asset

"To fight and conquer in all our battles is not supreme excellence; supreme excellence consists in breaking the enemy's resistance without fighting."
- Sun Tzu[xix]

O ver the course of the last few millennia our thinking on identity has gradually evolved. In recent years, however, the pace of change has been astronomical. This new "digital twin" of our online selves is unprecedented. The external forces guiding, nudging and steering this digital you are unprecedented. In more recent history, our online and offline world started to merge, and what identity is and is not has become less defined and more complex. All with major consequences. Many of these consequences are unintended by-products of how technology is put to use, and, as we will see, not all are good. In this chapter we will first discuss why privacy matters, then quantify the sheer extent of data floating around about you and how this data is being used in profit games, after which we will briefly examine how nation states optimise aggregate behaviour to achieve good citizenship, using the Chinese social credit system as a case study. But before we jump into the chaotic complexities of the 21st century, we will first travel back in time.

The History of You

Identity has changed before. Try to retrace someone's family history back to Europe and records will likely become opaque around the early 19th century. Although family names existed many centuries before then, most notably for nobility, recording a family name only became obligatory under the French Emperor Napoleon Bonaparte. Starting in France in 1804, Napoleon issued a decree in all occupied territories making the documentation of family names compulsory and the paternal name binding.[xx] A pioneer in bureaucracy, Napoleon realised that in order to govern one needs to be able to identify who one is governing. Ensuring taxes are paid is easier if you know where your loyal subjects live.

During the immigration waves to the US in the late 19th and early 20th century, many immigrants arrived without documents. Sometimes people took new names to live new lives. At other times, English-speaking immigration officers simply misheard exotic-sounding names, and subsequently spelled out a different name altogether. Because there was no global standard for identifying documents this was not only possible but even relatively painless. The concept of a worldwide passport standard is fairly new and closely related to the events that unfolded during the First World War. At the beginning of the war passports began to modernise, partly to keep track of aliens and, of course, potential spies. The first modern British passport, product of the British Nationality and Status Aliens Act in 1914, consisted of a single page, folded into eight and held together with a cardboard cover.[xxi] Next to a photo-graph and signature, it featured a personal description of the bearer as well as the wife of the bearer. Forehead: high. Eyes: grey. Nose: aquiline.

The aftermath of the First World War was defined by chaos. Numerous governments fell and national borders were redrawn. In some countries unrest boiled over into civil war, as happened with the Russian Revolution, forcing many to flee their homes. The upheaval resulted in many people's being without passports, or even nations to issue them, which in turn interrupted international travel. The international chaos could only be managed by an international response, and in 1922 this responsibility was carried by the League of Nations. The "Nansen passport", named after Nobel Peace Prize winner Fridtjof-Nansen, was a stateless person's passport that gave the owner the right to move more freely across national boundaries.[xxii]

As the structure of civilisation evolves, so does the role and function humans play in that system. Methods of identification and categorisation advance in parallel to rising societal complexity. A reference point signalling who you are in the sea of almost eight billion people. Sometimes change emerges via a direct reaction to unfolding events, such as the Nansen passport in response to the Russian revolution. At other times change builds gradually, for example the progression from descriptions of large foreheads in the 20th century to biometric data in the 21st century. With the rise of the Internet, how we see ourselves and how our governments see us have stopped being the only identity inputs available. Gradually, subjective behaviour was codified and added to previously objective rights. And not just governments, but also companies granted themselves the licence to tell you who you are.

Privacy Phases

In the 21st century it is widely accepted that our identity extends well beyond what is logged on our passports. How we feel about this fact, however, is less straight forward. For example, not every thought is shared out loud. *Am I ready to start a family? Why do I feel sick? Should I settle for this relationship?* Ask any given person wandering the street if they care about privacy and the answer would likely be a non-committal yes. Yet, when pressed on what privacy means, no answer would be the same. An elusive concept, privacy is a feeling, and feelings are experienced differently. There are three distinct phases to processing what privacy means to a person. First *Denial*, then *Resignation* and finally *Confrontation*.

The first dimension is Denial. For starters, human capacity to care about privacy is limited because the human brain is limited. Over time memories fade. As the years pass, the impact of previous experiences flattens. When adults play peek-a-boo with babies, the two players experience the game differently. The adult hides their face behind large hands while the baby sees the adult magically disappear. This is how humans tend to interact with data. Nobody *wants* Big Brother in their room, but if he is invisible blissful denial comes easy. Because homo sapiens, the apex predator, has limited memory and computing power, it takes comfort in the fallacy that nothing does. *If I do not feel it, I guess it is not there.*

Search engines, on the other hand, are not burdened with limited computing power. Data is definitive. Computers are more trusted than friends, and online queries resound with unspoken worries and desires: *Early signs of pregnancy; How do you know if you have cancer; What does love feel like.* After acceptance that data is painfully permanent and computers do not work like the human brain does, there is the second dimension of denial. *I am not doing anything wrong — why should I be concerned about privacy? I am not a criminal. I have nothing to hide.*

But is that really true?

Would you print your browser history? Maybe tattoo recent online purchases on your face? When facial recognition is sufficiently advanced, this is the type of information that will be shouted into the world. Digital tattoos will survive our bodies.[xxiii]

People behave differently if they think nobody is watching. In a now deleted CNN interview, Google chairman, then CEO, Eric Schmidt famously quipped *"If you are doing something you do not want people to know, maybe you should not be doing it in the first place."*[xxiv] In his 2014 Ted Talk, journalist Glenn Greenwald explains how the same Eric Schmidt told his employees to stop speaking to the news website CNET, after the magazine posted personal details about his life exclusively obtained via open information available on Google products.[xxv]

Maybe shame is not a motivator, but fear might be. How far will your piece of data travel? Information could be used by a host of actors, for a host of agendas, over an indefinite period of time. Data is infinitely replicable. Lose control of the data and lose control of the narrative. History is rife with cautionary tales. Bar Mitzvah photos on Facebook are innocent when there is freedom of religion. In the Second World War, however, it would have put a target on your back. Freedom to love is another human right in most Western countries in the 21st century, yet homosexual activity was illegal in Britain not too long ago. Alan Turing, a British codebreaker who during World War II arguably turned the tide in favour of the Allies, was later subjected to chemical castration for homosexual activity. He received a royal pardon nearly 60 years after he committed suicide. What you are really saying is: *I am going to give up my rights because I do not think I will need them.*

Empathetically, privacy is not measured by current rules of society. Privacy is measured by *the accumulation of societal rules in the past, present and future, and the actors with an interest in enforcing those rules.* Current data granularity and enforcement potential is unprecedented. This kind of power never existed before. It could empower totalitarian and authoritarian regimes, surveillance capitalistic companies, or malicious rogue individuals and communities to do things that were technically impossible before.

The cost of privacy might be unexpected and its timing surprising. This was the case for the actor and artist Shia LaBeouf. After President Trump assumed office in the White House, LaBeouf started a four-year art project called "He Will Not Divide Us" (HWNDU). It lasted six days. The art project pointed a camera towards the White House inviting people to chant the mantra: "he will not divide us". Almost immediately, the project drew the ire of the notorious 4chan community, and trolls showed up. At some point things reportedly got heated, and LaBeouf was arrested and charged with assault and harassment. The exhibition moved to Albuquerque but shut down when gunshots were reported in the area. The third and last act of HWNDU is the most extraordinary part of this story. All which was communicated about the new location was a livestream of the HWNDU flag, gliding against the backdrop of an undefined sky. Trolls analysed the flight patterns of airlines overhead to pinpoint the general area: Greeneville, Tennessee. Then, someone took it upon himself to drive around the area, honk his horn, and see if it registered on the livestream. It did. The flag was captured and replaced with a signature red "Make America Great Again" hat.[xxvi]

After denial follows a shrug of Resignation, the second phase. As Tim Cook stated, surveillance has become the norm. People tend to be never more than three feet from their phones. Giving up data to interact online is assumed. Faced with the prohibitive effort of not being online, most resign themselves to the status quo. *Why bother?*

However, it serves to assume that over a long enough period of time any data given to third parties will be made public — whether or not this happens intentionally is irrelevant.[xxvii] From high profile data leaks, such as Marriot and British Airways, to the Cambridge Analytica Facebook controversy, this loop has run its course countless times. To this date shards from broken privacy violations can still be found online. Again, it is impossible to know which actor, with what agenda, at what point in time, will capture or use such data. This is why it is important to over-invest in privacy: once lost it is painstakingly difficult to recover.

When the stakes are this high, ignorance is not an excuse. Resignation is just not good enough. Bad cyber hygiene habits could follow a person their entire life. Which of the two will be more important for a sixteen-year old's career prospects: reciting the Greek alphabet or ensuring their potentially embarrassing pictures do not end up on the Internet? Cyber hygiene should be a mandatory skill at schools. New habits need to be internalised. Privacy is a right, owed to the people. Exercising that right is a duty of the people.

After denial (*I have nothing to hide*) and resignation (*Why bother*) comes the third and final phase: Confrontation. People need privacy. There is a real difference between limits to privacy necessitated in modern society and imposed intrusion. Short-term this is the difference between being an agent or a tool. Long-term this is a trade-off between freedom of speech and hyper individual accountability. Words can, and will, be used against you. A particularly dangerous trade-off, shaving the edges of critical thinking. If privacy can no longer be assumed, should people not know?

It is time to come to terms with what has happened: privacy is dead.

Digital Twins

On some level, the fact that privacy is dead is tacitly accepted by a large majority of us. To many, giving up data is simply required to interact in the modern world. The majority of Americans do not think it is possible to go through life without both companies and governments collecting data on them.[xxviii] Few want to live without Google's search engine, Amazon's one day delivery or Facebook's newsfeed. Through a system of clever mechanisms, websites and applications condition us to spend as much time as possible within their world. This digital dependency is collateral damage in the quest for social capital and status. On the Internet we compete for attention with everyone, everywhere. In response, we willingly share our every thought, and although in the back of our minds there is a little voice of caution, we press that button anyway. Almost a quarter of children begin their digital lives when parents upload prenatal sonogram scans to the Internet.[xxix] We want to see others, and we want to feel seen. Humans want to be online.

The basic relationship between being online, cookies, and behaviour somewhat being tracked is relatively well known. However, the sheer extent is stunning. Investigative journalists reported one instance of a person's location being sold over 14,000 times a day.[xxx] That is approximately 15 times per waking minute. The journalists argue that even though companies claim location data is anonymised, the sheer quantity of it made it not only possible to "narrow it down", but to exclusively identify somebody. Where do you live? Where do your friends live? Do you ever spend the night? What neighbourhoods do you frequent? What kinds of shops do you go to? How long do you stay at work? Do you go to religious buildings? For context, when presented with a dataset of more than 12 million Americans containing over 50 billion location pings, journalists from The New York Times discovered that they could identify people with relative ease. From military officials with security clearances as they drove home at night to high-powered lawyers (and their guests) as they travelled from private jets to holiday properties, the journalists were able to track them using just location data.[xxxi] Most shockingly, the team could track someone in the entourage of President Donald Trump.[xxxii]

7.10 a.m.
Mar-a-Lago, Palm Beach.
9:24 a.m.
Playing golf with Prime Minister Shinzo Abe of Japan at Trump National Golf Club, Jupiter.
1:12 p.m.
Private lunch at the Trump International Golf Club, West Palm Beach.
5:08 p.m.
Working dinner with President Shinzo Abe, Mar-a-Lago. Palm Beach.

Location is merely one of many targeting variables. From behavioural data on location movements to biometric data on how firmly you press the keys on your screen, the accuracy of the likelihood you will convert into a paying customer is worth something. This is the foundation of algorithmic advertising.

Recently it became possible to request a copy of the data library Facebook has collected about you. Downloading this file will probably take a while for the body of data a company like Facebook gathers is not merely related to direct activity on the platform. Specifically, the mosaic of information includes access to platforms where you have used the Facebook Social Login (one of the three identity proxies in Chapter 5), third parties who have installed the Facebook market-ing tracking "Pixel", plus all content you have ever given a "like". In isolation, the quantity is merely shocking. In aggregate, it is staggering. A facial recognition profile could be derived from photos and videos. Likes and search history signal preferences and values. A bulk analysis of posts, comments and chats would provide insight into use of language, typing patterns and vocabulary. Combine logs of calls, location, and relationship status, and Facebook might have a better overview of your fidelity than your partner. As you are holding your memories in your hand, I offer the following: the aggregate of these data points reveals a digital you, and this digital you can be targeted "whole" by advertisers or broken up into tiny pieces for machine learning purposes. At which point becomes the mapping of your personality a gross violation of your privacy? Do you know who knows who you are?

The backlash against these so-called "Web 2.0" companies can be ascribed to the discrepancy between what people think they consent to and which terms and conditions are actually accepted. The arbitrage between what you think data is worth, and what it is actually worth. If something is free, there is a hidden cost. To use the Internet we pay with data and attention. The magnificent market capitalisation of web giants underscores the efficiency of behavioural modification via advertising, at its essence simply a soft glove method of manipulation. These widely successful business models are based on the appropriation of user's behavioural data, viewed as a free resource. Facebook "likes" and Amazon "clicks" enable algorithms to better assess someone's personality than their friends ever could. Which confronts us with the question, do we truly trust companies like Facebook more than our friends?

What is more, the data shared with one party runs the risk of being re-shared with other third parties. For many companies, selling data directly ("monetisation") or indirectly ("targeting") is their business model. More often than not, the buck does not stop at its primary collector using it for primary business purposes. Rather, data is frequently repackaged and resold, leading not only the source (an individual) to lose visibility on the end-to-end data trail, but even the entity capturing and aggregating it. For example, Acxiom, one of the largest data brokers, reportedly has approximately 23,000 servers scrutinizing the data of millions of individuals.[xxxiii] Your phone is not your friend.

Even more concerning, this sharing is not always planned. The first rule in hacking is that it takes the path of least resistance. The weakest link which can be exploited. Marriott International revealed that hackers had breached its Starwood reservation system and had stolen the personal data of 500 million guests, including credit card and passport information from Sheraton, Regis and W hotels.[xxxiv] Discovered in 2018, the leak was open since 2014. December of that same year saw a mass leak of 202 million Chinese resumes, containing details such as mobile phone number, email, marriage, children, politics, height, weight, driver licence, literacy level, salary expectations and more.[xxxv] Origin unknown.

Fathoming the magnitude of information referring to you stored on online databases around the world is too much to take in for one person. Because the human brain is not wired to readily comprehend bytes and bits this information asymmetry has largely developed unchecked. We are already at a point where people are creating more data than they could possibly process. This is why a greater awareness of exactly why data is collected and what it is used for is long overdue.

Invisible Hand

Algorithms increasingly make decisions, and I would argue that we owe a responsibility to ourselves to understand what role we play in those decisions.

In the digital world, past behaviour influences future options. Past behaviour of others, and past behaviour of you. The majority of dating apps (Tinder, Bumble, Hinge to name a few) make use of "collaborative filtering".[xxxvi] Once you sign up, recommendations depend entirely on what other users think. Over time, the app becomes more personalised. If you consistently match Asian women between 25-35, it is more likely those matches will be suggested in the future – which makes you more likely to go on dates with them. Using historical data to feed and train algorithms that decide yet-to-be-formed outputs could quickly result in a self-fulfilling prophecy. A snake eating its own tail: all that is, is all that will be. Choices today affect choices tomorrow. Habits are not destiny. But it is also true that once a loop is established the human brain defaults to autopilot and stops fully participating in decision-making. A smoker for many years who finally decided to quit will not be spared advertisements listing discounts on favourite brands. We could be increasingly defined by old habits, pounding harmless preferences into hardened convictions.

But what if the algorithmic input is not a conscious decision at all? In 2018, researchers at Cornell University found that setting a user's gender to female resulted in them being served fewer ads for high-paying jobs in the Google search engine.[2] Algorithms can be biased, mirroring prejudices that already exist in society. Combined with self-fulfilling prophecies, prejudice bubbles can grow fast. If you are a female technologist, today's negative correlation between gender and pay could directly affect future exposure to opportunities, systematically decreasing the likelihood of breaking the cycle.

---

[2] To their credit, Google sponsored the research.

As authority shifts from humans to algorithms, assumptions, methods and goals of those controlling the algorithms begin to matter a great deal. It is important to realise that actions taken by companies based on these information asymmetries are completely self-authorised.

What if you have a secret, a secret you are not ready to tell others, and a company is going to great lengths to find out, uncovering hidden meanings in your behaviour to fill in the blanks? That secret could be that you are pregnant, and the company in question could well be the retailer Target. In 2012, Target infamously distributed targeted coupons based on pregnancy prediction scores.[3] The New York Times reported that one year after the scheme was launched, a man walked into a Target outside Minneapolis and demanded to see the manager.[xxxvii] Clutching pregnancy related coupons that had been sent to his daughter, the father was angry. Later the father apologetically confirmed that his daughter was due in August. To the daughter this was an intrusion of privacy in true form; Target effectively told her father, completely unsolicited, that she was pregnant. To keep your pregnancy a secret today demands a spy worthy operation. You would need to avoid search queries on the topic, be mindful of the products you order online, and convince friends not to share any giveaways on social media. The costs of keeping a secret online are prohibitively high.

In sum, the perceived control over our data is no real control at all, and conclusions drawn are outside our field of vision. What this means is that our data is not

---

[3] The first step was the creation of a "pregnancy prediction" score, based on the combination of buying behaviour across 25 products. To make the baby ads look random, Target started mixing in ads for things they knew pregnant women would never buy: an ad for a lawn mower next to diapers or a coupon for wine glasses next to infant clothes.

only viewed as an unlimited free resource, but also that the right to analyse and even act on the former is decided without involving us.

From the moment the browser opens we are bombarded with invisible nudges, flashy links and advertisements posing as news, all pushing different agendas. This algorithmic invisible hand is by no means limited to advertising, but has penetrated all types of sectors, from insurance to banking, from education to politics. This makes you wonder: what happens when algorithms know you better than you know yourself?

Computational Values

History has always been a battle of ideologies. Some conflicts were settled on the battlefield, others in courts. In the 21st century, the battle of ideas is taking place on the Internet. Data is used to break down profiles to increasingly deeper layers. From likes to preferences, from preferences to opinions, and from opinions to core values. Just as past behaviour influences future options in the online world, values guide future behaviour. Our core values are not static but grow with us over our lifetimes. Today, with our beliefs out in the open, this is a public process.

Identity is no longer just an input into algorithms, but also an output. The argument goes: if values can be identified they can be changed. There are multiple techniques to manipulate a person's core beliefs. "Identity reinforcement", the tendency to agree with people you identify with or want to identify with, is one of them. This explains why influencers are so effective. "Negative social reinforcement" is another. In this version, content is shown to people who will harshly criticise it, serving as a nudge to tone down your views. "Positive social reinforcement" is its upbeat twin. Here, everybody, may they be bots or people, overwhelmingly agrees with you. When "sampling bias" is applied, it creates situations where an Internet user encounters only information and opinions that conform to and reinforce their own beliefs. A personal information universe. When encountering a perspective we agree with, we press that like button. If the algorithm in question is optimised to maximise engagement, more content will be presented we are likely to interact with. Consequently, we become more and more convinced that our world view is the right one, and more and more blind to any alternatives. Information fragmentation minus quality controls quickly spirals in utter disaster. The last tactic is arguably the most dangerous of them all; "argument personalisation". A granular profile of personality, passions and perceptions to generate maximally effective content from scratch, tailored to convince, of all people, you specifically. Human minds are rife with vulnerabilities which can be exploited to game the system and the digital invisible hand is extending to our autonomy of thought and reason (Chapter 7 and 8).

In the darker corners of the Internet influence campaigns propagate ideologies justifying "the new normal". Politics can be argued with, but common sense is much trickier. The grey area between nudging and outright manipulation through a combination of disinformation ("fake news") and echo chambers has proven to be a potent, dangerous mixture. A domain of hidden agendas, hackers and trolls. Identity is becoming a battlefield in the war for "normal", and 2016 saw the first casualties in the political field (Exhibit A: the American presidential election. Exhibit B: Brexit).

Real opinions can be based on fake news. One of those stories escalated within a few weeks from a post on Facebook to a shoot-out in a pizzeria in Washington. The American Edgar Welch pleaded guilty to opening fire in a family-friendly pizzeria that inauthentic news reports claimed to house a child sex ring linked to Democratic presidential candidate Hillary Clinton in its basement. The pizzeria did not have a basement. Welch told the police that he was investigating a conspiracy theory known as "Pizzagate". The Pizzagate story found its way from mainstream social media such as Twitter, Facebook and Reddit to niche platforms such as Alex Jones' Infowars conspiracy website, eventually landing Welch in jail.

Conspiracy theories are nothing new. Before the Internet came into existence political discourse was as partisan and diverse as it is today. What has changed, however, is the feeding of these anxieties via precise curation. Online influence is becoming a numbers game, and these types of games tend to be the playing field of those with the largest resources.

Arguably, the stakes for "identity politics" have never been higher, and the tools to feed division have never been more powerful. Political scientist Francis Fukuyama explains identity politics as people adopting political positions based on their ethnicity, race, sexuality or religion rather than on broader policies.[xxxviii] Identity politics hits its stride when it can prey on anxieties and prejudices for optimal political advantage. It does not take much to feed the seed of division if the ground it is planted in is already fertile.

In only 15 days of existence, the Pizzagate subreddit had attracted 20,000 subscribers. When the subreddit was banned, Pizzagate-believers verbally attacked Reddit moderators, believing them to be part of the conspiracy as well.[4]

---

[4] The subreddit r/Pizzagate is now banned. After verbal abuse along the lines of "fuck u/spez", the username of the Reddit CEO Steve Huffman, Huffman wrote a script to change his username to prominent members of subreddit "The_Donald". The incident became known as Spezgiving:

Micro-targeting identifies who is most susceptible to which nudges, and then activates those trigger points via a calculated combination of environmental re-affirming. Welch built his opinion on what he knew to be true: Hillary was a crook, and in his mind, her running a sex ring in a pizzeria was not that much of a stretch. As futurist Yuval Noah Harari noted, in liberal democracies we make our decisions based on feelings, and if somebody can hack our feelings, democracy is at risk of becoming a puppet show.[xxxix]

Even with sincere intentions, it is becoming harder to filter and break through the online pollution. Fake news is increasingly being propagated by "fake people". Coordinated by hackers and bots, these "people" leave online reviews, create fake social media profiles and send tweets. Rolling Stones Magazine estimates that Pizzagate was shared roughly 1.4 million times by more than a quarter of a million accounts in its first five weeks of life – from the first tweet to the day Welch showed up at the pizzeria.[xl] Many of these accounts were not actual humans.

As it is becoming easier to game the system, it is becoming more difficult to use the system. Online pollution is clouding the border between what is "real" and "fake". Fake news, people or videos are limited in their effectiveness by the willingness of people to believe they are true. However, detailed research demands resources and time, scarce goods for people who have lives to live, things to do and places to be. Web browsers currently load a grey mix of well-researched news, promotional content, earned content and fake content. In today's 24-hour news cycle it can be a challenge to filter information. Exhausted by the

---

see Andrew Marantz, "Reddit and the Struggle to Detoxify the Internet," The New Yorker, 12 March 2018.

media exhaust, people are, frankly, tired. The Washington Post estimates that President Trump has made approximately 13,500 false or misleading claims in the first 1,000 days of his presidency.[xii] As truth becomes a scarce resource, so does trust. When people cannot trust existing institutions they end up trusting either nothing or anything. Who benefits in low trust environments? In an environment of perpetual distrust, the message repeated most frequently might well win out.

Humanity is stumbling into a situation where past behaviour is influencing future options, and it is unclear which of those options are informed, biased or malicious. For humans to remain a functional part of the system for the long run, we first need to understand how the system works. How do people feed the system? How is our identity being interpreted? Do people still have full autonomy over their options and opinions? Who gets to decide who you are? Yet to fully understand what data privacy will mean in the 21st century another element is missing still: power games.

Good Citizenship

Just as the ultimate goal for corporations is optimising individual human behaviour to maximise profits, the ultimate goal for nation states is optimising aggregate behaviour to achieve good citizenship. Traditional incentives and disincentives include indirect tools such as subsidies or taxes. Today different strategies are available to governments. But what does good citizenship mean? Interpretations differ. At a minimum, history, culture and overall wealth play a role. Take China for example. China has a rich long history where the collective tends to be placed above the individual, and a relatively new tech-savvy rising middle class. This renders a mindset where decision makers adopt a long perspective, demonstrating a willingness to make controversial decisions in the short-term as long as the end result positively affects the majority of its citizens in the long-term. One of the approaches China has decided to use to keep its population of nearly 1.5 billion people in line is the social credit system.

Starting with the end in mind, the social credit system is meant to judge the behaviour and trustworthiness of citizens and companies alike. Perhaps poorly named the social credit system, the actual implementation is more similar to a permanent record linked to the ID of an individual or entity. To date, implementations are mostly tested on a regional rather than the national level. Local municipalities have implemented rules such a "credit" deduction for jaywalking or disturbance of the public order. Judgement is not just a private affair: jaywalkers have been publicly shamed on billboards. In a similar vein, companies are encouraged to be mindful of certain standards, such as restaurant sanitation. More serious consequences arise if these "transgressions" involve the government. Owing the government money could result in loss of rights. For example, a late tax payment could result in not being able to book flights, buy property or get into a reputable university. Poor reputation on one service could trickle over to another. Sesame Credit, also known as Zhima Credit, is a private credit scoring and loyalty programme system developed by Ant Financial Services Group, an affiliate of the Internet giant Alibaba Group. It crunches data from Alibaba's services, such as its giant marketplace, to compile its score. Sesame Credit infamously paired up with the dating site Baihe to display the social credit score of a potential suitor. Gaming is bad. Donating to charity is good. Stealing electricity is bad. Being a parent is good. According to China's own National Public Credit Information Centre the results for 2018 were as follows: 17.5 million people have been banned from buying flights and 5.5 million from buying train tickets.[xlii]

Fair or unfair, eventually the government system will be countrywide. To achieve this, private systems will be linked up to the uniform government ranking. That is a lot of data to be collected with little protection, analysed by opaque algorithms, to eventually arrive at a score which will determine someone's standing in society.[xliii]

An aspect many people do not know about is that governments enjoy greater data access than most companies, which is something we will examine in the next chapter. The social benefits gained through big data technology do not obviate the political downsides. The question is: just how "down" is the downside, and how "up" is the upside? Does technology ultimately enable or disable? Who will decide what is right and what is wrong? And where does that leave you?

Identity Must Evolve

On the Internet, individuals are playing on the losing side. Over its lifetime, data autonomy and privacy have been lost, and equity was never part of its design. Vulnerabilities are exploited to attack core values. Humans cannot feel data, but are beginning to feel the consequences of the situation we are all currently in. In light of advancing artificial intelligence and algorithms, security hacks and privacy scandals, it is becoming glaringly obvious the present situation is untenable.

As profit and power games extend deeper into our personal lives, it is indisputable that our identity is worth something to others. Now, we must realise it is worth something to us. Identity spans our online and offline world, serving as a beacon for banks, bots, bureaucrats, lawyers, landlords and lovers to verify us, measure us, and ultimately interact with us. Personal data is not merely a form of individual property but central to personhood. I argue that identity is the most valuable thing that humans own, and we need to start treating it as such.

The answer is not to throw your smartphone in the toilet, spill coffee over your laptop and to unplug the Internet cable. Nor is the answer the end of all data, algorithms and artificial intelligence – far from it. In fact, a knee-jerk reaction vilifying technology such as AI would be an immense mistake. We want to be online, but on terms that respect the self-sovereignty of our identity. To make use of the many beneficial break-throughs in machine learning, even support it, without fearing abuse of the data we provide to feed these efforts.

In order to imagine something new, we first need to examine how we got here, warranting a harsh look at the break down of the privacy realm, which is the focus of the next chapter. Because identity lies at the very root of our online and offline interactions its context is multi-dimensional, touching long-running debates ranging from interpretations of human rights to human dignity. A lot hinges on these debates. The situation has spiralled out of control, and there is only one response to the chaos. Identity must evolve to save the Internet. Just like identity adapted to the 19th and 20th century, it must evolve to fit our digital age.

3. House of Surveillance

*Ils doivent envisager qu'une grande responsabilité est la suite
inséparable d'un grand pouvoir.*[5]

Collectively, humanity is sleepwalking into the, what I call, *House of Surveillance*. No matter where you live in the world, online interactions in the 21st century come at a cost to privacy. A privacy tax. As connectedness expands in all directions, the price of privacy rises in tandem. There are many, but the most prevalent ones are the *Privacy Tax of Messaging* and *Privacy Tax of Payments*. Next to passive privacy taxes on online interactions, people actively seek to quantify and automate their lives. In pursuit of convenience, people push IoT devices through the front door, cause for the *Internet of Worrying Things*. Meanwhile, governments assumed the key to the house via mandated

---

[5] "With great power comes great responsibility". Originally thought to be born in the French Revolution, variations of this quote have been attributed to Roosevelt, Churchill and Spiderman.

Government Backdoors in both software and hardware. Leaving the house for the wider garden of the world in pursuit of a resemblance of privacy will meet another dead end. *Facial Recognition* is becoming ubiquitous, and advances in technology will make it possible to effectively use faces as trackers. In this chapter we will cover each of these technologies in turn.

Privacy Tax of Messaging

The raison d'être of the Internet are online interactions with anyone, anywhere. The two most popular interactions are with people ("messaging") and services ("payment").

The first privacy tax is messaging. It is impossible to talk about messaging without mentioning the company that owns the popular platforms Messenger, Instagram and WhatsApp. Facebook's pivot towards a privacy-first company graced global headlines. The magic word Mark Zuckerberg kept repeating in his public statement was "encryption". In one form or another, encryption was mentioned 24 times.[xliv]

What is encryption? Encryption is like a lockbox. Any type of data can be stored inside, but access is subject to predefined rules. Do not follow the rules and the content will be in a form or code that will make no sense whatsoever.

Tempting as it might be, equating encryption with privacy would be a comforting mistake. One could be forgiven to forget that Facebook controls an immense body of information from a pre-encryption era, three world leading messaging platforms with abundant "metadata" inventories (data about data), as well as a substantial data trove bought from third parties. Between historic data, metadata and third-party data, metadata is the biggest danger to privacy. If content is what you say, metadata is what you do. Metadata is generated automatically: it is the diary entry you did not mean to write. Metadata is key because its interpretation can be automated. To understand the menace of metadata, it is essential to first understand the concept of "triangulation".

At its essence, triangulation is a technique which uses more than one source on the same subject of interest to infer from the visible information what the invisible might hold. Like mapping the dark side of the moon based on the available information on the side rotated towards the earth. When applied to humans, available data is used to make predictions about who you are, what you will do, and how you will react to certain prompts.

Triangulation could take place within one platform. For example, even though location data is turned off, cross-referencing events someone signed up for to determine where they are, even if they did not give explicit permission. Triangulation could also be cross-platform. For instance, imagine Sarah shares a picture on WhatsApp. WhatsApp is encrypted so this transaction is completely private, right? Not quite. Triangulating metadata, such as cross-referencing phone numbers associated with Facebook profiles, in addition to Facebook's own data together with data it obtains from data brokers could result in an educated guess that the contact in question is in fact her mother. Reportedly Facebook makes 29,000 categories available to ad buyers based on 52,000 unique attributes. Nearly 600 of the categories were described as being provided by third-party data brokers, including offline sources.[xlv] Okay, but the content of messages is private, correct? Maybe. Nearly all smartphone pictures are embedded with location data, also a form of metadata. Here inferring Sarah is in fact at the local hospital. Knowing she has repeatedly searched for baby clothes for the past nine months (cross-referencing social login), explicit content is not required to guess her needs. Brazenly, Zuckerberg himself even admitted as much in his privacy letter: *"People should be able to use any of our apps to reach their friends, and they should be able to communicate across networks easily and securely."*

Not so subtly, this makes the case for deeper integrating Messenger, WhatsApp and Instagram, further combining associated profiles to perfect the aforementioned targeting techniques. An early signal of this desire was cross posting WhatsApp status to Facebook and Instagram "Stories". Strikingly, Facebook's CEO guaranteed the EU during the acquisition evaluation of WhatsApp that linking data across the two was impossible and would never happen. In 2017, under the leadership of Commissioner Margrethe Vestager, the European Commission fined Facebook €110 million ($122 million) for providing incorrect and misleading information during the Commission's 2014 investigation.[xlvi] Privacy is as strong as its weakest link, and the weakest link is metadata. Pushing encryption as a privacy solution whilst using triangulation to build data profiles is false advertising.

Privacy Tax of Payments

Payments are another dead giveaway of who you are and what you are up to. One cannot disconnect identity from communication, and the most prevalent and essential communication method is payment. Transactions are interactions. *Who are you paying? What are you paying for? Where are you?* Inferring detailed relationships through payments is entirely possible. As Hollywood movies like to say: follow the money.

Every non-cash payment logs an identifiable data point and every online payment spawns a wealth of data. Pay with your face applications carry even larger information profiles. Pay online and pay a privacy tax. Arguably, payments are the holy grail of data. Online payments in China outweigh the US fifty to one.[xlvii] According to AI expert Kai-Fu Lee, the overwhelming tendency of Chinese to pay online and the treasure of data that is created as a result is sufficiently significant that it could even result in a lead in artificial intelligence. Now imagine a data-hungry multinational with considerable cash reserves looking for new data points. What do you do? You enter the payment space.

Currencies are among the strongest geopolitical tools of countries. Imagine a company such as Facebook issuing a new dollar. How to feel about that? We will soon find out. Facebook is developing a cryptocurrency called Libra. Imagine two billion people united under one store of value. Reach would be unprecedented. If adopted across its two billion users, Libra would be more broadly used than the US dollar or the Chinese Yen. Assembling 100 custodians, for which the likes of Uber and Visa volunteered before the latter dropped out, Libra's reach would be greater still. The new oligopoly deciding the level of visibility on the lives and likes of individuals and their spending patterns is notably dominated by Web 2.0 giants. At time of writing, Facebook claims it will not crosslink contacts or any of profile information with Libra but may ask if you wish to do so. Yet if the "constitution" is against the vested interest of those with the power to change the constitution, with limited checks and balances in place, do not be surprised if this promise will not hold up in the long-term. The long-term play could well be to earn more via higher ad prices for shorter route to conversion. Alarmingly, metadata is exposed to those 100 custodians running the "nodes", the rule engines of the network.[xlviii] Make no mistake, this is not a drawbridge towards individual empowerment, but rather the creation of impenetrable moats. At best Libra would result in digital inclusivity. The worst case scenario is voiced by the British historian Niall Ferguson: *"My nightmare would be that Amazon, Google or Facebook creates some hugely popular version of a digital dollar at which point every transaction is going to be monitored by the network platforms' big data and AI systems, to an even greater extent than is already true."*[xlix] My personal nightmare would be one entity owning data, identity and payment layers. In response to anti-money laundering probes Zuckerberg replied at the Libra House Financial Services Committee hearing October 2019: *"Our vision of this, our wallet is going to have a strong identity".*[l] Case in point.

The dollar and the yen are just common stories. History books are full of dead currencies. Currencies can be replaced. To rival the Chinese messaging giant WeChat (Tencent), entering the payment space is an obvious move for Facebook. Meanwhile, Amazon is in talks with banks, Google is working on current accounts, and China is working on a cryptocurrency.[6]

The Chinese DCEP (Digital Currency Electronic Payment) has been years in the making. China's Digital Currency Research Institute declared its desire for *"controllable anonymity"* and to *"protect monetary sovereignty"*, which translates to the desire to capture the wealth of information currently expressed in foreign currency transactions. Adoption of the Chinese cryptocurrency will start locally – boosting over one billion users, WeChat is reportedly among the parties committed – and export via tourism. Spreading from wallets for the 2022 Winter Olympics to the lure of Chinese tourists abroad, similar to the WeChat playbook. Although the groundwork already started in

---

[6] With messaging semi-saturated, payments will be the next battlefield for data.

2014, the threat of the cryptocurrency Libra going after the same market has sped up development efforts. In reaction to both, the EU has reportedly urged the European Central Bank to explore *"central bank digital currencies"*.[ii] Both companies and governments are in the payment race.

Internet of Worrying Things

Where the privacy tax of messaging and payments have become popular journalistic news items, there is another sleeping giant about to wake up. By inviting connected devices, effectively communicating sensors, into our personal space, we have invited strangers into our homes. Many feel suspicious when seeing ads related to what was seemingly discussed in private quarters. In a nutshell, the inability of AI to distinguish between conscious wake-up prompts ("Hey Siri") and casual conversation ("Hey Sarah") makes it natively prone to eavesdropping. For example, three other wake words for Alexa are "computer", "Amazon" and "Echo". In 2018 an Alexa-enabled speaker owned by an American family recorded a personal conversation and promptly sent it to a contact in its linked address book. Alarmed, the husband's co-worker who received the message immediately called: *unplug your Alexa devices right now, you are being hacked*. After meeting initial scepticism, he continued: *you have been talking about hardwood floors*. This is no isolated incident. A journalist from MIT Technology Review found that her Alexa switched on unprompted, recording mundane details about her life, such as *Mommy, let's go to the car*, forwarding it to the Amazon cloud storage. You might own the device, but the company owns the data.[iii]

Recent revelations that the teams behind Siri, Alexa, and Google Assistant used human workers to manually review real voice samples for quality purposes unleashed floodgates of pent-up public discontent. Recordings were transcribed, annotated and fed back into the software. Contractors were forced to sign watertight non-disclosure agreements barring them to speak publicly about the programmes. Under public pressure these practices were suspended. The trickle that started the stream originated in Belgium, where the public broadcaster VRT NWS received over 1,000 Google Assistant recordings from a Dutch language reviewer. The recordings detailed addresses, medical conditions and even a woman in distress. In case of the latter no guidelines were provided. Over 150 recordings were reportedly activated accidentally.[liii] Worryingly, the snippets contained enough information for the research team to identify the people behind the voices. Depressingly, this is just a small segment of a subset of the linguistic market.

Facebook's Messenger and Microsoft's Skype admitted to also using contractors to review audio clips.[liv] The big differentiator is that where Alexa, Siri and Google Assistant listen for prompts to execute the services they were bought to do, Messenger and Skype facilitate direct and private communication between people. There is a reasonable expectation of complete privacy. Facebook claimed to have paused human review and Microsoft claimed to take reasonable measures to de-identify the samples. Of course, not linking these fragments to an identity is a moot point if the recording itself includes identifiable information.

Thinking of voice assistants such as Alexa as digital minimalism is a typical fallacy of the human brain. Amazon recently reported that Alexa now has 80,000 "skills" and thousands of integrations with third-party products, ranging from the actual Echo hardware to car dashboards.[lv] You could ask a virtual assistant anything from "Is it kosher" to "How to mix a Manhattan". Thanks to these integrations the number of people talking to

Alexa each day doubled in 2018. Nowadays IoT devices in homes tend to run into the double digits. As online and offline worlds blend, telling a voice assistant to order bread is more or less a fact of life. What do these devices actually record? Video or voice? Do the "listen" or "see" when "asleep"? Most pressingly, what happens to the data? Where is all this data processed? How is all this data analysed? By who?

Data captured in voice packages is different from clicks in browsers. Futurist Amy Webb speculates that voices carry emotion. Voices echo. Are you happy or are you sad? Have you been crying or are you aroused? Is the room you are in small or large? Are you standing close to the wall or in the centre of the room? These are all categories machine learning could be applied to.[vi] But that is not all. After it is bought, how are products, services, hardware and software being used? Once connected to one central point (for example a voice assistant), for the first time ever, it will be possible to map life inside the home. If someone has made their home "smart" it would be possible to infer, for example, how often they do laundry, what time they boot up the microwave, or when they turn off the lights to go to bed.

This data is not just vulnerable to the ethics of those companies creating such applications. A group of researchers discovered vulnerable patterns in Alexa and Google Home.[vii] For example, invoking the command "rap game" (attack skill), instead of "rat game" (Alexa skill) activated a rogue command. Another example is faking that the device is turned off whilst continuing to listen in ("faking termination attack"). Frequently placed in the living room, kitchen, bathroom or bedroom, these devices could witness the most private moments of people's lives. From family dinners to going to the toilet.

After the Internet browser, devices have become less and less neutral. It started with mobile, after which the user interface of IoT devices has become increasingly minimalistic. In a voice-only interface, dependence on the integrity behind the machine increases in spades. Although devices have changed, human relationships with devices barely has: we buy it, install it and never check settings again. When it controls the consumer endpoint, what will companies like Amazon, Facebook, Microsoft, Apple or Google use it for?[lviii] If you own something, should you not control it?

The total body of these IoT devices is expected to total 10 billion by 2020 and 22 billion by 2025.[lix] Although exact estimates vary, there is consensus that by 2025 the data gathered by IoT devices will run into the hundreds of zettabytes.[7] Part of the proliferation is deceptive for the same things are recorded in greater detail, such as pictures. The ocean of data bits and bytes broadcasted by the many billions of IoT devices every day is also, unsurprisingly, not entirely useful. Still, one finding of the technology consultancy IBM is particularly arresting: 90 percent of IoT sensor data is never used.[lx] This even has a name: "dark data". Such statistics unveil a bitter contradiction. If more than 90 percent of data is never used, why does it exist in the first place? As IoT becomes ubiquitous, what does this mean? Increasingly, the devices we make and the platforms we build have real, lasting, even permanent effects on the individuals and communities who use them. Trust placed in a device should be linked to the interests behind the device. Accountability when any sensor could capture information about anyone is a tale with no end. But not only corporate strangers are keen to sit at your table. Where privacy taxes and the Internet of Things mostly exist for profit purposes,

---

[7] 1 Zettabyte is 2^{70} bytes. If a byte is one grain of rice, a zettabyte fills the Pacific Ocean. 25 zettabytes of rice would easily cover the earth.

governments are interested in these information flows for wholly different reasons.

Governmental Backdoors

A truism for China, the US and many others is that a company is only ever allowed to do business within the desired borders if it concedes to the general conditions set by the government governing those borders. To keep those borders safe governments adopted a new philosophy: to find the needle in the haystack, collect the whole haystack. Because actors cannot always be controlled, the result is that entire infrastructures are sometimes controlled by states.

Google received over 121,000 user data requests and nearly 262,000 user account requests from government agencies, courts and parties in civil litigation in 2018 alone. Reportedly 67 percent resulted in the production of some data. Requests ranged from subpoenas to search warrants to wiretap orders. Facebook received more than 214,000 of such requests, complying just over 73 percent of the time.[xi] Apple publicly refusing to unlock the iPhone used by one of the attackers in a 2015 shooting in San Bernardino, as demanded by the FBI, and the corresponding fallout which ensued underscores just how rare it is to say no. The government dropped litigation after investigators got into the phone with a contractor's help. Russian authorities blocked Telegram due to its refusal to make encrypted data accessible to the Federal Security Service.[xii] The deputy director of the National Security Agency (NSA) claimed during his appearance at the TED 2014 conference: *"Every industrialised nation in the world has a lawful intercept programme where they are requiring companies to provide them with information that they need for their security, and the companies that are involved have complied with those programmes in the same way that they have to do when they are operating in Russia or the UK or China or India or, you know, France, any country you choose to name.*[xiii] Pressure on technology companies to create so-called backdoors mounts.

"Should governments continue to encounter impediments to lawful access to information necessary to aid the protection of the citizens of our countries, we may pursue technological, enforcement, legislative or other measures to achieve lawful access solutions". Words from the now-deleted 2018 memo by the Australian government issued on behalf of the "Five Eyes", the intelligence coalition of Australia, the UK, the US, Canada and New Zealand. Another letter, drafted on 4 October 2019, obtained by The Guardian, explicitly urged Facebook to build backdoors in all its messaging platforms. It was signed by government officials from the UK, Australia and the US, with one of the signatories being William Barr, acting US Attorney General.[lxiv]

Under the current profit-oriented model under-pinning services such as Messenger or Gmail, content is decrypted in-transit for targeted advertising, making parent companies like Facebook and Alphabet vulnerable for court-ordered interception. The amount of data companies would be able to collect is dwarfed by the mandates governments could issue to gather and use information. For example, India's new privacy bill poses GDPR-like expectations on companies, whilst including an exception clause for government: *"Exempt any agency of government from application to act in the interest of sovereignty and integrity of India, the security of the state, friendly relations with foreign states* (and) *public order."*[lxv] With the risk of stating the obvious, service providers are legally obligated to decrypt messages at the order of governments in order to do business in certain countries.

As NSA (US National Security Agency) whistle-blower Edward Snowden uncovered in 2013, electronic communication records of US citizens were being monitored indiscriminately and in bulk via a FISA court order (US Foreign Intelligence Surveillance Court) forcing the telecommunications company Verizon to share records of 120 million subscribers – regardless of whether they were suspected of any wrongdoing. The PRISM programme, the second scoop by the investigative journalist Glenn Greenwood, reported data collection directly from servers, including email, chat, photos, VoIP, video conferencing, file transfers and special requests. Firms included Microsoft (added 2007), Yahoo (added 2008), Google (added 2009), Facebook (added 2009), Skype (added 2011) and Apple (added 2012). Global firms, with global users. One device targeted was the smartphone of the German Chancellor Angela Merkel. Mind you, the NSA is part of the military. The military had been granted un-precedented access to civilian communications inside and outside the largest democracy in the world.[xvi]

Over fifty years in, it is easy to forget that the Internet had military origins, birthed at the US Defence Advanced Research Projects Agency (DARPA). Although backdoors can be mandated in software, such as direct data requests to social media platforms, and hardware, as alleged against the Chinese 5G telecom communications platform Huawei, there is a third way to obtain access to information. This is at the place where data is stored. When governments insist that both data centres and physical infrastructure are hosted on their own soil, there is a strategic reason to do so. India famously pushed for data localisation, reportedly citing Google rejecting 55 percent of the government's requests for data as a strong point of proof for the government to pursue storage of data locally. Reportedly, China, Russia, Vietnam, Nigeria and Pakistan have already instituted data localisation requirements. Instead of building the house, governments took a short-cut and mandated the key.[8]

The justification? National security. According to the founding document of the social credit system, released by the Chinese State Council in 2014, the scheme should *"allow the trustworthy to roam everywhere under heaven while making it hard for the discredited to take a single step."*[lxvii] The result? Harmonious lives in a harmonious nation. A fine principle as long as one is prepared to presuppose its rightness. Lacking a crystal ball, nobody can predict who will sit in the White House for the next four-year term, or the one after that. The upside or downside of optimisation of human behaviour hinges on the parameters for which it is optimised.

Voluntary opt-in needs a persistent enemy. Some go as far as saying all "publicly available data" should in fact be classified as "open-source data". This open-source data is to be used for real-time monitoring by the intelligence community (Chapter 10). Now facial recognition comes of age, this open-source umbrella graduates from listening to seeing.

Facial Recognition

Consider the following three scenarios. The British government capturing the average Londoner on camera over 300 times a day for law enforcement purposes. A high-end retail store capturing your likeliness over 300 times a month for targeted advisement purposes. Your neighbour capturing your morning shower routine on camera over 300 times a

---

[8] An increasing number of countries insist on localised data storage. The Freedom on the Network 2018 provides a detailed list.

year for entertainment purposes. Even if the latter is a multitude of factors less frequent, it feels infinitely more intrusive.

The underlying implication is intention: what is data used for? If data about a person exists, but it has no use, its legitimacy should be questioned. If it exists, and it has a use, its legitimacy hinges on the intention behind that use. Is the use known to the subject in question? Is the use authorised by the subject it affects? Nowhere are these questions more visible, and more pressing, than in the domain of secondary video data.

Amazon's surveillance technology service, which is marketed to various US law enforcement agencies and entities, boasts that it can identify up to 100 faces in a single image, tracking people in real-time through surveillance cameras and scan footage from body cameras. The accuracy of these models is inconsistent. When applying "Rekognition", the name of Amazon's service, to all members of the US House and Congress with a dataset of 25,000 publicly available arrest photos, the non-profit organisation American Civil Liberties Union found that nearly 40 percent of false matches included people of colour, even though they only made up 20 percent of input. Joy Buolamwini, a researcher at the MIT Media Lab, reiterates this bias. She found that when the person in the photo is a white man, Rekognition delivers a near-perfect result of 99 percent. Changing gender or skin colour measurably increases errors — up to nearly 35 percent error rate for images of darker skinned women. AI bias disproportionately affects those who are underrepresented. Is it scarier if this technology is accurate or not accurate? Which lives would be better or worse off in the case of the latter?[lxviii]

Amazon shareholders wrote Bezos in the summer of 2018 that they were concerned that the technology would be used to unfairly and disproportionately target and subject people of colour, immigrants and civil society organizations to surveillance. Over 450 members of the academic community further signed a letter to warn against supplying government and law enforcement agencies with facial recognition technology. Two Amazon shareholder votes took place in 2019 on non-binding recommendations to stop the programme. Both were voted down.[lxix]

At the top of the Oriental Pearl Tower in Shanghai, the first ever picture running into the billions of pixels was created.[9] A beautiful 195-billion-pixel super panorama stretching out to every corner of the city. Shanghai is a busy city, so let's assume that there are over a million people captured in this photo. Now imagine how long it would take to identify every single person pictured. Assuming access to the right data-bases, it would take the latest cutting-edge GPUs, computer vision, and advanced facial recognition algorithms only a few seconds to identify every single person in the picture. Bringing us full circle, to intention.

China counts over 200 million CCTV devices, one for every seven people.[lxx] These capabilities are put to use to keep the country's population in check, starting with its 11 million strong Uighur Muslims minority in the region of Xinjiang. According to the New York Times, the local facial recognition network looks exclusively for Uighurs based on their appearance and keeps records of their comings and goings for search and review, a practice which makes China a pioneer in applying next-generation technology to watch its people, potentially ushering in a new era of automated racism.[lxxi] As many as one million Uighurs are currently in *"re-education camps"* according to the United Nations.[lxxii] Human Rights Watch found that a wide array of information

---

[9] View the 195-billion-pixel super panorama at: sh-meet.bigpixel.cn.

was monitored to ensure that those *"who ought to be taken, should be taken"*. External observations such as *"unusual use of electricity"* and *"excessive trip length"*, biometrics such as blood type, voice samples, DNA, fingerprints and height, and personal convictions such as *"religious atmosphere"* and political affiliation.[lxxiii] Meanwhile, south-east of Xinjiang, Hong Kong protestors fighting to protect the city's special legal status within China have been filmed destroying facial recognition towers and pointing high-powered lasers to confuse the machines and prevent detection.[lxxiv]

The same argument relevant to video surveillance could be applied to drones or any other video graphic sensors: facial recognition capabilities are only limited by the databases they are linked to. According to the Centre on Privacy and Technology at Georgetown Law, the US facial recognition database which can be searched by police departments without warrant counts 117 million people. That is half the US population, or one in two Americans. This was in 2016. The UK home office reported July that same year that over 16 million searchable images had been enrolled in its own facial recognition gallery. When crossing borders, some countries require photography upon exit and entry, enriching the database of faces with foreigners. The US proposed, and retracted, to make this mandatory for all US citizens too (who now still have the option to opt-out).[lxxv] There is a whole generation of biometrics that are being experimented with.[lxxvi] Anyone anywhere translates to everybody everywhere. Biometric data can now be captured without consent, raising questions which need answers. Do we want to use biometrical data? And if so, under which supervisory and legal conditions?

The city of San Francisco publicly condemned this trend, following words with black on white legislation making it one of the first US cities to require a warrant for facial recognition applications. I argue that companies and governments have an information fiduciary duty, and if governments do not lead by example, the private sector will not follow.

An Offer You Cannot Refuse

The ultimate proxy for freedom is deceptively simple. Can you opt out? Opting out from the Web 2.0 realm, avoiding the likes of Facebook and Google, is time intensive and difficult, if not impossible. The fact that there are no real alternatives is exactly what makes the house of surveillance acutely alarming. It suggests that the privacy taxes of messaging and payments are unavoidable. Inviting IoT devices into our homes remains a choice at discretion, for now, yet transparency is direly needed. Meanwhile, governments have adopted backdoors in private infrastructure. Finally, opting out from the secondary data realm, such as facial recognition and other indirect data, is impossible. We have seen that because legislative frameworks for secondary data are lacking, consent is self-authorised.

The good news is that all these networks are not connected. The bad news is that all these networks are not connected, yet. We find ourselves at a very early stage of something few of us can fully comprehend. The house of surveillance illustrates that visibility in the lives of individuals rapidly escalates. Visibility used for optimisation towards either profit or power. And in this pursuit artificial intelligence plays a starring role. Data is the building block of AI whilst AI lends meaning to data; this tug of war will be the focus of the next chapter.

4. Benevolent Gods

"I believe it is universally understood and acknowledged that all men will ever act correctly, unless they have a motive to do otherwise."
- Abraham Lincoln[lxxvii]

In and of itself, data is worthless. That data is becoming ever more important has been pounded into everyone's mind to such an extent that we seldom pause to re-examine why. To understand the growing hunger for data, we must discern when, how and why data crosses the threshold from being a worthless scramble of 1's and 0's to being a sought-after commodity. Data only becomes valuable when combined, processed and analysed in a way that drives actionable insights. The field of AI studies the general problem of creating intelligence in machines. In true chicken-egg fashion, AI lends meaning to data whilst training AI requires data. The universal takeaway? Whoever amasses a critical body of data quickest could win the AI race.

Yet a step in thinking is missing. In this chapter we will see that the great data arms race is, rather surprisingly, not actually about data, but about the potential benefits of AI. The biggest corporate success stories of the past decades took this wisdom to heart.

All valued at over hundreds of billions of dollars, Facebook, Microsoft, Amazon and Google in the West and Tencent, Baidu and Alibaba in the East, are competing in the AI gold rush. To not get left behind data is collected indiscriminately and in bulk. The most efficient strategy to accumulate as much as possible is via centralised platforms. This centralisation of data honey pots is paired with centralised cyber vulnerabilities. Vulnerabilities which can be, and increasingly are, exploited. Additionally, and alarmingly, centralised data collection accumulates in centralised control over AI. This chapter will examine the ethical collateral of the AI and data race. Then, refocusing on the endgame, explore what the implications are of centralised AI across the power and profit spectrum. But first, to understand the dynamics between data and AI, it is necessary to understand how AI behaves.

Information Overload

In many ways artificial intelligence is the perfect student: self-learning, self-correcting, self-improving – as long as it is fed enough information. The words "artificial" and "intelligence" suggest performing tasks characteristic of human intelligence. The AI which exists today, however, specialises in one particular task and is called "Narrow AI". This task could be filtering spam, curating a music playlist, or optimising the daily commute. Its big brother "General AI" is more elusive. General AI would master the cognitive abilities and general experiential understanding of its environments similar to human qualities, but enhance it with the ability to process this data at much greater speeds than us mere mortals.

Narrow AI is already great at a lot of things humans are generally not good at. Humans are not wired to perceive slow, visual changes; AI can watch plants grow. After a while, humans become bored of repetitive tasks and start demanding lunch breaks; AI is always alert and ready to do the required calculations without skipping a beat. From retail to banking, significant efficiencies could be (and are) achieved through AI-enhanced optimisation, planning and forecasting. By refocusing resources, most notably human resources, AI could be humanity's partner in innovation. Data crunching could greatly accelerate the discovery of new medicines for rare diseases. An AI could crawl every history book in the world and access relevant information in a split-second. This would help automate and even completely reimagine existing processes. Because machines do not approach tasks the same way as humans, there are many scenarios where applying AI logic will be far superior and efficient than a human brain will ever be. Other times, algorithms do not need to be perfect, just better than humans. Carefully applied, AI could do wonders for humankind. This is why the lifeblood of AI, data, is in high demand.

"Machine learning", a subset of AI, is a pattern recognition mechanism. It allows computers to learn without being explicitly programmed. "Deep learning", a subset of machine learning, is inspired by the structure and function of the brain, namely the inter-connectedness of neurons. To make sense of things, deep learning uses multiple processing layers where every layer has distinct logic attached to it. One layer could detect shapes, while another could detect combinations of shapes that form parts of objects, like a dog or a cat. The next layer could read colour patterns, followed by texture, and so on. The same method could be applied to voice or natural language processing. The depth of the network with its multiple layers is what allows it to recognise complex patterns in this hierarchical fashion. With each new data set it updates its models and the way it "sees" the world.

Conversely, to apply deep learning to recognise a cat requires a lot of pictures of cats. In 2012, it took "the brain" from Google three days to process 10 million cat video thumbnails to achieve just under 75 percent accuracy when identifying cats. An aspect many people do not know about is that "the brain" was not told beforehand what a cat was. It basically invented the concept of a cat. In deep learning, there is no data like more data.[lxxviii]

This was a pivotal turning point in how to solve problems. The new narrative went as follows. Amass enough data, throw it against an algorithm and let software automatically learn and improve. But how to achieve the first step? How to obtain the data we need? In contrast to the fixed value of gold, data is worth something different to everybody. This led to the next challenge: how to use data in a way which creates value? Companies across the board did a fairly decent job answering the first question. The last decade's modus operandi has been to hoard data with the idea that it will be useful one day. More often than not, data was obtained indiscriminately, not acknowledging that data comes in many shapes and sizes. A mistake at the cost of ethical collateral.

Why Data Is Not Oil

In 2017, the Economist magazine proclaimed that *"the world's most valuable resource is no longer oil, but data."*[lxxix] Calling data the new oil is misleading. For starters, oil is well defined whereas data is not. In fact, data has four dimensions: *Format*, *Type*, *Quality* and *Volume*. Because not all data is created equal, we first need to unpack the intricacies of the construct in order to form an opinion about how it should and should not be used.

The first data dimension is Format. Format informs which form of machine learning is best suited. Supervised machine learning requires labelled data. For example, an AI agent training on a database of cat images labelled "cat" in order to learn how to quickly identify cats. According to AI pioneer Kai-Fu Lee people unwittingly support these efforts: labelling data could also involve linking data to a specific outcome. *Bought vs. didn't buy. Like vs. didn't like. Share vs. didn't share.*[10] According to a recent survey, data preparation and engineering tasks represent over 80 percent of the time consumed in most AI and machine learning projects, which explains why data labelling efforts are often outsourced to countries such as India.[lxxx] Unsupervised machine learning, on the other hand, can process unlabelled data. Here, the focus is to extract as much value as possible, uncovering hidden patterns along the way. Unsupervised machine learning is less focused on output and more focused on maximising the value of its input. If you are the input, what do you look like in ones and zeros?

This is the territory of the next data dimension, Type, which is roughly split into three sub-categories: "personal identifiable information", "pseudonymous data" and "anonymised data". When it comes to personal identifiable information (PII), the term itself is already a matter of hot debate. If information could be used to exclusively identify an individual it tends to fall in the PII bucket.[11] This extends beyond more obvious

---

[10] All online actions take place at a certain place in time, and these actions (or lack thereof) can be recast as input for labelling. Like vs. did not like. Share vs. did not share. Click vs. did not click.
[11] Definition as used by the Information Commissioner's Office: the UK's independent authority set up to uphold information rights in the public interest, promoting openness by public bodies and data privacy for individuals.

expressions such as first and last name or date and place of birth. Information which on its own may not be able to identify a person, but when combined with another piece could identify, trace or locate somebody could be regarded PII as well. For example, as the only woman in a male dominated team, reporting gender on an anonymous survey will immediately exclusively identify you. Pseudonymisation, the second category, is a form of de-identification, where information remains personal data but "linkability" is reduced. The last group is anonymous data. If it is impossible for any party handling the information to re-identify the individual it would probably pass the anonymisation threshold. These are all shades on a spectrum, and in practice this ambiguity is used as an error margin in data capturing strategies.

The third data dimension is Quality. If input is flawed, resulting insights will be flawed also. Garbage in, garbage out. High quality data is *Clean*, *Machine-Readable* and *Fresh*. In contrast, "dirty data" is burdened by inconsistencies, missing information or even errors. As competition intensifies, pressure to capture the largest volume of relevant, high-quality data mounts. The less diversified company revenue streams; the more aggressive its data collection practices. For context, about 99 percent of Facebook's income arises from selling advertising – $14.9 billion in the first quarter of 2019 alone.[lxxxi] Lucrative yields beckoning, in the rush of not wanting to get left behind the temptation to cut corners increases.

One such initiative to mine Clean data is the now-deactivated "Facebook Research" app, which paid participants aged between 15 and 35 years $20 per month to install a VPN on their mobile devices in order to obtain near limitless access. Next to recording all phone and web activity, the app also captured biometric data and extracted sensitive information from third parties such as period cycles. For those short on cash, like the teens and young adults the app targeted, the monthly payment could tempt them to sell their privacy at bargain prices. In this scenario, humans actively trained an AI agent to improve performance. However, the question remains if these participants really understood what they consented to. In 2030 we will quite likely find it incredible that anyone would ever share limitless access to their device for as little as twenty dollars a month.[xxxii]

In addition to being "clean", high-quality data is also Machine-Readable. For example, a side by side comparison of two photos of the same face within a fixed time frame, a phenomenon popularised on social media, such as the "10-year challenge" on Facebook. When humans passively train AI agents we enter debatable ethical territory. Think of monitoring employees at work, sentiment analysis across status updates or behavioural driving data. Is passive consent adequate in such circumstances? Even deliberate, direct human-agent relationships are not without footnotes. Direct training requires an awareness of human and algorithmic bias. An incident which Google would prefer to stay deeply buried took place in 2015. A software engineer pointed out on Twitter that the image recognition algorithms in Google Photos were classifying his black friends as "gorillas." The fix? Removing "gorilla" as a label.[12] The technical equivalent of duct-taping a leaking boat, instead of acknowledging it needs a new plank.

The last characteristic defining high-quality data is "Freshness". Data collected today is worth more than

---

[12] The bug was identified by software engineer Jacky Alciné. Loss functions in AI represent the margin of error and are always strived to be minimised. The problem starts when AI attributes equal risk to similar labelling mishaps, i.e. equating the relative cost of mislabelling a human as a gorilla on par with confusing a tree with a table.

data collected last week, or last year. Old data stinks a little. In the early days, Google famously used CAPTCHA, an acronym for "Completely Automated Public Turing test to tell Computers and Humans Apart", for training their in-house artificial intelligence. Humans named word clouds, solved puzzles and identified objects at the threshold of what AI could do. By 2014, the computer got the test right 99.8 percent of the time, while humans stranded at a mere 33 percent.[lxxxiii]

Live data is terribly tempting. Roboticist Rodney Brooks proposed back in 1990 that *"the world is its own best model"*, emphasising *"ongoing physical interaction with the environment"* (live sensors).[lxxxiv] Too bad there are people in it. Governments like fresh data too. The British tax authority collected over five million records via its controversial Voice ID system. Only 1.5 million customers consented. The civil liberties and privacy non-profit Big Brother Watch found that since January 2017 HMRC had been taking voice recordings from those who call the helplines to identify future callers with the following prompt: *"Please say my voice is my password"*. There was no opt-out. Although the British Information Commissioner's Office (ICO) found HMRC in breach with GDPR, it got off with a slap on the wrist.[lxxxv]

Following format, type and quality, the last data dimension is Volume. Big data is getting bigger. Google research shows that AI performance increases logarithmically with training data volume.[lxxxvi] Data volume could elevate a moderate model over an excellent model. For all these reasons, the default is to hoard data.

As Charlie Munger, long-time business partner of billionaire Warren Buffett, maintained: *"Show me the incentive and I will show you the outcome"*. In a way, capitalist markets are like a game of poker. Play your hand the best possible way in keeping with the rules of the game. Break the rules and you will be disqualified.

Companies optimise resources based on the rules of the market. If the goal is to maximise profit, high-quality data will be hoarded to optimise advertisement conversion. If the goal is to maximise ad conversion, click-bait will be pushed to maximise user stickiness and engagement. If the goal is to build a long-term competitive edge, data is captured centrally to train AI systems to stay one step ahead of rivals. The gravitational pull of data lends it so well for centralised business models: more data; better recommendations; more users; more data. Under these conditions, we have seen some favouring brute strength over deploying a targeted data strategy and cutting corners over well-considered ethics.

As attractive as this approach might be to companies and governments up high, it is not as kind to the individuals on the ground. The great hoarding of data has come with unintended consequences. As automation spreads, responsibility centralises. Yet, as we will see, this responsibility is not adequately met. Centralised systems are vulnerable, and the scent of data honey pots draws hackers.

The Trust Chasm

The Cambridge Analytica scandal from 2016, where data of tens of millions of Facebook users was captured to create targeted influence campaigns intended to manipulate the US presidential election, is important for a couple of reasons. According to Facebook, Cambridge Analytica used a simple quiz-app called "thisismydigitallife" to acquire detailed profiles. Although the initial group who used the app was relatively small, running in the hundreds of thousands, a loophole in the API exposed the Facebook friends of the quiz-takers as well, suddenly growing the data breach to include millions of users. According to whistle-blower

Christopher Wylie, each "seeder" exposed around 160 "friends".[xxxvii] Your privacy decisions extend to those closest to you. Additionally, the illegally collected data was used to not only feed targeted dis-information, but also to buy real advertisements. Facebook not only failed to flag that data was stolen; it was misused on their own platform. The Mueller report mentioned Facebook more than 80 times in relation to Russian interference in the 2016 presidential election. The report found that the Internet Research Agency, an election interference group affiliated with the Russian government, paid Facebook over $100,000 for more than 3,500 advertisements.[xxxviii] The honey pot attracted the Russian bear.

This is not an isolated incident. A white hat hacker discovered similar API exploitations in yet another Facebook quiz app, NameTests.com. By displaying personal data of its 120 million active users in a JavaScript file, this information was unprotected to any further third-party website the user would visit. Sharing information for targeting purposes was intentional, the fall-out was not.[xxxix]

Can we really blame the Facebook of 2004 for not foreseeing a world of deep fakes, influence campaigns and identity theft? Over a decade later, when making the world more open and connected is sounding a little hollow, we can surely judge inaction. Cambridge Analytica is a cautionary tale, but only the visible tip of a drifting iceberg. Privacy breaches due to unsecured architecture are embarrassing. Privacy breaches due to wilful blindness are insulting. And privacy breaches by design are deeply worrying. Some argue we cannot reasonably expect these companies not to act in their own interest. There is a counterargument to this line of reasoning. When a company grows to a certain size, say passing a billion users, it could be argued to be a public utility. In that case it carries an ethical as well as a commercial responsibility. Those ethics extend, as a minimum, to protect identifiable information of people.

Regulators echoed this responsibility three years later. Counting two breaches of the Data Protection Act, the British ICO concluded that Facebook failed to safeguard its users' information and that it failed to be transparent about how that data was harvested by others. The fine was set at £500,000 ($650,000). In the first quarter of 2019 Facebook took £500,000 in revenue every five and a half minutes.[13] The Italian data protection watchdog followed with a 1.1 million dollar penalty in 2019, citing that even though only 57 Facebook users downloaded the quiz-app in question, over 214,000 Italians were affected.[xc] In preparation of the US Federal Trade Commission (FTC) fine for privacy violations Facebook set aside $3 to $5 billion.

How did the market react? The stock went up five percent. The market treated the fine as a fee. The difference according to philosophy professor Michael Sandel is that fines register moral disapproval, whereas fees are simply prices that imply no moral judgement.[xci] Perceived litigation risk appears to be a poor match for balance sheet resources. The FTC finally decided on $5 billion, nearly 30 times the FTC's largest-ever civil penalty to date, to serve as a signal to radically rehaul company culture.[14] To underline this decision, later that year the FTC also issued a statement that it found Cambridge Analytica to have *"engaged in deceptive practices to harvest personal information from tens of millions of Facebook users for voter profiling and targeting"*.[xcii] On the other side of the Atlantic Marriott's

---

[13] $14,900 million revenue per quarter gives roughly $115,000 revenue per minute. £500,000 approximates $650,000. Hence Facebook would earn back a fine of £500,000 in around 5.5 minutes.
[14] The second largest FTC fine was $168 million, levied on Dish Network in 2017.

Starwood data breach was penalised $126 million under GDPR, less than 24 hours after British Airways received a record fine of over $220 million for jeopardising personal data of 500,000 customers.

We need to decide what attitudes towards privacy we want to promote. There is no ethical violation to being hacked. The ethical violation occurs when non-reasonable efforts are made to protect people. The now battle-tested ability to impose a fine of four percent of annual revenues under GDPR suggests that we might begin to care after all. However, while this might seem promising, the reality is still less rosy. In 2019, the UK Parliament published a damning report, establishing that Facebook continues to choose profit over data security, taking risks and prioritising revenue from user data, concluding that Facebook needs to significantly change its business model and practices to maintain trust.[xciii]

Trust is the crucial concept in this context. When you trust a company like Google to protect your privacy, you actually place your trust in various versions of Google at the same time. You trust that "Google-the-company" will comply with existing legislation, and that this legislation is relevant. Secondly, you trust that "Google's employees" act in line with the goals and values of "Google-the-institution". And lastly you trust that "Google-the-platform" is secure enough to not be breached by malicious third parties. The question then turns to how much do we trust profit-maximising centralised platforms to protect our privacy? And if databases are breached, what happens next?

Happy Hackers

Few people are aware that, when large centralised databases are compromised, hackers have roughly three options.

The first is to illegally sell the data in question, a prolific practice on the dark web. Here, Facebook logins sell for five dollar each while credentials to PayPal accounts go for an average of around $250.[xciv] An entire digital identity, including PII and hacked financial accounts, can be bought for roughly $1,200. This makes what happened December 2019 all the more striking. More than 267 million Facebook profiles were found on the dark web (probably collected via a technique called scraping, which is illegal), leaving unique Facebook IDs, names and phone numbers of one in ten Facebook users exposed.[15] This is but the tip of the iceberg. An individual hacker or group called "Gnosticplayers" has been responsible for a sequence of enormous data breaches in 2019, bordering one billion records, hitting companies such as the family genealogy service MyHeritage (92 million records, 0.55 bitcoin), the interior website Houzz (57 million records, 2.9 bitcoin) and the video sharing platform Dubsmash (161.5 million records, 0.55 bitcoin). If hackers are selling, who is buying?

An alternative to the dark web, and this might sound strange at first, is for hackers to sell the data back to the company or government from whom they stole it. Companies and governments can be extorted. When hackers stole personal data of 57 million customers and drivers from Uber, the company concealed the breach for more than a year. Instead of informing those affected that licence numbers and addresses had been compromised, the company paid the hackers $100,000

---

[15] 4 December: The database was first indexed.
12 December: The data was posted on a hacker forum.
14 December: Bob Diachenko discovered the database and immediately sent an abuse report to the ISP managing the IP address of the server.
19 December: The database is now unavailable.
Paul Bischoff, "Report: 267 million Facebook users IDs and phone numbers exposed online," *CompariTech*, 19 December 2019.

to bury the scandal. Only when the episode became public one year later, one of its top managers was promptly and publicly fired. Just as there are teams for legal breaches, there are also teams set up to deal with data breaches. Accepting the external appeal of data honey pots falls within the margin of error that is part of the inherent make-up of these organisations.

For example, a well-known white hat hacker discovered that a massive database exposing over 275,000,000 records of Indian citizens was left unprotected on the Internet for more than two weeks, containing detailed personally identifiable information (such as date of birth, gender, email, phone number, education details, employer, current salary). Why this database was created is as of yet unclear. After the white hat hacker reported his findings to the authorities, another hacker group called Unistellar deleted the whole thing and dropped the following message: *"Restore? Contact: unistellar@hotmail.com".* [xcv]

The third option at a hacker's disposal is to use the data for him or herself. Once data falls into the wrong hands, identities can be stolen, cloned or proportionally appropriated. If identity is a collection of claims that allows you to do things, this means other people with access to those claims can do things on your behalf.

One of the largest Western privacy breaches in recent memory is the Equifax hack of 2017. According to the US House Oversight Committee, hackers gained access to the US consumer credit reporting agency Equifax mid-May 2017 and attacked the company for 76 days. Equifax noticed "red flags" late July, allowed key figures to sell significant stock in August, and waited until September to inform the public of the breach. The hack compromised the information of 148 million people, leaking PII such as names, social security numbers, birthdates, addresses and driving licence numbers. Two factors amplified public outcry. Firstly, Equifax knew and did not immediately inform the public. Secondly, according to the US House Oversight Committee the hack was entirely preventable, citing *"a culture of cybersecurity complacency"*, outdated technology systems and Equifax's failure to patch a *"known critical vulnerability"*. The class-action lawsuit details Equifax used the username *"admin"* and password *"admin"*. Two years later Equifax conceded to pay a stunning $700 million fine, of which $300 million set aside for the victims.[xcvi]

The AdultFriendFinder hack easily exceeds Equifax in size, and depending on how you look at it, sensitivity. The breach exposed 412 million accounts related to the *"world's largest sex and swinger community"*, reportedly including around 8,000 US military email addresses and approximately 5,500 US government email addresses. Almost every account password was cracked due to poor security practices.

Unlike a password or account name, you cannot change your fingerprint or face. This makes biometric data extremely sensitive. No government is immune to being hacked. The US Office of Personnel Management repels upwards of 10 million attempted digital intrusions per month, but when the name of the Avenger Steve Rogers (Captain America) blinked on screen there was a reason for panic. Avenger names are the trademark of a hacker group rumoured to be affiliated to China. Data at risk included: *"Over two million background investigations per year, involving everyone from contractors to federal judges"*, *"a 127-page questionnaire for federal security clearance"* including probing questions about an applicant's personal finances, past substance abuse and psychiatric care, data on applicants for some of the government's most secretive jobs, ranging from *"lie detector results"* to notes about *"whether an applicant engages in risky sexual behaviour"* and over 5.5 million government employee fingerprints.[xcvii] Reportedly in the aftermath of the hack the CIA preventatively withdrew a number of officers from the US Embassy in Beijing.[xcviii]

With access to biographic, behavioural and biometric data, imagine the damage somebody could do pretending to be you online. Americans are more worried about being a victim of cybercrime than being a victim of a violent crime.[xcix] Identity fraud is the unauthorised use of someone's personal information for illicit financial gain. Spending money could be the least of your concerns. If a credit card rating is ruined beyond your control, long-term consequences could vary from obstacles to renting an apartment, complications to obtaining a bank loan or even being denied for employment. Early red flags are irregular withdrawals on credit card statements, suspicious bank emails or unusual transactions on unsafe websites. "True name identity theft" is when a real person's identifying information is used without modification. The thief actually poses as the victim. Examples include "medical identity theft", to acquire medical services, and "criminal identity theft", to commit a crime. The latest iteration is "synthetic ID-fraud". Synthetic IDs are created by applying for credit using a combination of real and fake, or sometimes entirely fake, information. Fraud rings sometimes establish thousands of synthetic IDs, all waiting to default. One of the largest synthetic ID rings detected to date racked up losses for banks of $200 million from 7,000 synthetic IDs and 25,000 credit cards.[c] We find ourselves in an odd situation, where we co-exist with fake news, fake people and sometimes even fake versions of ourselves.

In pursuit of profits centralised platforms have not been diligent data stewards. Corners have been cut obtaining data, as shown in the previous chapter. Corners have been cut protecting the data obtained, as this chapter illustrates. And corners have been cut by governments and corporations alike when using data, as detailed in Chapter 2. The realisation is dawning that it is in fact the people who drew the short straw. In the 21st century data and control are inseparably linked. Data gives the capacity for control.[ci] The volume of data under control is unprecedented. Its associated power is unprecedented. The logical next question is what this power will be used for.

Artificial Endgame

Maximising the gains of artificial intelligence has been overwhelmingly commercially focused, with important societal implications developing largely unchecked. Many missed the gathering storm. Centralisation of data via centralised platforms masks a deeper trend: centralisation of artificial intelligence.

Artificial Power

Artificial intelligence is a potent tool, conveying power to its wielder. Because access to high-quality data demands significant resources, these critical capabilities are increasingly limited to a handful of companies: Facebook, Google, Microsoft and Amazon in the West and Alibaba, Baidu and Tencent in the East. These companies are headquartered in two countries: the US and China.

If the power spectrum runs from good to bad actors, the natural question becomes: how "good" is good and how "bad" is bad. Take Mark Zuckerberg's proposed Facebook "privacy pivot" for example. The good news? A little step towards the good actor side of the spectrum. The bad news? It remains disproportionately within the decision power of one individual to guide the direction of privacy of a platform covering over a third of the world's population. Bigger than most countries, the course of action of corporations is steered by capitalism, not politics. Now, it is highly unlikely that a tech giant like Google would turn evil overnight, yet "do not be evil" and "cannot be evil" are two entirely different things. And if it would, an evil-Google would be a thing of terror. An evil Google could publish the search history of politicians it did not agree with. Historically close to the Democratic Party, imagine Google deciding to publish President Trump's search history. An evil-Google could choose to wiretap all Android devices, with video. Capacity for control can exist without an explicit exercise of that power. Voluntarily electing to do no harm, Google is a benevolent god. And artificial intelligence exponentially increases this capacity for power.

These are the early beginnings of what AI can do. From a historical perspective we are only seconds in, and already it is not a pretty picture. At the moment, AI is mostly based on digital interactions. In the future, its body of data will include secondary data also, expanding in breadth, depth and volume. Google's parent company Alphabet is already making headway in the IoT space via its Nest thermometers (home), Fitbit fitness trackers (health), Internet service providers (Google Fiber) and Waymo connected vehicle arm (transportation). Acquisition patterns of the tech giants point emphatically towards the IoT sector. Facebook is trying this route for drones (Ascenta), fitness trackers (ProtoGeo Oy), virtual reality (Oculus) and its video hardware Portal – a Facebook endorsed camera and microphone for the living room. Snugly positioned within Amazon's ever-expanding product range, the doorbell Ring is experimenting with facial recognition using the Rekognition stack. More likely than not, AI will be the technology of domination in the 21st century. Those left behind could be exploited or even conquered by those who forge ahead.[cii] Nobody wants to stay behind.

When it comes to artificial intelligence, China and the US are arguably light years ahead of the other 195 countries. By extension, the ethical decisions that will matter most in the next few decades will orbit these two countries. Breaking this hegemony is squarely in the interest of the other 195 making up the world ranks. If this does not come to pass, only big countries and big platforms will have skin in the game. And those not in the game will be forced to play by another's rules.

A single point of power is a single point of failure. Morally, but also politically. A great unknown remains how AI-run societies will treat outliers. Less than a century ago, AI in the German Third Reich would have been able to easily identify people it deemed unwanted. Now consider that the social credit system in China will be rolled out nationwide in 2020. If the system decides on a perfect model citizen, it also has the ability to identify those not fitting that description. Certainly it could spit out a list of the top one percent "anomalies". The data to arrive at these anomalies will be based on the quantification of the lives of millions. Remember also that certain governments demand a backdoor in exchange for the right to do business – near-monopolies are particularly vulnerable to this non-negotiable request.

In response to the posed danger of these massive datasets and unprecedented associated logic, governments are taking sides. The German government proactively took a position against a potential data merger of Facebook Messenger, WhatsApp and Instagram. The Bundeskartellamt, an independent competition federal authority whose task is to protect competition in Germany, convicted Facebook for combining user data from different sources: *"In* [the] *future, Facebook will no longer be allowed to force its users to agree to the practically unrestricted collection and assigning of non-Facebook data to their Facebook user accounts."*[ciii] Although the order got kicked down the long halls of the court system and is expected to take years to resolve, the ire of the technology world was swift. Germany hinders progress. After all, the argument goes, the ultimate benefit of AI is improving lives. From the mundane, such as effortless shopping, to the essential, such as personalised medicine. Do the pros not outweigh the cons? The zero-sum proposition presented is an impossible choice between centralised data paired with centralised AI or discarding artificial intelligence and its benefits altogether. Today's systems are not setup to accommodate anything else. But what if there was a third way?

Artificial Benefits

If we truly believe in deploying AI for the betterment of humanity, why would we want to restrict access? Do the remaining 195 countries unquestionably accept the dominion of China and the US? If training data pools remain siloed, the many potential benefits of AI will remain siloed also. Companies are cementing their centralised positions. Recent leaks revealed that Facebook treated user data as leverage with external developers and spun anti-competitive manoeuvres as privacy improvements.[civ] This unequal benefit distribution stands in sharp contrast to Silicon Valley slogans of making the world more open and connected.

Continuing down this path means substantial benefits will be skewed towards a tiny elite while most will suffer from data exploitation and, finally, irrelevance. In the near-term, humans will complement machines and machines will complement humans. In the long run, however, human input in the form of manual or mental work will relatively decrease in importance, while human input in the form of data will increase in value. Artificial intelligence superpowers are created on the back of your data, your identity. This is why giving your data away for twenty dollars will seem incredible in 2030.

Overall, the whole situation is unsustainable and will eventually lead to instability in the political and economic spheres (Chapter 10). National and corporate competition is intensifying. *"The one who becomes leader of AI will be ruler of the world,"* observed Russian President Vladimir Putin.[cv] The new Cold War will not be about counting missiles, but networks. Centralised data and centralised AI are two sides of the same coin. One reinforces the other. Both are not in the long-term interest of humanity. Similar to the nuclear arms race: no matter who wins the AI arms race, humanity at large loses.

If this is one of the most pressing issues we face, one of the most personal ones, can we do something about it? Unethical data hoarding has been an efficient strategy, albeit not a sustainable one. Based on what we see now, it will not survive the 21st century. Data without consent never can and never will be the new gold. As humans are part of the input of AI, individuals have a role to play in the democratisation of its benefits. What if the world's response to centralised AI was localised access controls? What if those involved in the process would have a stake in the outcome? In other words, what if data was decentralised? In later chapters we will see that the use of data and AI in a distributed and decentralised environment will not only make it more useful, but also more equitable, scalable and sustainable. But first, if individuals hold the key to the future, what type of identity proxies are currently available for individuals to navigate society?

5. Identity Proxies

*"Think about what people are doing on Facebook today.
They're keeping up with their friends and family, but they're
also building an image and identity for themselves, which in
a sense is their brand. They're connecting with the audience
that they want to connect to. It's almost a disadvantage if
you're not on it now."*
- Mark Zuckerberg[16]

Millennia ago, humans outgrew their local communities and started to organise at increasingly larger scales. Anthropologist Robin Dunbar believes that the evolutionary structure of social networks limits humans to 150 meaningful relationships at a time.[17] *I know you are who you say you are, because my family has hunted with your family as far as we can remember.* As human interactions be-came more complex humanity needed a more scalable method to distinguish friend from foe. In the identity

---

[16] Interview with a younger Zuckerberg. In 2009, Zuckerberg was already trying to rewrite Facebook's founding story from the "Hot or Not"-like app to "When I started Facebook from my dorm room in 2004, the idea that my roommates and I talked about all the time was a world that was more open": Fred Vogelstein, "The Wired Interview: Facebook's Mark Zuckerberg," *Wired*, 29 June 2009.
[17] This is known as Dunbar's number.

world, the equivalent of *why, why, why*, is *who, who, who*. Who backs up your claims? Today, three dominant identity proxies exist: the *Passport* issued by governments, *Social Login* like the Facebook login, and *Reputation* build on platforms such as Airbnb and Uber. In this chapter we will discuss each identity proxy in turn and evaluate their suitability for the complex needs of modern-day society.

Passport Proxy

Three main flaws hunt the passport proxy. Firstly, although its content is standardised, interpretation is not. Secondly, if a centralised entity, namely a government, has a monopoly on the issuance of passports, the vulnerabilities of this government become the vulnerabilities of all associated identity. Trust is derived from its root. Vulnerabilities include the questions of who to turn to when a central institution goes rogue or, what will a passport mean when the issuing government collapses. Lastly, the passport is a relic from the early 20th century, and its physical origin not equipped for daily use in an increasingly digital world.

The first passport proxy flaw is voluntary interpretation. You could claim you are you whilst waving your passport, which a government issued, because an administrator signed off on it, based on laws politicians created, representing nations whose borders were shaped in wars and changed at least once over the last century. If that sounds a bit arbitrary, maybe that is because it is. Arbitrary enough to leave room for interpretation. Extending the question game, we could ask; who is leading your government? Does the government as a body, and the officials making up that body, adhere to an ideology the verifying party agrees with? If not, how much value is placed on the government's attestations? In some cases, it can even be a red flag. Syria, Lebanon, Libya, Kuwait, Iran, Iraq, Pakistan and Saudi Arabia are all among the countries that do not accept passports with an Israeli stamp in them. Two countries could look at the same passport and see either a friend or a foe.

Centralisation is the second flaw. Thinking about potential implications of a monopoly on issuing passports is not something most do on a daily basis. That is, until they are affected. Take the conflicts in Syria, for example. Before the bombs started to go off March 2011, Syrian citizens – like many of us – would have taken government-issued passports for granted. However, the multi-sided armed conflict in Syria is still ongoing at time of writing, and civilians are caught in the middle of the various domestic and foreign allies and forces. What does their passport mean now their government has collapsed?

In September 2015, German chancellor Angela Merkel famously reacted to the European-wide refugee crisis by opening the German borders to Syrian refugees with the words *"wir schaffen das"* – we will manage. This eventually meant that Germany welcomed over one million refugees.[cvi] Of course, due to one of the founding principles of the EU being freedom of movement, this had implications for the rest of the European member states. To get to Germany, many refugees had to travel through mainland Europe. Often on foot, routes started in Greece or Italy, leading through the Balkans and Austria before arriving at their destination. At every border, identities needed to be verified.

Several things happened all at once. When it became clear Germany could not manage after all, a call for solidarity was made to other EU members to take in Syrian refugees. Meanwhile, the appeal of the European opportunity and welfare system spread beyond refugees. Economic migrants from countries such as

Afghanistan and Iraq also became part of the mix. Because those with a Syrian nationality experienced better odds of getting accepted, many falsely claimed to hold Syrian nationality. This kick-started a prolific black market in Syrian passports. Those who could not get their hands on a falsified passport simply claimed their papers were lost. The Syrian government was not functioning as it ought, and was therefore not in a position to respond to the volume of these claims. This is why when genuine Syrian refugees applied for asylum, many cruelly had trouble proving that they were actually entitled to refugee status, and deserved protection.[cvii]

Another complication was that economic migrants sometimes altered their final destination mid-journey, deciding the odds were better in for example France instead of Germany. Lacking verified information to go on, European countries responded in one of two ways: accepting, or rejecting, all. The identification crisis frustrated proper handling of the refugee crisis. This resulted in brutal generalisation, politically, but also in public opinion.

After the horrors of war, those Syrians who were granted asylum tried to rebuild their lives. However, facts about themselves they knew to be true did not always translate to these foreign environments. From doctors whose diplomas were not recognised to professors not allowed to teach at schools and lawyers who could not obtain a licence to practice law, many refugees struggled to prove they had the qualifications they claimed to have. Because the root of their identification – their passport – was "corrupted", any attestation they build on top of it also decreased in value.

This problem is wider than just Syria. Over one billion people worldwide have no documents.[cviii] Without a formal identity you cannot vote. Without a formal iden-tity you cannot get a job. Cryptography pioneer

Christopher Allen visualised this conundrum as follows. The French philosopher René Descartes famously said *"cogito ergo sum"*. I think, therefore I am. The previous highlights the absurdity of the identification question. It suggests a person can lose his or her very identity if a state revokes credentials. I think, but I am not. No papers, no prospects.[cix]

Another example of what could happen when a government is not functioning as it ought is Venezuela. After the new President Nicholás Maduro assumed power in April 2013 instability in Venezuela imploded. Faced with sky-high inflation many tried to leave. A scramble for passports ensued. The wait was months, sometimes even years. The process is complicated, expensive and sometimes illegal. Many have reported being asked for bribes up to $1,000, which could rise to $5,000 if the applicant had urgent reasons to leave, such as wanting to visit a sick family member abroad. Once a passport expires when abroad there is no route to extending it, leaving searching Venezuelans stuck in limbo.[cx]

When the government says no, who do you turn to? In Myanmar, nationality is based on membership of one of 135 "national races" that are said to have lived within the country's boundaries before the British invaded in 1824. The law, created by Myanmar's military dictatorship in 1982, excludes others from full citizenship but allows them to apply for two lower tiers with fewer rights. The result can be years of waiting for those who do not fit obviously into the list of national races, including ethnic Chinese, Indians, Nepalese and people with a foreign parent or grandparent. Humans Rights Watch reports restrictions on freedom of movement, discriminatory limitations on access to education and arbitrary confiscation of property. The UNHCR warns that over 12 million people worldwide are stateless. These extremes again illustrate how foggy our notions of citizenship really are.[cxi]

Millionaires, however, are rarely stateless. Actually, there is a legal market for passports. For example, countries like Malta and the US essentially sell citizenship — the former currently for upwards of $700,000, the latter for significant investments. In the US one green card category includes foreign nationals who have invested or are actively in the process of investing one million dollars in a new commercial enterprise (or $500,000 in targeted employment areas) that will benefit the US economy and create at least 10 full-time positions for qualifying employees.[cxii]

All in all, identity is a measure for rights, and the examples above show that today just governments alone are not reliable enough to base those rights on. Governments can collapse, as happened in Syria. Governments can deteriorate, as shown in Venezuela. Governments can openly target minorities, as is happening in Myanmar. Governments can have financial motives, as evidenced by Malta and the US. Because nobody can predict the future, nobody can know with certainty which parts of the world will find themselves in these situations in 2050 or 2100. Depending on country of origin, a passport may grant us extreme privilege or extreme distress. To this day, these flaws have been ignored, or at best insufficiently addressed. A recent development, however, cannot be ignored, bringing us to the third and final flaw.

The way we live and use our identity has changed rapidly – too rapidly – to be reflected by a system of identification that was set up a century ago and has in essence remained unchanged. During the First World War, the passport emerged as the international standard for people, nation states and companies to determine if somebody was who they said they were. Even though the methods of verification were centralised, top-down and opaque, trust in nation states was high enough for this approach to enjoy wide acceptance. Up until the late 1980s, that was the way the cookie crumbled. The passport system kind of worked, and there was little reason to change the system. But as we have transitioned from handling transactions in the "physical" world to the digital world, it has become necessary to add another layer to our identities. How can we prove that we are who we say we are – and protect our own digital identities at the same time?

The Missing Layer

Because our world has changed so rapidly, these questions have become a matter of urgency: we are on a deadline. Filling the identity gap in the Internet cannot be put off. Markets are growing more connected every day and transaction speeds quicken rapidly. The volume of transactions is already immense: the payment network Visa handles an average of 150,000,000 transactions a day.[cxiii] On the 10th edition of Chinese Single's Day, or "Valentine's Day for singles", Alibaba grossed $30.8 billion, of which $1 billion was hit in one minute and 25 seconds. Just a year later, the 11th edition grossed $38.3 billion (268.4 billion yuan).[cxiv] As transactions increase in volume and complexity, trust becomes a crucial factor. For those transactions to be trusted, the identities behind these transactions must be trusted. Adding further urgency, as the Developing Countries enter the computer age, digital citizenship becomes a route to greater access to human rights and to the global economy.

As in the physical world, we need proxies to function in the online world. The wild success of the tech giants underscores just how urgent, lucrative and important filling the Internet's identity gap really is. The race of proxies is the race to (exclusively) capture elements of you. The motivation behind the scenes varies with players and applications. While governments issued passports in the early 20th century to keep track of people, Facebook and others introduced social login to ultimately increase advertising revenue. Shortly after, the likes of Airbnb introduced the concept of reputation to more efficiently share high-value assets. The world right now is making do with an odd mix of 19th, 20th and 21st century identities. Today's situation is not clear-cut, and as a consequence confused nations and corporations conflate driver's licences, social security cards and online data profiles with identity.

Social Login Proxy

So, what precisely is it that makes online identity so different and difficult? Because the Internet cannot identify people, websites and applications must do that job. A void never stays a void. The first initiative to fill this void came from Microsoft, back in 1999. The "Microsoft Passport" first introduced the concept of "federated identity". Federated identity allowed users to utilise the same identity on multiple sites. Today, there is a Facebook-you to log in on your dating app, a Google-you to log in on your Gmail and a LinkedIn-you to apply for a job. These login proxies are called "social logins". The social login method comes with promising benefits, but also structural limitations.

Why the Facebook social login, first introduced in 2013, took off, is obvious in hindsight. The promise of better user experience, speedy onboarding and customisable data permissions was an unprecedented and unbeatable combination. Yet the main ingenuity was the need to only remember one password. On average, people have up to 90 online accounts. Joint-research by MasterCard and the University of Oxford found that a quarter of Internet users forgets at least one password per day and one third of online transactions are abandoned at checkout due to forgotten passwords.[cxv] To stop forgetting, many opt for passwords that are easy to remember, like a birthday or a dog's name. Cybersecurity expert Kevin Mitnick discovered that the domain user password of the CEO of Sony (hacked in 2014 by North Korea), Michael Lynton, was "sonyml3".[cxvi] On the other hand, even a high-complexity password is pointless when cross used across every service. LinkedIn was hacked in 2012, and what initially seemed to be a theft of 6.5 million passwords turned out to be a breach of 117 million. This "minor" detail was confirmed in 2016, four years after the fact. Tumblr had a similar episode, where three years in it turned out that over 65 million unique email addresses lay exposed, now floating on the dark web.[cxvii] Using one social login, such as Facebook, was arguably safer than this Wild West patchwork of username-password systems. Of course, Google and others followed suit with their own solutions. Today, millions of applications offer social login as an option, and many more millions of people choose this option on a daily basis.

Next to speedy onboarding, personalisation and standardised data collection, trust is another benefit. According to University of Oxford fellow Rachel Botsman, the real perk of social login is its ability to unlock value of already established connections. *Who do you know that I know?* Trust in one group or context can spread to another. The degree of separation on Facebook is merely 3.5 people. It illuminates why dating apps such as Tinder and Bumble have such strong ties to the Facebook social login. The same social validation is applied to LinkedIn. *Who do I know that works here?* Trust in a friend could then transfer to trust in their ability to pick a desirable, ethical company to work for. Or, inversely, a company to avoid at all costs.

However, using social log-in comes with its own risks. Users and applications alike are now depending on the parties offering the infrastructure behind social logins. When there are unforeseen changes, issues arise. In 2018, for instance, Tinder crashed when Facebook updated its data policy. This can lead to widespread problems when today social login is so prevalent that without it many apps do not work. In fact, many apps offer this option only, limiting your choice of logging in to choose between Facebook, Twitter, LinkedIn or Gmail.

All reasons to closer examine how social login works. Facebook login is marketed as *"a secure, fast and convenient way for users to log into your app, and for your app to ask for permission to access data"*. For example, an app can request access to a name and profile photo. Social login is based on the logic behind "OAuth 2.0". Typically, OAuth 2.0 works with tokens. When an app uses the respective API to authenticate someone it receives a temporary "access token".[cxviii] What is omitted is that by connecting login patterns via its API, "Facebook-the-platform" knits a detailed be- havioural network beyond the reach of any individual app. This holds true for most social login platforms; may it be Facebook and Microsoft's LinkedIn in the West or Tencent's WeChat and Sina's Weibo in the East. In some nations like India, where Facebook has a whopping 260 million users, Facebook also gathered passport and Aadhar details, the government-run identity database, alongside phone numbers.[cxix] This is important for two reasons. For many of these people the internet *is* Face- book. Also, it is illustrative of how social login providers carefully and deliberately extend their reach further and further into the identity realm.

Although convenience, outlined above, is the domi- nant narrative, there is another which warrants our attention: fragmented identity. Under social login, our identity only exists when we are logged in. LinkedIn-you is only accessible when logged onto LinkedIn. Stop using the application and the associated digital existence becomes meaningless. The model is funda-mentally context dependent. To the platforms de-ploying these social logins this is a good thing, creating "lock-in" effects. The user, however, is left with fragments of themselves scattered across different organisations.

Withdrawal of access is another symptom of fragmentation that users face as a consequence of using social logins. Recently, users successfully fought for the right to download existing data. But even as you download the data surrounding the Facebook-you, you cannot easily copy it to the Snapchat-you. We can access data, but not move it. If we struggle with this, how can we even start untangling personal information from the web? You cannot unscramble a cake to retrieve an egg. Let's pause on this for a moment: you cannot easily find what you are looking for, or move what you need to move, or delete data you might prefer to delete, because the infrastructure is not built around you. Surprisingly, the infrastructure is also not built around companies. The duplicated costs of collecting, storing and protecting data in parallel to the liability associated with holding such data runs into the many millions and billions.

Noting the above, there is one more narrative to be considered, and this happens to revolve around the most powerful argument against social login. Social log-in fails to capture one crucial, but often overlooked factor: if the people behind the users are real. On their development website Facebook outlines, *"when people choose to login with Facebook, they can share their real identity through their public profile."* People *can* share their real identity. Facebook does not deploy thorough background checks, or any checks for that matter, when a "person", or rather a new user, signs up. The only exception and hard requirement is a check against duplicate email addresses. If the Russian interference in the US presidential election taught us one bitter lesson, this is that it is entirely possible to create fake profiles on Facebook or any other social platform. Social login merely shifts the burden of authentication to another centralised point, making the generous assumption that information hosted there is true.

The combination of these limitations with the pay-off of getting it right, is why Apple's announcement early 2019 that it intended to compete in the identity trenches caused quite a stir. "Sign in with Apple" is a decided break with its predecessors in one way, and a tired continuation of the status quo in another. The proposed features read like a user-friendly best practices list: two-factor authentication is automatically enabled, frequent reauthentication, data collection is limited to name and email address, no cross tracking and the possibility to verify real personhood. The critical difference with its peers is this: users creating accounts have the option of using a unique email address per service, breaking that key link to their data profiles wherever they are housed. This is a deliberate, strategic move, as Apple is not dependent on advertisements to make a profit. It again illustrates that incentives shape outcomes. The most exciting part is that, because of the edge processing (on-device processing, Chapter 9) of biometric data, Apple could verify personhood. Lastly, two-factor authentication (2FA) is a security tool that requires a user's password as well as an additional form of authorisation. This combines something you know; – your password – with something you have; such as your phone). Despite its advantages, penetration for 2FA remains low: Google, for example, reports that over 90 percent of Gmail users do not use 2FA. Making this native to Sign in with Apple could be a gamechanger and jump-start adoption. On balance, Sign in with Apple could be a more privacy-compliant solution for users, developers and companies.[cxx]

However, there is a footnote to this remark. Apparently, Apple is going to leverage its monopoly position as app provider on the iPhone to force app developers (who currently use 3rd party solutions) to integrate. Centralisation as a strategy. Furthermore, it is a conduit, not a complete, portable identity proxy. Moving data across services will still meet friction. Lastly, apps installed on iPhones are still connected to the cloud. Addressing linkability over underlying practices, Apple is making a noble effort to solve the wrong problem. In sum, Sign in with Apple is a silo of a different sort, minus the exploitation. Instead of trying to make a centralised login service more privacy-friendly, why not do away with the "man in the middle" model altogether?

We have seen that a free flow of data is impossible when silos are a key part of social infrastructure. The more frequently a certain social login is used, the more useful it becomes, the more data is captured centrally, and the more likely a centralised artificial intelligence capability becomes. Recalling privacy and security vulnerabilities of centralised control from the previous chapter, this is undesirable when looking to maximise social good. But social login is not the only digital identity proxy on offer. At the core of the success of the sharing economy lies the ability to inspire millions of individuals to trust each other. If federated identification is social login under OAuth 2.0, distributed identification is reputation as a proxy. But what does our reputation say about us?

Reputation Proxy

A core ingredient to share high value assets, such as a car on Uber or house on Airbnb, is trust. Can I trust you if I do not know who you are, and if so, what is that trust based on? The true innovation of the sharing economy is the concept of distributed trust. In lieu of comprehensive background checks, trust is outsourced to a large number of people to determine each other's trustworthiness. This means offloading individual cognitive power in favour of collective trust.[cxxi] Also called reputation, this is the coordinating mechanism which allows companies to organise communities of strangers at scale. However useful, it is important to keep in mind that reputation is not a perfect proxy. Reputation is *Subjective*, subject to fear of *Social Retribution*, *Free*, *Unforgiving* and *Not Portable*.

Let's consider these aspects one by one. First of all, reputation is Subjective. Similar to social login, sharing platforms tend to use an email address as a base line. Actions in the offline world impact online reputation scores. Are you a "good" passenger? Five stars. Is your house "clean" and banter "chippy"? Four stars. Did you deliver the food in a "speedy" manner? Five stars. Where reputation starts to fall apart is that all assessments like "good", "clean", "chippy" and "speedy" are subjective assessments. What peer-to-peer reputation really means is: *How much do I like this person*? What is left is an emotion-driven popularity contest. The default becomes: the more "likes", the more likely you are right.

A second characteristic is the fear of Social Retribution. When completing an Uber ride, a frequently heard phrase is *I will give you five stars, if you give me five stars*. Not holding up your end of the bargain could result in a rancorous, and much dreaded, one-star rating. This fear of retribution is why holiday-goers sometimes rate messy Airbnb's as "five-star clean" or reward rude drivers with "five-star service". As a result, a high reputation means increasingly little. Uber drivers with high ratings have committed crimes ranging from rape in India to murder in America. Across 2.3 billion US Uber trips in 2017 and 2018, there were 1,150 instances of *"Non-Consensual Kissing of a Non-Sexual Body Part"*, 575 occurrences of *"Attempted Non-Consensual Sexual Penetration"*, 2,875 reports on *"Instances of Non-*

Consensual Touching of a Sexual Body Part", 766 cases of *"Non-Consensual Kissing of a Sexual Body Part"*, and 460 situations of *"Non-Consensual Sexual Penetration"*, or rape.[cxxii] In addition to the total of 5,826 sexual assaults, *"Fatal Physical Assault"*, or murder, was recorded 19 times. The cost of relying on incorrect or incomplete reputation can be high. Once the rater is anonymised, like on the holiday hub TripAdvisor, there is a noticeable uptick in brutal reviews. No social retaliation; no consequences.

A third limitation is that reputation is Free. There is no cost to gaming the system. Drove your Uber rating through the floor? Simply sign up with a new email address. Uber has been stripped of its London licence after authorities found that more than 14,000 trips were taken with drivers who had faked their identity on the firm's app.[cxxiii] With the perceived value of reputation increasing it is also becoming more attractive to give it a little push. Buying fake reviews is one example. On TripAdvisor, a non-existent restaurant called "The Shed" was temporarily the highest ranked restaurant in London. Absurdly, "The Shed" was an actual shed. All reviews were faked and the photos of delicacies on the menu included a photo of the prankster's heel dubbed as a loaf of white bread.[18] What connects all these observations is that reputation is not, and can never become, the only identity currency, because the system can be gamed.

Fourth, if perfectly equal, reputation would be meaningless as a differentiator, but if you cannot leave unfavourable reputation behind, reputation can be un-

---

[18] The bizarre account of how prankster Oobah Butler made his shed the #1 restaurant on TripAdvisor: Oobah Butler, "I Made My Shed the Top-Rated Restaurant on TripAdvisor," *Vice*, 6 December 2017. Next, Butler worked on a fake fashion brand, Georgio Peviani and, through a talent for SEO and theatre, managed to get it into Paris Fashion Week.

comfortably Unforgiving. Creating winners and losers is part of the system by design. Add to that that reputation is backward-looking with forward-facing consequences and bad reputation trails could follow someone for the rest of their life. Experiments such as the Chinese social credit system are already attaching hard consequences to soft values. To be fair, the social credit system takes into account more than just peer-to-peer based assessments, and by interlacing binary variables such as repayment terms it is arguably more reliable and robust than its Airbnb or Uber counterparts. However, according to University of Oxford fellow Botsman, the gamification of obedience could lead to social pressures not seen since the Cold War, stamping out individualism and leading to more sameness.[cxxiv] The app Xeuxi Qiangguo (which roughly means "Know Your Strong Country") promotes party leader Xi Jinping and the communist party, and is used by more than a hundred million Chinese citizens to rack up points.[cxxv] When reputation is linked to eligibility, the stakes are raised. And when the stakes are raised sufficiently, there will come a point where people will start pretending to hold onto their rights.

Finally, for all its benefits and flaws, online reputation is Not Portable across platforms yet. Reputation exists within platforms, reminiscent of the previously mentioned centralisation and lock-in effects of social login strategy. A ban means lost access to services and social capital, as experienced by a man named Jackson Cunningham back in 2018.[cxxvi] A bad Airbnb review resulted in a life-long ban for Cunningham. The review in question was contestable and the holiday-goer did not agree with the conclusion drawn, but to no avail. The Airbnb response included language such as *"we are not obligated to provide an explanation"* and *"this decision will not be reversed"*. What this story illustrates is that not only there is no appeal process to contest the input of reputation scores, there is also no mechanism in place to contest actions taken based on those scores. If access to the reputation proxy is disabled by the provider, all value associated with that identity is lost.

The reputation-based approach is not doomed, but most certainly incomplete. As it stands, neither the passport, social login nor reputation proxy are equipped to deal with the complexities of modern-day identity. Firstly, the passport proxy is plagued by voluntary interpretation, a single point of failure, and a physical nature not equipped for the digital world. Secondly, the social login proxy is characterised by silos, fragmented identity, limited checks and balances and limited data ownership. Thirdly, the reputation proxy is by nature subjective, vulnerable to social retribution, free, unforgiving, and not portable. Since the status quo is inadequate and unsustainable, this gives us the licence to reboot identity.

A Blank Canvas

These three proxies were not designed to serve individuals, but to realise capitalistic gains in the case of companies and to exercise control in the case of governments. They are not meeting the basic pre-conditions of 21st century identity: data autonomy, equity and privacy. Autonomy is left wanting across the board, the underlying incentive structure is fundamentally misaligned and the privacy burden to use the Internet is unfairly placed on people. The confusion between identities such as driver's licences, pictures of passports and online equivalents contributes to the chaos and reinforces the status quo.

These proxies are not merely insufficient; the institutions offering these tools are also impermanent. Governments are impermanent. Companies are impermanent. Platforms are impermanent. The pressures of modern-day identity force companies, regulators and people alike to become experts. Today's chaos gives us the licence to take a blank canvas, remember what we learnt, and pick the proper brush for the job.

Part One of this book, *Chaos*, discussed power and profit optimisation games. Based on the challenges identified in *Chaos*, the identity meta-system must adhere to the following solution requirements. Firstly, all humans must be able to identify themselves in a way which is portable, secure and robust: autonomy of being (Chapter 6: The Sovereign Individual). Secondly, all humans must be able to access independent information of high integrity in order to form an opinion: autonomy of thought (Chapter 7: Information Wars). Thirdly, all humans have the right to consent, recourse and discourse when faced with algorithmic decisions: autonomy of reason (Chapter 8: Algorithmic Truths). Fourth, data must be collected, processed and combined in a manner which is beneficial to society and the individuals compromising that society in equal measure: data equity (Chapter 9: Liberating Data). And fifth, as data resides at the heart of societal and geopolitical trade-offs, the weighing of these dilemmas needs to be explicitly discussed: data privacy (Chapter 10: The New Social Contract).

As the next part will showcase, the unrealised potential of decentralised identity is vast. What should identity look like in an increasingly online world? How will this influence how we interact (Chapter 6)? How can we combat the toxic stew of fake news, fake people and deep fakes? Is coordinated inauthentic activity merely a nuisance or something more (Chapter 7)? What happens when humans lose the monopoly on reason? What can and should we do when "the computer says no" (Chapter 8)? How can we stop paying the privacy taxes dominating our online interactions? Does humanity need personalisation or privacy (Chapter 9)? Who will win the battle for human preferences, predictions and actions? How will values clash geopolitically, and what are the stakes (Chapter 10)?

Part One showed that mistakes have been made. An unprecedented problem requires an unprecedented solution, including a rethink of certain dynamics of society. With that in mind, Part Two, *Reboot* aims to navigate these uncharted waters to explore: *what might an identity meta-system for the 21ˢᵗ century look like?*

II

REBOOT

Who will win the battle for
human preferences, predictions & actions?

*What happens when humans lose
the* **monopoly on reason**?

Does humanity need
personalisation *or* **privacy**?

6. The Sovereign Individual

"If modern society has always been supposed to be individualistic, only now perhaps is the individual emerging as a social force to be reckoned with."
- Keith Hart[xxvii]

In the feudal system, those who worked the lands shared their yield in exchange for the protection of those who owned the lands. In the 21st century, those browsing the web receive proxies from the platforms owning the most complete versions of their online identity, i.e. social login and reputation. Land exploitation and data exploitation, both necessitated via an offer impossible to refuse. Eventually the feudal system weakened when the farmers migrated to cities, searching greener pastures. The digital parallel is different: rather than migrating to other websites and services, I propose that individuals should be able to use those same services, but detangle their identity. You do not need a proxy if you own the whole thing. What if we could create a form of *Self-Sovereign Identity*? Self-Sovereign Identity (SSI), as used in this book, is based on five laws.

1. *Digital identity is a human right;*
2. *Digital identity is a public good, provided without profit to all members of the society for the well-being of the public;*
3. *Governments are responsible for foundational identity;*
4. *The private and public sector provide value through contextual identity;*
5. *Things must have an identity to be accountable.*[19]

A self-sovereign individual has the power to project attestations about him or herself, reimagining identity as a web of relationships. You are different things to different people, so why should the person to connect the dots not be you? Re-centring the human model of identity around the individual promises a radically different paradigm of interaction. Accepting this shift implies that profit and power optimisation games must also evolve. Acknowledging this principle would not only mean endorsing a new way forward, but would inversely imply, looking back, that mistakes have been made. Nobody wants to be on the wrong side of history. Vested interest is behind justifying the status quo: the combined market capitalisation of the AI leaders Google, Microsoft, Amazon, Facebook, Tencent, Baidu and Alibaba far exceed the nominal GDP of every country in the world, save China and the US. Luckily, facts do not stop being facts just because they are

---

[19] When proposing the first draft of the Identity Meta-System in 2005, Kim Cameron proposed 7 laws: 1: User control and consent. 2. Minimal disclosure for a constrained use. 3. Justifiable parties. 4. Directed identity. 5. Pluralism of operators and technologies. 6. Human integration. 7. Consistent experience across contexts. The value-add of this summation for the work on SSI which followed cannot be overstated. Now, over a decade later, the 5 laws proposed in this book are focused on how SSI could work in modern society.

inconvenient, and all signs point to the fact that data privacy needs to be reimagined for the 21st century.

A reimagined system has to be global, open and extend in all directions, with the appropriate configurations for every relationship. For a long time, building this solution was too complex and required too many resources. This was true – until now. The time has come to do better. This chapter will focus on the first building block of the identity meta-system: the autonomy of being. In turn, we will first discuss a mechanism for self-sovereign identity, followed by breaking down its components (identification, authentication, authorisation), and finally we will focus on the identity of things.

Digital Keystone

The Caribbean island of St. Maarten (St. Martin) has not been the same since Hurricane Irma breached its shores on 6 September 2017, bringing winds of 180 miles per hour (nearly 300 kilometres). All in all, Irma caused as much as three billion dollars in damage and losses. This storm, the strongest hurricane since hurricane Wilma in 2005, upended the daily lives of many of its residents. International relief came pouring in but distributing relief to those who needed it proved challenging. Food vouchers took the form of slips of paper and were physically distributed. Errors, both human and bureaucratic, carried unpleasant consequences. Lose your piece of paper, lose your right to eat. You will get another chance next week.[cxxviii]

Restoring human dignity in these types of crisis situations lies at the heart of self-sovereign identity. What if you, the individual, could create and control claims about yourself? Let's examine the following example. John is a resident of St. Maarten (claim) and owner of a fish restaurant (claim). Imagine that John writes these facts on a piece of paper and stores these in a secured vault. Naturally, such unshared information is of limited utility, particularly if the only person backing up these claims is John himself. However, the more parties confirm these claims as facts, and the higher the trustworthiness of these verifiers, the more weight John's claims carry. What if John could open the vault to verifiers he chooses to assess the validity of his claims? This way, when the Red Cross or any other relief agency distributes aid, John could prove without a doubt that he is indeed eligible for food vouchers and could even claim damage compensation for his restaurant. Building a digital version of this solution is already possible today. The answer lies in the much discussed, and often poorly understood, distributed ledger technologies, widely known as blockchain.

The solution to this and similar challenges is a blockchain powered self-sovereign *Identity Triangle*. The three sides of the triangle are attestations, authentication and authorisation.[cxxix] More often than not, blockchain explanations are guilty of being long-winded and inaccessible. A shame, and furthermore completely unnecessary. It is especially regrettable because blockchain applications in the identity field are straightforward and clean-cut. In a nutshell, if claims (attestations) are verified (authenticated), this empowers somebody to do things (authorisation).

It is key that these verifiable attestations are fully under the control of the identity owner, independent from any centralised registry or authority.[cxxx] In other words: decentralised. In a decentralised system, many parties offer many features, granting many individuals the power to make many verifiable claims. This multitude of verifiable claims unleashes the right of self-determination for everyone. Self-sovereign identity could become the keystone for human interaction in the 21st century.

Do You See What I See?

Of course, this is a large claim which requires a deeper understanding of the three sides of the triangle. First is a closer look at attestations, followed by authentication and authorisation.

There are three kinds of attestations, or claims, that need to be differentiated: *Inherent*, *Assigned* and *Accumulated*.[cxxxi] The first kind, Inherent, describes those attributes that cannot be altered. Such inherent attestations are permanent, just like the date of birth is inherent to every individual. This also applies to place of birth, age and fingerprints. Either a claim is true, or it is not. A student is old enough to drink, or she is not. The elderly couple qualifies for reduced transportation fares, or they do not. Because these types of attestations never change there is little room for conflict in their authentication process.

Assigned attestations, however, describe relationship -based attributes. A government might, for example, assign citizenship. A person tends to be a citizen of at least one country. That is not to say this country cannot change. After immigrating, new citizenship can be requested according to the rules of the new home country. On verification, the old claim is then severed. Assigned verified claims thus need to be portable and robust but not necessarily permanent. In the words of the author Gertrude Stein: *"What good are roots if you cannot take them with you"?*[cxxxii] In an ideal scenario, multiple parties underwrite the same attestation to reduce the risk of a single point of failure. For example, multiple verifiers would make the forced displacement of citizens an easier target of international criticism and, hopefully, more preventable.

Behavioural claims fall in the last category: accumulated attestations. Throughout life you make meaningful choices and experiences that are specific to you. These choices or encounters include elements such as education and healthcare. Some behavioural claims are built up over time, such as moving through the schooling systems to obtain diplomas. Others are with us for shorter periods. For example, there might come a day when smoking becomes part of somebody's health record. There might also come a day when the last cigarette has been put out.

The sum of these claims or attestations is stored in an "identity portfolio". Every assigned claim in an individual's identity portfolio is either explicitly given or purposely requested. In the blockchain world, these identity portfolios are called "wallets". Wallet rules are customisable and extensible. For example, a wallet could be set up to hold multiple phone numbers for one person, but only one nationality. Another configuration could be to store multiple addresses, but only one spouse. Because the logic in wallets is extensible, like building with Lego blocks, codeable functionality makes combinations of countless expressions possible.

Wholly unprecedented, self-sovereign identity grants individuals the opportunity to hold the complete body of attestations relevant to them at their fingertips. Portable sub-identities, tailored to the situation at hand, will disrupt established interaction patterns. The spoke-like structure of these sub-identities creates the opportunity for themed applications, such as credit scores or medical history, allowing for selective data sharing. Disclosing medical information on blood pressure when applying for a job sounds preposterous, because it is obviously completely irrelevant. When the relevant requirements have been met, why provide redundant information at all? Need-to-know disclosure could push open the door to colour-blind, gender-blind and age-blind opportunities. If requirements are hard-coded in a service, self-sovereign identity could serve as a merit-based digital megaphone free from discrimination. When eligibility criteria are transparent, the path towards meeting these criteria is clearer (and less intimidating) than as to when they are obscured. Just as humans have a right to be forgotten, they have a right to be seen.

Interestingly, a multitude of identity satellites could live in the same identity universe. Demonstrating eligibility for a subsidy programme and opening a bank account are clearly different actions. A single relying party, like the bank extending the subsidy, will want to accept more than one kind of identity, and a user, like the subsidy applicant, will want to understand his or her options to select the best identity for that context. Having this option invites dreams of easy to navigate bureaucracy, fair process and reduced overcollection of information.

However, because of its broad application base – human resources, healthcare, e-commerce, and education, to name a few – all claims must constitute of objective, verifiable facts. While some claims, such as your place of birth, phone number or university degree can be easily verified, this does not always apply to reputational claims. There is a big difference between inalienable rights, as set forth in the US Constitution, and an opinion about your eligibility for a right, as the Chinese credit system proposes. Reputation could inform eligibility, but it always needs to be as part of a larger set of requirements. This distinction is essential as it serves as a reminder that identity is closely related to rights. As a citizen of the US, you would not expect to lose your right to vote without an explanation. Yet this is exactly what happened in 2016, when the New York City Board of Elections confirmed that more than 125,000 voters in Brooklyn were removed from voter rolls. The Board of Elections offered no adequate explanation as to why.[cxxxiii] This example illustrates why blockchain technologies can add immense value to otherwise flawed systems. Because data on the blockchain is shared, the verification of eligibility is auditable. Consequently, malicious intent will be exposed in the harsh light of transparency. Again, facts will not stop being facts just because they are inconvenient to powerful gatekeepers. But how can we separate fact from fiction? This is where the second side of the self-sovereign identity triangle comes in: authentication.

Stamp of Approval

Before a stamp of approval is given, two pieces of information are needed to authenticate the claim. Does the individual actually hold the verifiable claim (attestation) in question? And has this claim been authenticated?

Think of a medieval castle, owned by you, a respected knight. In every room of the castle, you hide one verified attestation, a piece of parchment that proves when pieces of land were conquered by your family over the decades. Every room is locked individually, and the castle gate is locked with a master key. However, there is one particularly annoying neighbouring knight who challenges your claim to some of your lands. Luckily the proof is safely locked away in room #1. What do you do? Do you hand over the master key to your rival so he can examine the room by himself? This would tie all attestations together, immediately exclusively identifying you by exposing all the lands that you own. Alternatively, you could only provide the key to room #1. If your rival then shares the key with your enemies, anyone holding the key could unlock the room. A dilemma presents itself: how can you share a secret? The answer, surprisingly, does not just require one key, but four.

Suddenly, your medieval castle becomes virtual. You now own two digital keys: one is public, one is private, and so does our rival. These keys come with two rules: your private key is extremely private and never shown to anyone, while your public key works as your digital signature, visible to everyone looking for it. Together, both keys are part of your personal encryption arsenal. When the goal is to share a secret, you can now do so in several steps. The first step is to exchange public keys. You now hold your rival's public key and your own private key. Next, you retrieve the verified attestation of the land deeds and encrypt this with your rival's public key and your own private key. Once you have encrypted your claim, you share it with your rival. Now the magic truly begins. The knight takes his private key to decrypt the message and verifies that it originated from you using your public key. The result is success on both counts. Congratulations! You just proved that you own the claim, while keeping the claim secret, because it is only visible to your rival. And, coincidentally, this just so happens to describe one kind of cryptography among many.

Now that the claim in question has been attributed to the individual (you just successfully shared your claim to the plot of land), the next question is if the shared claim has been authenticated (is the claim verified). Claiming something with confidence does not make it true. In the First World War, the Germans disguised one of their ships as a British ship, the RMS Carmania, and sent it out to ambush British vessels. In a hilariously bad stroke of luck, the first ship it encountered was the real RMS Carmania, which promptly sank the German imposter ship.[cxxxiv]

It is also worth stressing that "identification" does not equal "authentication". Identification is the process of establishing who an entity is within a given population or context, while authentication proves that a claim is verified. For example, consider the statement: *Sarah Zhou* is a *medical student* from *Shanghai*. For Sarah to prove she is indeed Sarah Zhou from Shanghai those claims need to be authenticated in turn, but to authenticate the claim *"I am from Shanghai"*, the "I" is irrelevant. Or consider a puppy; to prove the puppy is vaccinated, his name is irrelevant to the validity of that statement. If stamps of approval are selectively given, they can be precisely used. This approach is the opposite of how authentication is currently done. Common authentication methods, such as passwords, face or fingerprints, tend to be set up to exclusively identify a person before they are authenticated. For example, for Sarah to buy medical books online the site first verifies her general identity ("Sarah Zhou"), instead of the more precise claim ("medical student"). Blockchain takes an altogether different approach. To be exclusively identified all claims must be authenticated, but it does not require exclusive identification for a claim to be authenticated. One room does not unlock the entire castle.

Those entities who verify claims are the providers of the identity. In decentralised systems, there are many institutions and organisations that could be called "identity providers". Think of insurance companies, universities, medical practices, governments or any other entity playing an important role in the lives of many. When looking beyond those traditional means of proving identity, integrity is one crucial condition that has to be fulfilled. Here, blockchain technology has a clear advantage over other alternatives as it also comes with a distinct set of rules that ensures everyone plays nice.

Blockchain encourages collaboration because it is built on coordination: the rules that organise data cannot be circumvented, and each new data entry is connected to previous ones. In other words, blockchain is a collaboration tool because it is a coordination tool. The logic behind blockchain ensures that all involved parties work together in an organised, constructive way. Firstly, there can be no conflict with data already in the "database" (or, in blockchain terms, the "ledger"). The claim that somebody was born both in Korea and

Italy is mutually exclusive and thus inadmissible. Secondly, information stored is append-only. Every iteration is time-stamped, allowing anyone with the right permissions viewing the entries to understand changes over time. Data cannot be changed without recording the alteration, adding transparency that might be missing from more traditional systems. This immutability adds another layer of trust. Finally, everyone agrees on the state of the database (consensus) without a central party (decentralised). This effectively means arriving at a shared consensus on the data "state" without crowning a king. This decentralised nature bolsters censorship resistance. The combination of these characteristics earns blockchain the status of a foundational technology for the future.

This rule engine is critical.[20] Get it wrong and the alternative would be worse than merely "garbage in, garbage out". On blockchain, once garbage is in, garbage stays. Output and input require a logical, transparent correlation. Because this output is binary, i.e. something is either true or false, there is no excuse for two verifying parties to arrive at different conclusions.

This has several important implications for some of the most challenging issues in the current system. What would it mean for society if we could reduce identity fraud? How would our lives change if we could increase the reliability of identity at large? What would the Inter-

---

[20] In general, most blockchains have the following characteristics: 1) no conflicting entries, 2) append-only, and 3) decentralised consensus. The governance layer (the blockchain rule-engine), is where such and further characteristics are captured. The governance layer is comparable to a "constitution of the network". It frequently includes rules on how to vote to change the "network constitution".

net look like once we successfully remove fake users and fake reviews? These examples illustrate that the potential upside is massive. The commercial value and social benefits of verifying real personhood at scale cannot be overstated. One reason is that the current system cannot eliminate errors creeping in. On average, organisations suspect that nearly 30 percent of current customer or prospect data is inaccurate in some way. At the same time, identity fraud is increasing. Roughly three-in-ten Americans reported suffering from at least one of three kinds of major identity theft problems in the previous 12 months at the time of a 2018-2019 Pew survey.[cxxxv] Another issue is that some opportunities come with an incentive to lie. Over 85 percent of employers in the US report that they have caught candidates lying on their applications.[cxxxvi] Some data even suggests that, one-in-five job applicants falsely claim to hold a college degree. This is where the current system leaves room for foul play, as the ingredients for faking a diploma are known to be as simple as minor spelling alterations (for example "Stamford" instead of Stanford University), dubious accreditation institutions, and fake validation via fake faculty testimonials.[cxxxvii] There is a big difference between claiming to be a Harvard student, and Harvard University confirming that you did indeed graduate from this renowned institution.

Now, what would change if such claims could be verified by the educational institution in question? This would benefit the student, as it formally acknowledges their investment of time, effort and funds, as well as benefiting the university, as it combats false claims, protects institutional integrity and mitigates potential reputational damage. Likewise, companies profit from increased certainty if hiring managers can trust the data without the shadow of a doubt, reducing the need for circumstantial data greatly. This is a win-win-win situation. Finally, reducing fraud might also mitigate one of the main reasons used to justify the overcollection of data. If it becomes easier to use data for good, it will be easier to spot when this is not the case.

So far, we have established that next to being a right (Law 1), identity is a public good (Law 2). Based on this premise, foundational identity should be provided by the government to all citizens for the well-being of the public (Law 3). The private sector provides value, ranging from health care to education, through contextual identity, priced for functionality (Law 4). The combination of verified ownership of verified attestations is uniquely useful, as will be discussed in the next section on the final side of the triangle: authorisation.

The New Gatekeeper

Authorisation is the rule engine of the identity triangle. It grants individuals the autonomy to build their own relationships, as well as to determine the scope of those relationships. Likewise, the authorisation capability allows companies to set qualifying criteria for demonstrating eligibility. The result is an equilibrium of consent in a decentralised system. The ensuing balance makes the decentralised identity meta-system functional.

It encompasses several dimensions. The first dimension is relationships. As outlined in the previous chapter, currently used models represent and use relationships in diverging ways. In the federated identity model (using social logins for identification), Facebook and other social login solutions embody the spider in the web of interactions, observing the breadth, depth and width of all of your relationships through their many spider eyes. In the reputation model (in which distributed trust drives identification), relationships are limited to the platform, with few protections in place, as the Airbnb story illustrated. In the future, a blockchain-powered system could empower the identity holder to keep interactions with one party completely separate from any other party. This means that you become the spider. Rather than allowing an organisation which provides identity proxies to watch your interactions, you can take back the power to keep them as private as you would like. It is as if you, the spider, get to wear a different (spider-sized) hat in every relationship, displaying a selected version of yourself in every interaction. This illustrates the technical equivalent of being something different to every person. Additionally, and of great interest to both the public and the private sector, the information that is shared will most likely be updated accurately and in real-time because the root of trust will be on an individual level. This great separation of relationships is only one part of the story.

The super-power of revocation is the other part, making relationships multidimensional. Unlike the previous two models, in which cancelling your account severs your connection with every service where the proxy was used, revoking relationships under self-sovereign identity is at your discretion. Every self-sovereign identity solution includes some form of "revocation registry". The registry functions as a two-way black book. Identity providers and identity owners alike can use it to retract claims. For example, when a recently married woman takes her husband's last name and updates her "last name" attestation, the "root of trust" of all parties with approved access to this claim reflects this change. From her bank to her local council, this would save all involved hours and hours of paperwork. Or, when a data scientist loses her job at Google, Google then revokes its authentication of her employment status. This could be instantly communi-cated to tax authorities, or serve as a digital record for her next job. Identity becomes a two-way street.

The "Known Traveller Digital Identity" programme, an initiative born from the World Economic Forum, combines many of the solution components discussed in this chapter. The first pilot phase will focus on passport-less travel between Canada and the Netherlands. Selected partner organisations, such as airlines, receive a public identifier on the ledger. The passport authority reviews the traveller's attributes and issues an attestation to their digital wallet – kept on their phone for now – signed by the passport authority's private key. To verify this identity, participating organisations use the issuer's public key. The ledger also includes a revocation registry. The traveller can revoke participation at his or her discretion.[cxxxviii] If successful the programme is slotted to roll-out more broadly.

In addition to the great separation of relationships and the direction of identity (i.e. becoming a two-way street), its magnitude matters too. Some applications will require that third parties are authorised to access data selectively or to act on your behalf. These per-missions are then logged, as well as the terms, conditions and potential compensation. For example, providing access to health data might be granted to improve medical services while access to behavioural driving data could be exchanged for reduced insurance fees. Permissions can be tracked and revoked if necessary, expediting legal repercussions and encouraging compliance.

In sum, the identity triangle equips us to answer a series of questions. What must be true about an individual to complete the desired transaction (authorisation)? Can said eligibility be proven (authen-tication)? And, do the attributes presented genuinely belong to the entity that is presenting them (identification)? If the current forms of proving identity work like forcibly fitting a square peg in a round hole, the extensibility of self-sovereign identity bears closer resemblance to Play-Doh: it can be molded to the problem at hand. Fittingly, the same principles can be applied to tangible assets, bringing in the fifth and final law: things must have an identity to be accountable.

This Is Mine

If a person claims they own something, as described earlier in the example of the knight and his claim to a plot of land, there are three qualifying questions that have to be answered. Who is the person claiming ownership? What is the asset? And, what is the relationship between the two? Having already answered the first question above, we need to add a new piece to the identity puzzle for the second and third question: the identity of things.

Perhaps intuitively, to digitally prove ownership of a piece of land that land first needs to be represented in the digital realm. Just as a person is connected to his or her inherent attestations (such as age), a piece of land has inherent attestations as well (e.g. geographic coordinates). Assigned attestations are equally diverse. Yellowstone, for example, is a national park, designated as such by the federal government of the US. Similarly, blocks in Manhattan, New York City, are assigned to be residential areas, while, across the pond, areas in the busy city centre of London are assigned as retail ventures by the local council. Across the world, governments assign a variety of attributes to tangible assets in a similar fashion. Lastly, just as decisions and encounters shape the lives of people, events also affect the life cycle and value of things. Over time, a piece of land could "receive" the right to develop real estate, increasing its cumulative value. By layering inherent, assigned and accumulated attestations, the asset's history shapes its worth and, arguably, provides an identity of its own.

The third question addresses the relationship between the person and the asset. Just like individuals hold identity attestations about their person in their identity portfolio or wallet, they can own and hold digital representations of things. Based on this model, ownership would become portable and universally acceptable, no matter where you are in the world.

The authentication of this relationship also relies on cryptography. The blockchain equivalent to who owns the land is who owns the cryptographic keys to its digital counterpart. Just as sub-identities make self-sovereign identity functionally extensible, different key solutions are the technical counterpart for things. The public transfer of land ownership would, for example, require a specific exchange of keys, where the private key is the signature for all operations of an identity. Key management is an event-driven infrastructure, logically allowing for many different interaction options. Does the individual own or lease the land? Can you access it or even build something on it?

Thrillingly, the proposed permission structure extends beyond simplistic owner-thing relationships. As opposed to land, which is relatively static, this becomes even more apparent when an asset is decidedly more dynamic, such as a car. What is the relationship between the jeep parked on the side of the street and the individual approaching it? Does the individual own the car or are they just driving the car (attestation)? Is the person eligible to unlock the driver's door or just the trunk of the car to retrieve something from the back (authorisation)?

Identity could become a starting point for collaboration. Imagine that a smart device like Alexa had an "identity" similar to the structure proposed in this chapter. Hardware would fall under inherent attestations and serial numbers would be assigned (for example, both could be recorded in the factory or by the parent organisation). Third-party integrations could complete the identity triangle with accumulated attestations (e.g. all third-party integrations with your Alexa are logged, as they are now, but would fall under a revocation registry giving you further control over your data). Following this logic, approved stakeholders could add to the identity, creating a "living" digital twin of the asset which represents reality.

The whole premise of decentralised identity is a web of trusted relationships. To interact, this ecosystem must include both humans and things. Merely living in the same neighbourhood is not sufficient. To truly create ongoing relationships between the two, identities need to be readable by both humans and machines.

To build such an identity, all parties need a central address to "talk" to. This address can be public or private. If identity is a mechanism which allows you to do things, organisations could hold a blockchain based identity as well. Let's take the Known Traveller Digital Identity programme again as an example. The traveller stores a selection of private claims, here verified by the passport authority, in his digital wallet. To help the traveller move from point A to point B, participating organisations (airlines) use the public key of the issuer (passport authority) to cross-reference the authentication of the claims. Two things are important. Firstly, the traveller retains his privacy in the process. Secondly, all claims and subsequent verifications must be trusted for the system to work. To satisfy the second condition in this set-up, this means that some central "addresses" must be public. The passport authority needs a public identifier to help stakeholders cross-reference if the entity is allowed to verify the claim in the first place, or in other words, if the verification carries "weight". Additionally, to participate and gain access to the verified claims selected airlines also need public identifiers on the ledger. In contrast to private identities, public identities are omni-directional. Where open collaboration makes sense, open identities could make sense, as demonstrated by the Known Traveller Digital Identity programme.

Depending on the situation, the appropriate identity configuration is either public or private. Because the connectedness of devices is rather new and expanding rapidly, things do not yet have a default privacy expectation. Today, there is no GDPR for things. Three schools of thought exist around this concept: things must be owned by humans (private). Things must be open (public). And lastly, things must own themselves. The last category falls in the science fiction category for now, but not indefinitely so. The possibility of a thing holding its own ownership claim in its wallet would make fantasies of self-owning autonomous vehicles and public interest commons, such as self-owning, shared energy grids, a reality. Identity of things opens the door to self-owning economic actors. Thus, making the fifth and final identity law perhaps the most important one of all: things must have an identity to be accountable (Chapter 8 and 9).

In conclusion, identity owners control inherent, assigned and accumulated attestations following customisable rules, which can be decentrally verified and multi-directionally used. Just as humans will manage their own identity and sub-identities through a wallet, people will likewise manage the identities of things through cryptographic keys.

Identity & Autonomy

Self-sovereign identity is the natural evolution of an ecosystem which has moved faster than its supporting capabilities. Now that self-sovereign identity is possible, it seems inevitable.

Following the five laws, decentralised identity systems will mend the gap in the Internet, finally empowering individuals to know who to trust and to be seen as trustworthy in turn. The gap it will fill is widely felt all over the world. The autonomy of being would have made all the difference in the world to a Syrian refugee migrating by foot into Europe. It would have contributed to restoring self-respect and self-determination of the uncounted minorities of Myanmar. Although it empowers citizens of all countries, its capabilities will assume a special role in the developing world, paving a more direct route to human rights. Those fleeing violence or oppression, survivors of natural disasters, or any number of life-altering circumstances often have one thing in common – the ability to prove who you are is essential to rebuilding a sustainable existence.

Today, the world's population counts nearly eight billion. The impact of extending tools for robust identification is immense. Each of us exists in different contexts simultaneously: as citizens, customers or employees, as travellers, shoppers or parents. A universal identity meta-system must accommodate all those contexts.

Next to its clear potential to restore dignity and autonomy to the lives of millions, if not billions, across the globe, the potential to combat fraud across sectors and geographies suggests a clear commercial reason for its existence. There is also reason to hope that data overcollection will be reduced if the legitimate pur-poses for that overcollection are more easily met. Reimagining the rights and relationships of eight billion people is a non-trivial task, but over the past few years scientists, researchers, mathematicians and politicians have been fighting to make self-sovereign identity a reality. Now the wheels have been put in motion they will not be easily stopped.

Identity is a multi-layered problem and demands a multi-layered solution. In this chapter we have discussed that the power to make verifiable attestations is possible, feasible and relevant to humanity. Now the foundation is laid for the autonomy of being, the next layer of autonomy involves a different set of rights: the right to make up your mind.

7. Information Wars

*Who controls the present controls the past, and who
controls the past, controls the future.*
- George Orwell[cxxxix]

Amongst the many impressive paintings in the
Louvre museum in Paris is a particularly striking
one: amidst a cloud of smoke, a woman carrying
the French flag leads the revolutionaries into battle. The
painter Eugène Delacroix called his creation "Liberté
Guidant Le Peuple" or "Liberty Leading the People". The
scene depicts the July revolution of 1830 as a protest
against the restored Bourbon monarchy, yet the seed
for this revolt was planted decades earlier, when the
French Revolution of 1789 questioned centuries of God-
given monarchy. Like other radical departures from the
status quo, the French Revolution followed a pattern,
evolving from an idea, to hope, to a movement. Along
the way, ideas need oxygen and room to grow. Ideas
are typically quite fragile, especially if they challenge
the status quo. This is particularly true in the 21st
century, when two types of "digital weapons" can target
and kill unwanted ideas: flooding (the *manipulation of
information*) and withholding information (*censorship*).
Before further looking into remedies against them, we

will discuss each of these digital weapons in turn. To restore the damage of manipulation and censorship on our information infrastructure, and to prevent further harm, this chapter will end with suggestions on how to strengthen the provenance of information and how to replenish the health of our information distribution ecosystem.

Manipulation

Propaganda, the manipulation of information to achieve a desired outcome, dates back to the Pharaohs. On his self-issued memorial temple, a giant-sized Pharaoh Ramesses is depicted crushing ant-sized enemy Hittites single-handedly with his imposing sceptre, serving as the version of the Battle of Kadesh that will go down in history.[cxl] Ramesses is larger than life and the Hittite threat is negligible. That the victory nearly cost the entire Egyptian army did not fit in the frame. But who dares doubt a god? This story, among many others including Delacroix's painting, illustrates that history is written by the victors. The manipulation of information is as old as time, limited only by the technology available at the time.

Then, the Internet arrived on the scene, changing the nature of information both significantly and permanently. As data exploded from petabytes to zettabytes, the age where a human brain could process all information directly is long behind us.[cxli] With well over one billion web pages indexed today, humans *must* rely on technology to filter the information for us. If filtering is a necessary force, trust in those doing the filtering is forced. Once filtered, information is no longer fully *Independent*. The result? Constructive participation in discussion, debate and deliberation becomes biased by default. Further, to form a well-founded opinion, a person must be able to access independent information of high *Integrity*. A report prepared for the Council of Europe distinguishes between mis-information (falseness), mal-information (intent to harm) and dis-information (falseness and intent to harm).[cxlii] Refining the concept of manipulation further, we will first seek to understand how the act of filtering undermines information independence and then how malicious intent can attack the integrity of information.

Filtering vs. Independence

The ability to curate information is incredibly powerful. It gives you the power to make the call on what is newsworthy and what to leave out. Everything that is considered "not fit for purpose" is not served. Until quite recently, this was decided by journalists and the interest of the outlet they worked for. In the digital age, journalists are counterbalanced by crowdsourced information, editors are mirrored by algorithms, and guiding interests are often embodied by the business models of the platforms which provide the content. This opens up a much broader spectrum and volume of opinions and interests, while the human brain conse-quently is able to process a smaller and smaller fraction. Filters have become more fragmented, at the same time as they have gained unrivalled importance.

Filtering and targeting techniques work hand in glove. Facebook's Mark Zuckerberg even went so far as to argue that fragmentation and personalisation are two sides of the same coin.[cxliii] If so, who will be served what information, why, and, more importantly, who gets to make that decision?

Remembering the influencing tactics of Chapter 2 (identity reinforcement, negative social reinforcement, positive social reinforcement, sampling bias and argument personalisation), it is crystal clear that targeting is becoming ever more precise, while the interpretation of said content is becoming ever more burdensome.

Take "false balance", for example. Traditionally, every argument had two sides, implying that the truth is somewhere in the middle. False balance, however, completely turns this approach on its head. Consider a debate between a climate change believer (supported by the vast majority of scientists) and a climate change denier (supported by a small minority of scientists). Giving both the same platform implies that both arguments deserve equal consideration, potentially pulling a centrist position to the extremes.[cxliv] Platforms do not wish to be seen as arbiters, shying away from the mere suggestion of partiality, and have often ended up rationalising themselves into inaction.

To many, living in a bubble in which you are always right is terribly tempting, especially if you can forget that the bubble even exists. But when facts are suddenly subjective, someone will always appear to be lying.

As former US President Barack Obama put it in his farewell speech:

> The rise of naked partisanship, increasing eco-nomic and regional stratification, the splintering of our media into a channel for every taste—all this makes this great sorting seem natural, even inevitable. And increasingly, we become so secure in our bubbles that we accept only information, whether true or not, that fits our opinions, instead of basing our opinions on the evidence that's out there.[cxlv]

There appears to be a trade-off between personalisation and nuance. Between the familiar and room for doubt. Is this personalisation self-selected or externally imposed? If filtering is inevitable, who benefits from it? And what does it mean if the ultimate benefactor of your information environment is not you?

Intent vs. Integrity

Even though it is notoriously tricky to unequivocally capture intent, the distinction between mis-information (falseness), mal-information (intent to harm), and dis-information (falseness and intent to harm) is helpful because of its contextual emphasis.[cxlvi] A computer generated Instagram influencer might be a false re-presentation of reality without an intent to harm, whereas a fake Twitter user might be purposefully created to play a role in a malicious influence campaign. The deep fake video of the Speaker of the US House of Representatives, Nancy Pelosi, was clearly not intended to flatter.[21] Also "DeepNude", an app that digitally undressed women without their consent, was widely considered a case of dis-information and subsequently banned from GitHub.[22] The aftermath is crowded, confusing, chaos.

The flood of mis-information results from the combination of the 24-hour news cycle and mass access to the Internet. Although mis-information is false, there is no intent to harm. Even a journalist with the best intentions could find herself stuck in a sticky web of websites quoting other (erroneous) websites, all the way down to mainstream outlets.[23] Coordinated net-works of fake reviews and followers are mushrooming. Shopping for fake profiles on the dark web yields three options: "soft reg" (no history), "boosted" (some

---

[21] The deep fake of Nancy Pelosi gained popularity when President Trump shared the video on Twitter. The video was slowed down to 75 percent, which normally lowers the tone of voice. Yet, in addition, Pelosi's pitch had been corrected, to draw attention away from tell-tale signs of alterations. The result is apparent slurred speech and accusations that Nancy Pelosi appeared drunk.
[22] Taking a clothed image of a woman, the app swapped the clothes for naked breasts and a vulva using generative adversarial networks (GANs).
[23] I call this "reputation fallacies".

activity) and "aged" (looks organic). The latter is notoriously difficult to spot. In one large sweep, Facebook removed over three billion fake accounts between October 2018 and March 2019. The reported 99.8 percent success rate implied that, due to Facebook's gigantic scale, millions of fake accounts remained at large.

Are you confident that you can spot what is real? When it detected another coordinated inauthentic behaviour ring in December 2019, Facebook deleted a network of over 900 Facebook accounts, pages, and groups as well as Instagram accounts. Mostly spreading pro-Trump messages, the pages alone attracted over 55 million followers. On the Internet, one bad apple can easily spoil the barrel, especially when combined with advertising. In this case, over $9.5 million was spent on advertising.[cxlvii] Facebook's partner Graphika, which examined the sources, found that even though a small portion constituted of real people, the overwhelming majority, sometimes including whole groups and all admins, were fake AI generated faces, mostly adopting an American presence. The technique that was used was the same as the app developers of DeepNude.[24] Graphika concluded it was the first time their team detected AI generated faked faces used at such scale for a social media campaign.[cxlviii] Another example is Lil Miquela. Sporting straight-cut bangs, a spatter of freckles and Brazilian-Spanish heritage, Lil Miquela had 1.6 million Instagram followers. It came as quite a shock to her devoted fanbase when, two years in, Miquela was exposed as a computer-generated character.[25]

---

[24] Try it yourself: create AI generated faces at thispersondoesnotexist.com.
[25] Calvin Klein commissioned a video where real human Bella Hadid kisses computer generated Lil Miquela. Non-human influencers will become a topic of hot debate. Reportedly, Balmain commissioned the former fashion photographer

Mal-information, on the other hand, intends to do harm but is not necessarily false. Revenge pornography is one expression, violating a person's privacy without public interest justification. Ironically, its perpetrators prefer to cloud themselves in anonymity. Mal-information feeds on impulsive emotion, yet it is often a violation of privacy that has lasting consequences on its victim. Some forms of hate speech fall in the same category. Mal-information also encapsulates deliberate leaks, such as hacking spoils consisting of vast databases of personally identifiable information or sensitive scandals saved for the optimal moment to achieve the maximum amount of political damage.

Dis-information, the third and final category, is the worst of both worlds. Both fake and intended to harm, it takes the shape of false context, imposter content, manipulated content and fabricated content. Dis-information includes the weaponisation of emotions, feeding fear and anger to divide the world further into "us" and "them". Deep fake videos of people saying things they have never said, standing in places they have never been, is a good example. As Pizzagate (Chapter 2) showed, dis-information preying on existing bias could carry real consequences for real people. Showing up with a gun in a pizzeria is a very real event. Due to its polarising nature and viral character, dis-information thrives on social media. This is further aided by the fact that the "real identity" behind any given social media account is easier to camouflage than in print publications which are strictly regulated. Another factor is the inferred trust pheno-menon referenced in Chapter 5. Even though research shows that nearly 60 percent of US social media users

Cameron-James Wilson to create a "virtual army" of digital models.

expect social media derived news to be *"largely inaccurate"*, it could be perceived as more trustworthy when shared by a friend.[cxlix] The consequences of such dis-information can be severe.

Examples of this can be found on both sides of the Atlantic Ocean. In the UK, the best remembered headline leading up to the Brexit vote in 2016 was likely *"Major leak from Brussels reveals NHS will be 'KILLED OFF' if Britain remains in the EU"* (464,000 interactions, The Daily Express). The 377-word article was entirely fabricated. In the US, BuzzFeed News reported that during the months leading up to the US presidential election, the 20 top-performing election stories from major news websites lost out to their dis-information equivalents in terms of interactions: approximately seven million Facebook shares, reactions and comments for mainstream journalists versus just under nine million interactions for dis-information agents. Among them were *"Pope Francis Shocks World, Endorses Donald Trump for President, Releases Statement"* (960,000 interactions, Ending the Fed); *"WikiLeaks CONFIRMS Hillary Sold Weapons to ISIS... Then Drops Another BOMBSHELL! Breaking News"* (745,000 interactions, The Political Insider); *"FBI Agent Suspected in Hillary Email Leaks Found Dead in Apparent Murder-Suicide"* (567,000 interactions, Denver Guardian). All were fact-checked. All were found false.[cl]

When TV changed the course of the Vietnam war in the 1960s, governments learnt an important lesson about public opinion: persuasion or dissuasion of public perception is a tactical objective in itself. The modern application of this lesson is China's reaction to the Hong Kong protests. Twitter disclosed that nearly 1,000 accounts were deliberately attempting to undermine the legitimacy and political positions of the movement. Furthermore, Twitter claims to have reliable evidence that this was a coordinated, state-backed operation. A larger spam network of 200,000 accounts was suspended as a preventive measure. One suspended account had already been created in 2007, suggesting a large dormant state-controlled network, steadily growing, waiting to be activated. Facebook confirmed similar activities on its own platform, banning posts comparing the protestors with ISIS fighters and cockroaches, and Google disabled 210 YouTube channels.[cli] Hong Kong protesters, on the other hand, reportedly raised nearly two million dollars in a matter of hours for an international ad campaign as they accused police of *"war crimes"* and using *"chemical weapons"*.[clii] Sometime between the events in Hong Kong and Vietnam, circa 2001, Osama Bin Laden's chief lieutenant, Ayman al-Zawahiri, lamented that *"we are in a battle, and more than half of this battle is taking place in the battlefield of the media [...] a media battle in a race for the hearts and minds of our Umma* (Muslim community)".[cliii] Since then, the ISIS propaganda machine has pushed out magazines, documentaries and even an a cappella song.[cliv] Now more than ever, truth is the first casualty of war.

The fear of automation of the creation of disinformation is precisely why OpenAI, a company focused on researching human-friendly AI, decided not to fully release its GPT-2 model.[26] The objective of GPT-2 is to predict the next word in a sequence of words, which in theory would allow for the fabrication of entire articles at a previously unprecedented scale, potentially resulting in dis-information. Unfortunately, OpenAI partners confirmed that extremist groups could do just

---

[26] Staged release of GTP-2: The smallest version contained 117 million parameters, the second had 345 million parameters, the third consisted of 774 million parameters, and the largest one at time of writing has 1.5 billion parameters: "GPT-2: 1.5B Release", OpenAI, 5 November 2019.

that, fine-tuning the model to ideological positions such as white supremacy, Marxism, jihadist Islamism and anarchism.

When information becomes weaponised, "keyboard armies" mobilise. In the Philippines, which is the most connected nation in the world with over 10 hours of screen time a day, such members reportedly could earn $10 a day creating content supporting President Rodrigo Duterte and attacking his political opponents.[clv] In Mexico, popular anti-government hashtags are quickly repressed by sock-puppet accounts with newer hashtags, or are alternatively pushed into oblivion by attaching a flood of irrelevant posts to the existing hashtag, a practice known as "hashtag poisoning". The estimated 75,000 automated accounts serving the interests of President Enrique Peña Nieto are collo-quially called "Peñabots". Further north in the Americas, the US Senate, Facebook and the Mueller investigations all found that the Russian Internet Research Agency's dis-information efforts were specifically targeted at communities of colour attempting to suppress minority voter turnout.[clvi] One of the campaigns implied that it was possible to vote for Hillary Clinton via text-message. No country is immune to the trans-border, trans-media, trans-lingual and trans-time nature of the Internet.

There is no doubt that profit and power optimisation games greatly contributed to the present-day situation, chasing likes and control. However, when it comes to the real architects undermining independent informa-tion of high integrity, web giants are merely puppets and governments are still the puppet master.

Censorship

Censorship, the second digital weapon, is more difficult to pin down because it becomes invisible when applied well. Starting with search, it is well known that the search term *"1989 Tiananmen Square protests"* – the bloody pro-democracy protests in Beijing – returns different results in China than in the rest of the world. People cannot read illegal content if there is no illegal content. Chipping away at everything that deviates from the party line, information is censored until a new narrative takes its place and the earlier version of the truth is forgotten.

Imagine that you need to create legitimacy for a certain narrative: dogs are the best pets in the world, cats are clearly inferior. One strategy could be to remove all negative dog-related content and all positive cat-related content. Over time, the "dogs-are-the-best-pets" narrative will be the only narrative available, thus likely the most widely accepted.

In the run-up to the 25-year anniversary of the Tiananmen Square protests, the messaging app WeChat intensified its censoring machine. Direct references, such as the iconic *"tank man"*, as well as indirect (*"twenty-five years"*) and remote (*"today"*) phrases were censored. WeChat reportedly even started using an image blacklist in the form of a hash index, giving it capabilities to censor images in real-time.[clvii] What is not seen is as meaningful as what is.

With more than one billion users, WeChat is the fourth most popular messaging app in the world. Because WeChat mixes social capital and utility it is near-impossible to opt-out. Citizen Lab, the inter-disciplinary laboratory of the University of Toronto, reports that in the past users received a notification when their message was blocked. Now censorship of chat messages and images happens without notice. This implies that you would not know if, and when, you are being censored on WeChat. Not knowing could lead individuals to over-correct, refraining from expressing ideas, just to be on the safe side, resulting in self-censorship.

To halt an unwanted idea to spread tomorrow, the Chinese government controls the apparatus to cut off the oxygen today. To remove the option. Internet controls within China reached new extremes in 2018 with the sweeping cybersecurity law which centralises all Internet policy. Hundreds of new directives followed – an average of one every two days – to fine-tune what its citizens can and cannot do online.

Reportedly, 55 percent of Internet users live in a country where political, social or religious content is censored or blocked.[clviii] China is currently in talks with 36 of the 65 countries surveyed by Freedom House about exporting its surveillance knowledge and products, amongst which is Iran. *"The use of paid commentators and political bots to spread government propaganda was pioneered by China and Russia but has now gone global,"* said Michael Abramowitz, Freedom House's president.[clix] Information, seen and unseen, is a direct route to power.

Information Infrastructure

If digital weapons like manipulation and censorship result in non-equal access to information, what does this mean for the health of our information infrastructure? The resulting democratic cost is hard to quantify, but it is clear that trust in institutions is waning. Under Article 19 of the UN Universal Declaration of Human Rights: *"Everyone has the right to freedom of opinion and expression; this right includes freedom to hold opinions without interference and to seek, receive and impart information and ideas through any media and regardless of frontiers."*[clx] Who is right cannot depend on who has the biggest megaphone (manipulation) or who can pull the plug (censorship). What can be done to restore these rights under Article

19? To bring back trust to the Internet, this trust needs to be earned.

Because it is not feasible to prevent the creation of dis-information, I propose that the goal should be to improve identification and reduce distribution. Because the Internet was meant to spread information, not to attribute, the first step is to launch efforts to verify *Provenance of Information*. Provenance is generally understood as the place of origin or the earliest known history of something. The previous chapter suggested that humans could not only issue verifiable claims about themselves, but also about the things they own. Could the same apply to information? The second bundle of initiatives centres around *Distribution of Information*. Because obscurity enables dis-information, its enemy is transparency. Together, this combination can serve as the foundation for a new infrastructure for freedom of thought, which is why we will look at provenance and distribution of information in turn.

Provenance of Information

The chief challenge in establishing provenance is overcoming distance to verification. In law, the burden of proof lies with the prosecution. Outside the courtroom the opposite holds true. Everything can be claimed, and debunking these claims is a tall order. On Twitter this is called Brandolini's law: *"The amount of energy needed to refute bullshit is an order of magnitude bigger than to produce it."*[lxi] This section will focus on how to reduce this distance to verification.

Sadly, the truth has become a luxury. In the very near future, just like luxury brands for watches and handbags have been going above and beyond to combat fake products, so will premium content creators. They will gladly go the extra mile to prove the quality of their work. I predict that the question will actually reverse direction. If the information shared is allegedly true, why is it not verified?

Because news is battleground zero, imagine a diligent journalist at a prominent newspaper writing a digital article including quotes from national politicians (attestations). Upon publication, this piece is time-stamped and its contents are vouched for by the newspaper in question (authentication). Because the "real" version of the article is time-stamped, direct subscribers can be confident that the version on their screen is the right one. What is more, both subscriber access and licenced partner distribution can then be managed and tracked by the editorial staff (authorisation). Provenance could be established by end-to-end verification of metadata logged on an immutable ledger, all the way to the root of the article.

Compared to the written word, photographs and videos suggest a false sense of objectivity. With visuals becoming powerful vehicles for dis-information there is a race against the clock to develop methods to spot manipulated images early. One provenance strategy follows the known-culprit approach, cross-referencing images known to be false. Another uses machine learning to assess if the image has been tinkered with, considering factors such as splicing, lighting, pixel inconsistencies and logical inconsistencies, such as excessive or non-existent blinking, features that should be symmetrical on the human face, and background details.[clxii] Providing context completes the ranks. For example, an image captured in 2007 in Vietnam of two young children clinging onto each other re-circulated seven years later[27], shared under the guise that it was a

---

[27] 2015 caption: "Two-year-old sister protected by four-year-old brother in Nepal". Actual story: *"I took this picture in October 2007 in Can Ty, a remote village in Ha Giang province (Vietnam)"*.

photograph from Nepal in the aftermath of the 2015 earthquake. When provenance is permanently logged in associated metadata, this enriches visuals with portable, verifiable context as they travel around the web.

"Deep fakes" are the next iteration of dis-information in the form of images and video, and especially complex to tackle. Deep fakes get their name from the deep learning algorithms that make them possible. The ingredients for a convincing deep fake include a combination of real audio and video to compute faked output, indistinguishable from the real deal. For example, real audio and video could be combined with a different face, or the other way around.

The dangerous thing about deep fakes is that they are easily accessible. The knowledge barrier is low. Knowing how to code is not a requirement; anyone with a handful of dollars can commission a deep fake online. The possibility of text-based editing on talking head videos will further democratise the creation of deep fakes. Data volume is not a meaningful barrier either. Image collection can come from any source. Russian researchers from the Samsung AI centre in Moscow set themselves an ambitious challenge: they wanted to make the Mona Lisa Talk. Using just one photo of this one painted portrait, the researchers succeeded in making realistic conversational movements. Marilyn Monroe, Salvador Dali and Albert Einstein reels followed.[clxiii]

All in all, using minimal funds and data it will enable practically anyone to do practically anything. Soon, you could make anyone say whatever you wanted. Stanford University has already created a credible deep fake of former US President Barack Obama. Imagine the perfect storm of a world leader making (fake) inflammatory remarks, attracting a flurry of polarising comments and reactions, trending on Twitter, and reaching any relevant targets in the span of hours.[28] From devastating high school bullying to fake terrorist videos: if deep fakes are not spotted early, they will not easily be stopped.

The technology to create a deep fake is surprisingly advanced, and improving rapidly. When the Apollo 11 mission was launched in 1969, two speeches were written: one in the event of success, one in the event of failure. Recently, MIT created a convincing deep fake of the second speech.[clxiv] Misapplied, deep fakes could create a version of history that never was. To protect independent critical thinking means to protect the integrity of information. If we are not extremely careful, the damage of deep fakes will exceed its written counterpart in spades.

Thankfully, there may be a solution. Consider the following situation: while browsing the web a suspicious video pops up. How can you determine its integrity? Early blockchain solutions suggest a path forward. When recording a video, hashes could be generated at regular intervals and could then get logged on the blockchain ledger.[29] Every hash is like a line within a fingerprint. When this digital fingerprint is public, it

---

[28] In 2018, a Belgian political party manipulated a Donald Trump speech in which the US president apparently calls on the country to follow America's lead and exit the Paris climate agreement. *"As you know I had the balls to withdraw from the Paris climate agreement. And so should you."* The speech continues, *"because what you guys are doing right now in Belgium is actually worse. You agreed, but you are not taking any measures. Only blablabla. Bingbangboom."* The Flemish Socialist Party claimed it was a stunt to start a debate about climate change. Again, it is technically possible to create deep fakes of anything.
[29] A major distinction between ciphers and hashes are that ciphers are (generally) reversible, while hashes are (generally not). A hash function mathematically converts data of arbitrary size to fixed size values. Hashes are convenient to cross-reference input data, while ciphers are useful to share a reversible secret, spy-style.

becomes easy to cross-reference for version control. If video or audio is partly or entirely edited, its linked hashes will be different, and the fingerprints will not match. It is like cutting an image into one thousand smaller puzzle pieces. If one piece is missing, or it does not fit upon reassembly, the puzzle has been tampered with.

Restoring provenance is not merely imperative to take comfort that opinion is based on fact, but also that those facts will be harder to deny. For example, a politician captured doing something they would rather not be caught doing could not simply claim that the video was fake.

Equally, verifiable provenance could ensure that information linked to you is true. Law enforcement is one of the sectors in dire need of such a solution. Most dashboard and body cameras have strong security systems that make it difficult to alter footage without leaving a digital trail. But the efficacy of these systems relies on open access: if courts and news outlets cannot access the original recording and digital record, there is no way to check that what you are seeing is unaltered. All starts at the source. Back in 2016, The Washington Post reported that 80 percent of Chicago PD dash-cam videos are missing audio due to *"officer error"* or *"intentional destruction"*.[clxv] Once sub-mitted into evidence it is near impossible to determine if images have been tampered with. Here detection would sit at device level: either the hash matches or it does not, and all is publicly verifiable.

As human self-sovereign identity is able to reduce fake users and identity fraud, so too can provenance of virtual content expose dis-information and deep fakes. Unambiguous identification, or provenance, is the first step to consistent treatment, bringing us to the second and final remedy of this chapter: how should we treat distribution of information?

Distribution of Information

Three actors in the information distribution ecosystem have emerged in this chapter: those controlling the conduits of content (often profit-oriented companies), the consumers of said content (often curious and entertainment-oriented citizens), and the creators of content (which can be a mix between the first two categories, or a third actor). This third actor, with a contentious role, is the government. Governments can create content, monitor or censor it. A natural tension exists between the three actors. Companies do not welcome dis-information because it erodes their reputation, yet interactions drive profits. Governments do not wish to have their citizens exposed to foreign influence campaigns, but the University of Oxford found evidence of organised social media manipulation campaigns in 70 countries in 2018 alone.[clxvi] Citizens speak out against dis-information, but six-in-ten news items shared on social media were not even read by those who re-shared them.[clxvii] Nevertheless, a healthy information ecosystem is critical for democratic societies to function. All three actors owe a shared responsibility to that democracy to keep it alive.

Currently, this responsibility has largely been ignored. Examining Twitter data from 2006 to 2017, University of Oxford researchers found that dis-information reaches more people and spreads faster than the truth, most significantly for politically charged information. Findings include that the top one percent of "false news" spreads to between 1,000 and 100,000 people, whereas the truth rarely circulates to more than 1,000 people.[clxviii] The following section will explore the reasons behind these observations.

Firstly, those who knowingly engage in the creation or spreading of dis-information make a conscious decision to abandon ethics. Next to political gain, money is an enticing motivator. The headline *"Pope*

Francis Shocks World, Endorses Donald Trump for President" originated from a small town in Macedonia called Veles.[clxix] The reported culprit was a group of get-rich-quick teenagers from Macedonia. A lucrative business, it is estimated that nearly a quarter of a billion dollars worth of advertisements is served on dis-information domains, with a generous majority coming from programmatic advertising.[clxx]

This serves as a reminder that content in algorithmic feeds is always paid for, may it be directly (ads) or indirectly (attention). Transparency on all levels of this process is vital. Facebook has taken a meaningful step in this direction by introducing its "Searchable Political Ads Library", providing information on ad sponsors, running details such as date and platform, and results such as impressions and audience. Unfortunately, even though those running political ads are now required to self-identify as government representatives, Facebook has also stumbled backwards by allowing false political ads to run on its platform as a policy – implicitly turning the platform into a paid-for dis-information machine.[clxxi] One step forward, two steps back. Twitter replied by banning all political ads.

The University of Oxford found that 56 of the aforementioned 70 countries formally organised computational propaganda campaigns on Facebook. In addition to transparency on funds of paid content (including where the content ends up being served), transparency on reach is needed. Researchers at Stanford University have suggested that, for all ads of a political nature, there should be a legal floor for micro-targeting.[clxxii][30] All this relates back to identity: the more information about you is floating online, the more

---

[30] Micro-targeting is the direct opposite of shared attention and shared reality.

precise the micro-targeting will be. There is a particular irony that the more you speak, the more you open yourself to potential third-party influence. This holds true for paid as well as organic content.

To achieve prioritisation of authentic organic content, Facebook is combining a host of techniques, among which are self-reporting by users and third-party identification by independent fact-checkers, temporarily slowing distribution until the verdict is in. Fact-checking is important because if ads appear next to dis-information, the former indirectly subsidises the latter. Like prioritising verified content, down-ranking of dubious content to de-fund dis-information via blacklists, while great in principle, should remain a transparent process in practice to stop censorship from becoming the norm. Even if fact-checked, the amplification of organic content, however, is decidedly not organic.

Even though all content is created equal, some content is more equal than other content. The structures underpinning commercially motivated platforms actually rely on the free amplification of "engaging" content, with scores favouring acceleration and velocity. Leading long, continuous and balanced conversations to lose out to the new, temporary and polarising news items in algorithmic feeds. Take YouTube, for example. YouTube has around one billion hours of video in total.[31] YouTube's CPO claims its recommendation algorithm generates more than 70 percent of total views, which would equate to 700,000,000 human hours, every single day.[clxxiii] Until 2012, YouTube focused on one metric only: view count. In response to the emerging clickbait problem, view

---

[31] In 2019, YouTube reported that two billion users watch more than 250 million hours of video per day on TV screens – more than households who own a television.

count was swapped for watch time (duration video) and session time (duration platform). YouTube published a white paper in 2016 to detail the role of machine learning in its recommendations. Roughly, it segments the viewer to serve content for "someone like you" (broad personalisation), and then assigns constantly evolving scores to videos, using a series of undisclosed variables, including newness, engagement and frequency of uploads.[clxxiv] In this set-up, transparency could be two-fold: transparency into how YouTube sees "you" and transparency into why certain content is amplified at the expense of other content, and how big this delta is. The former becomes open to individual discretion, the second open to political debate. All in all, dis-information becomes a lot less scary if it cannot choose its consumers.

Next to recommendation engines, automation is an oft-cited culprit, including three types of bots. "Scheduled bots" post messages based on the time, "watcher bots" monitor other Twitter accounts or websites and tweet when something changes, and "amplification bots" follow, retweet and like for clients who have bought their services.[clxxv] But how can you spot a bot? Bot activity can be detected through signals and patterns – not what it is, but how it moves.[clxxvi]

However, the same University of Oxford research cited above found that *"contrary to conventional wisdom, robots accelerated the spread of true and false news at the same rate, implying that false news spreads more than the truth because humans, not robots, are more likely to spread it."* Coordinated inauthentic activity just needs to seed an idea until it reaches an algorithmic tipping point, triggering recommendation algorithms, or a broad enough veneer of credibility for humans and mainstream media to believe and share it. Harvard researchers who conducted detailed research on information sharing patterns during the US presidential election echoed these findings.[clxxvii] This emphasises that citizens are as much a part of the solution as platform companies or governments are.

Enhancing human ability to assess content is therefore critical. I predict that within the next decade, real personhood will become a qualifying criterion when opening a social media account. If the account in question is a bot or computer-generated avatar, this should be clearly indicated. If reputation is put forward as a curation mechanism, as is the case for influencers, followers need to be verified. Making the Internet human friendly involves restoring the value of humanness.

Truth & Autonomy

In Alfred Huxley's novel Brave New World, the main character was drowning in useless information, where no one cares for facts, especially not unpleasant ones. In George Orwell's 1984, information was limited and controlled.[clxxviii] Manipulation (Huxley) and censorship (Orwell). Suffocation and obscurification. These science-fiction novels could not only be an extrapolation of what is happening now, but point to a deeper relationship between truth and autonomy. Memories can be constructive and reconstructive.[32]

---

[32] A folk story on how memories can be constructive and reconstructive: One evening an old Cherokee told his grandson about a battle that goes on inside people. He said, "My son, the battle is between two wolves inside us all. One is evil. It is anger, envy, jealousy, sorrow, regret, greed, arrogance, self-pity, guilt, resentment, inferiority, lies, false pride, superiority and ego. The other is good. It is joy, peace, love, hope, serenity, humility, kindness, benevolence, empathy, generosity, truth, compassion and faith." The grandson thought about it for a minute and then asked his grandfather: "Which wolf wins?" The old Cherokee simply replied, "The one you feed."

If we are the stories we tell ourselves, what does it mean if we find reason to believe someone else's story? *"If everybody always lies to you, the consequence is not that you believe the lies, but rather that nobody believes anything any longer,"* concluded the political theorist Hannah Arendt. *"And a people that no longer can believe anything cannot make up its mind. It is deprived not only of its capacity to act but also of its capacity to think and to judge. And with such a people you can then do what you please."*[clxxix]

Human capability for reason builds on autonomy of thought, which requires independent information of high integrity to exercise that capability. This chapter showed that provenance of information extends from journalists taking additional steps to bolster the origin of their high-quality content, to blockchain-based hashing solutions to combat deep fakes. Additionally, the three actors in the information distribution eco-system (profit-oriented companies, entertainment-oriented citizens, and national security-oriented governments) all have a constructive role to play in remedying the spread of dis-information. Because in algorithmic feeds content is always paid for, may it be directly (ads) or indirectly (attention), transparency should be introduced on the incentives behind each, and governments should protect against malicious incentives by empowering their citizens to restore the health of their own information environments.

Like the contemplative Immanuel Kant we met at the beginning of this book (*"have the courage to use your own reason"*), philosophers have long defended the innate human capability to exercise reason to distinguish between true and false, moral and immoral, as the one unchangeable constant in a changing world.[clxxx] Not just autonomy of being and autonomy of thought are in crisis because of inadequate identity proxies and digital information weapons such as manipulation and censorship, but autonomy of reason is under threat too. What happens if humans lose the monopoly on reason? Enter algorithms.

8. Algorithmic Truths

"Act in such a way that you always treat humanity, whether in your own person, or in the person of any other, never simply as a means, but always at the same time as an end."
- Immanuel Kant[clxxxi]

K ant thought moral action to be decided by reason and challenged the individual to not see himself as an exception to the rule.[33] He asked: what would the world look like if the logic that you just applied would be applied to every situation? In Kant's world, you are the moral endpoint. In his world, every single act of judgement, every single moral decision, creates a new reality. In the early 21st century we are not too far off from the world imagined by Kant in the 18th century. Except today, the rationalisation and enforcement of a narrow set of morals deemed best-fitted for the wider population is achieved through algorithms.

The topics today's algorithms are applied to are as diverse as Kant could only have imagined in his wildest dreams three centuries earlier. However, these same

---

[33] This Kantian principle is sometimes called "the universal law": act only on that maxim that you will to become a universal law. Exercising this capability for reason – pure reason – exceeds individual preferences.

three centuries have taught us that norms and values evolve continuously. In the US, for example, slavery was abolished in the 19th century. In most parts of the world, women only obtained the right to work in the 20th century. History shows us the story of a changing world, but also enlightens us that the very interpretation of that same story changes over time, holding up a mirror to what we believe to be true, then versus now.

According to William James, an American philosopher, how truthful an idea is depends on how useful it is. To the pragmatic James, truth is an adjective. True ideas, he argues, we can assimilate, validate, corroborate and verify. The same is not possible for false ideas. Rather than truth being stable, an idea is only confirmed to be true by events. Its validity is the process of its validation. In other words: you are more likely to accept an idea as true if that idea is useful to you.[clxxxii]

When we start hard coding our values, there is the assumption that these values are the ultimate, final version of what is right and what is wrong. If you believe in a clear distinction between the two, you probably believe in one version of the truth. If you agree with this basic concept, you are in good company and in agreement with the Greek philosopher Socrates. In ancient Athens, Socrates was known to wander around the city, asking people lots and lots of questions. What is love? What is death? What is happiness? He asked question after question, always assuming his own utter ignorance on the matter. He famously stated: *"One thing only I know, and that is that I know nothing"*.[clxxxiii] To him, in stark contrast to James, truth was a noun.

Now, what does this mean in the wider context of rebooting identity? We are facing three ingredients for a potent, unstable, dangerous concoction. One, humanity's values change over time. Two, humanity's interpretation of those values, our living truth, changes over time. Three, hard-coded algorithmic enforcement cements values with little room for nuance or uncertainty. The combination of the three is a warning sign for two equally undesirable outcomes. On the one hand, the value system of society and its living truth, enforced by code, could stagnate. On the other hand, the value system of society could remain stable, but its subjects (the citizens) would not subscribe to those values any longer. The first leads to stagnation of progress. The second leads to instability. There is an alternative value system, requiring consent, recourse and discourse on algorithmic accountability; foundations of such a system will be discussed in this chapter. Ending with avenues to accountability (consent, recourse, discourse), we will start with examining algorithms themselves.

False Equations

Many digital theorists believe the following statement to be true: decision rights will shift from humans to algorithms.

The overarching idea of algorithms is that they solve a problem exactly once, then replicate the method, and in some cases, learn from the output. Importantly, algorithmic enforcement creates decision distance (and consequently distance in regard to responsibility) between the algorithm's architect, its enforcer and any consequences which might impact the subject. As laid out in earlier chapters, human behaviour is increasingly an optimisation problem, and humans are providing the input that is being optimised for. As they represent a digital force to elicit and encourage specific actions, we might be forgiven for the knee-jerk reaction to vilify algorithms and artificial intelligence. Calling AI evil is an emotional response to a human problem. AI does not hate, nor does it love. Algorithms are nothing but an authorisation of applying logic to information. It could be the wrong *Information*. It could be the wrong *Logic*. It could be the wrong *Authorisation*.

Firstly, the perfect algorithm could lean on the wrong Information. In a world with data scandal fatigue, exposing more and more of the underlying iceberg, a larger issue is yet to enter mainstream debate. What data are all these algorithms actually trained on? How was this data obtained? And, who decided this was the right data to use?

An irony of studying history is that we often know exactly how the story ends, but have no idea how it began. To understand what caused the Second World War you need to understand the economy of Germany in the preceding decades. To understand why the German economy was in such an abysmal state, you need to examine the aftermath of the First World War and the Treaty of Versailles. To understand the decisions made at the Treaty of Versailles, you need to understand the political situation of France, the UK and the US at the time. And so on, and so forth.

History is a continuous chain of large and small events, in contrast, and by design, datasets are finite. Algorithms cannot take the whole story into account, just selective facts, composing in effect their own story and interpretation. Based on this already redacted baseline, data shows what is, not what ought to be. Additionally, past, present, or future, society is more than its laws; it is also based on unspoken rules and values. Finally, if humanity would build a digital twin of every event that ever took place, this quest would not stop until we arrive at a perfect digital copy of every-thing that ever was, a complete digital mirror world.

Which brings us to our second question: once selected, how is data obtained? More specifically, let's use the case of facial recognition as an example: where did the faces come from? One of the largest public facial recognition datasets in the world was published in 2016, created by scraping images off the web under a Creative Commons licence, which allows academic reuse of photos. The database counted more than 10 million images of some 100,000 people. The name of the database was "MS Celeb", and it was run by Microsoft. Next to Microsoft's own Research department, The Financial Times found that for-profit multinationals and even militaries had used the repository to test their own facial recognition software. Investigative journalists at Megapixel uncovered an even darker story. The people in the dataset were included without their knowledge, with plans to grow the total to include a million people. Instead of the declared Creative Commons sources, popular search engines were actually scraped, including copyrighted images. Adding more oil to the already blazing fire, other researchers were encouraged to download the remaining list of 900,000 names *"by using all the possibly collected face images of this individual on the web as training data."*clxxxiv

Equally concerning, but for different reasons, is a scandal starring a doll called Cayla. The American Federal Trade Commission accused this doll of posing an imminent and immediate threat to the safety and security of children in the US.clxxxv The doll, "My Friend Cayla", used speech-recognition to have conversations with children. These voice recordings were stored and used for a variety of purposes beyond the toy's functionality. You might wonder what kind of purposes these were. The FTC claimed that the products and services of the speech recognition technology provider included voice biometric solutions sold to military, intelligence and law enforcement agencies. In other words: children's voice samples were sold to the military as training data.

After the what and how follows the who. Take ten seconds to picture a CEO. Did you picture a man or a woman? Young or old? Beautiful or ugly? Tall or short? Just like your own mental image is based on what you are familiar with, algorithms use available information to extrapolate information. Ultimately, AI is a mirror. If we feed systems with data embedded with biases, those systems will reflect them right back at us, and, worse, magnify them out into the world. MIT researcher Joy Buolamwini retraced this bias to *who* is designing the systems. The reason for her fascination with facial recognition in particular is troublesome. Working with facial analysis software she noticed a problem: the software did not detect her face. When she literally put on a nondescript white mask to cover her dark skin, the software could finally "see" her. She observed that the people who coded the algorithm had not taught it to identify a broad range of skin tones and facial structures. *"Bias can travel as quickly as software being downloaded from the Internet,"* she warned. Non-representation could, quite literally, result in invisibility.

But even the perfect training data (information) does not stop algorithms from processing the wrong Logic. To what extent are algorithms an extension of their users and to what extent should they be neutral? Neutral tends to be confused with "the truth". As the philosophers Kant, James and Socrates heeded, weighing this question is a mammoth task. Currently, this task is carried by a small number of self-selected individuals. When Facebook acquired Instagram, the company had just 13 employees. When it was WhatsApp's turn, the team was comprised of 55 people. At the time of acquisition, the two platforms covered 30 million and 450 million monthly active users respectively. Can such a small number of employees really reflect the diversity of its users and find answers that have challenged philosophers for centuries?

What is bias? What is fairness? When is bias good and when is bias bad? These questions are going to be answered one way or another. And, right now, they are being answered by the corporate policies of Silicon Valley, and increasingly China's tech giants.[clxxxvi] Silicon

Valley, still predominantly white and male, is not renowned for its diversity in the workforce. On the other side of the Pacific, Chinese tech giants have to work with their government to remain operational, and, as WeChat demonstrated in the previous chapter, this means respecting the party line. Expecting a small, non-diverse group of decision makers to exhibit broad diversity of thinking, capturing the nuances of the lives of billions, is simply wishful thinking.

But as François Chollet, a renowned Google AI researcher, stresses, the stakes are high indeed: *"Applying machine learning inappropriately can potentially lead to simplistic, inaccurate, unaccountable, unauditable decision systems getting deployed in serious situations and negatively affecting people's lives. [...] It is not a hypothetical risk, it is a pressing concern."*[clxxxvii] As any action manifests at a specific place in time and space, some action aspects are inescapable, and automating judgement is oh so tempting. However, if these assumptions are biased, incomplete or incorrect, real harm could follow.

In Washington, one court case took such a turn. When a young man, agreed by both legal teams to be eligible for parole, received an unfavourable algorithmic score, the judge placed him in juvenile detention. Outraged, his lawyer insisted on seeing the algorithm. It was worse than she could ever have imagined. The algorithm in question was based on an unpublished thesis, written by a college student, and it had been in use for the past twenty years. It was not peer reviewed and included only a handful of variables.[clxxxviii] Later it turned out that one of the deciding factors of refusing parole was the young boy's dislike for the police, which was a subjective score entered by a human.

Such black box algorithms risk infantilising decision makers. Automated digital scores could have lasting real life consequences. In the case of the Chinese social credit system, it could be the difference between getting into a good school or a single ticket to the bottom. In the case of a female job applicant, it could be the difference between talking to a human being or receiving an automated rejection email. Apple's credit card algorithm made headlines recently when it was reported that men received higher credit limits than their spouses, running into the many multiples, despite the spouses submitting shared accounts, joint tax returns, the same residence and sometimes even higher credit scores.[34] If risk-mitigation and opportunity-maximisation are in everyone's interest, why is there no widely accepted process to provide feedback on algorithms?

Even if information and logic of the underlying algorithm have been perfected, there is still the third risk of carrying the wrong Authorisation. Algorithmic enforcement could be entirely self-authorised, both in the collection of information, conclusions drawn, and who those conclusions are shared with.

The latter deserve special attention: what happens if an algorithm discovers something about you that you might not know yourself? In 2017, researchers from Stanford University found that when presented with subject photos, their AI model could more accurately point to those who identified as gay or heterosexual than humans. The research team had built a real-life "gaydar".[clxxxix] This is just one example, and in the future, after crunching the numbers an AI might conclude you have diabetes, or that you are pregnant (like Target did in Chapter 2), or one of millions of other often very private deductions.

---

[34] Using Apple Card, women receive far lower credit limits than men. Apple co-founder Steve Wozniak said on Twitter that his credit limit was 10x that of his wife, despite the fact that they share all assets and accounts. See, for example, Evelina Nedlund, "Apple Card is accused of gender bias. Here's how that can happen," *CNN*, 12 November 2019.

Last but not least, the final step is what the entity behind the AI will decide to do with that newly acquired knowledge. For example, they might serve pregnancy related advertisements before you even considered taking a test, or could perhaps disclose your potential diabetes to the insurance company. What does it mean when meaningful information about you is not shared with you? And, what does it mean when these shared conclusions about you are distorted or even wholly untrue?[35] Portals of communicating those recommendations are narrow at the moment – for now devices are consciously turn on or off – but as devices capable of broadcasting those recommendations become more omnipresent, those recommendations become harder to ignore.[cxc] In these circumstances "moral singularity", a term used by the technology journalist Jamie Bartlett to describe the point when humans trust algorithms more than we trust ourselves, is particularly dangerous.[cxci] Ironically, we seem to be missing adequate rules to hold the rules engines to account.

Accountable Algorithms

Why is it that decision power is shifting towards algorithms, but that there are so few mechanisms in place to hold these algorithms accountable for those deci-

---

[35] Algorithmic bias could even extend to your very name. Professor of Government at Harvard Latanya Sweeney discovered that on Google, black-sounding names more likely associated advertisements for criminal background checks with that person's name. How did she find out? When the Harvard professor was using Google, she was served the following ad: *"Latanya Sweeney, Arrested?"* The Boston Globe writes that she found that names that sounded black were 25 percent more likely to trigger ads for criminal records than names that sounded white — even if, like Sweeney, the person had no criminal record.

sions? For now, it seems that the status quo is supported by market conditions and technology design choices.

Take, for example, Google's Search algorithm, which is a famous closely guarded secret. The algorithm's sophistication fuelled Google's rise to becoming the dominant market player. Open-sourcing Google's Search algorithm would go a long way in killing its competitive advantage over Russia's Yandex and Microsoft's Bing – now mere blips on its radar. In addition, full transparency would reduce friction for everybody, good and bad actors alike. Technology strategist Ben Thompson already noted back in 2013 that *"friction makes everything harder, both the good we can do, but also the unimaginably terrible. In our zeal to reduce friction and our eagerness to celebrate the good, we ought not to lose sight of the potential bad."*[cxcii] If information was like grains of sand it would be constantly in flux, but it is algorithms which shape its positive and negative concentrations. Malicious actors could utilise such knowledge to game the system, a risk highlighted in the previous chapter. Over-rotation towards total transparency might also not be the answer we seek.

Another factor for a potential algorithmic blind spot is design. Self-learning AI could lead to clever new approaches and strategies that humans would and could never even consider. For example, when AlphaGo, designed by Google's DeepMind, was playing the complex board game Go, it deployed a move no human would play, leaving the real-time commentators speechless.[cxciii] It won the game. Self-learning algorithms, like AlphaGo, create so-called "black boxes". Nobody knows how a black box algorithm actually arrived at its final decision. Inputs and outputs are known, internal processes are unknown. But what if something goes wrong and you need to understand why? As multiple journalists researching Brexit explained, it is actually quite tricky to find out who saw what and why. The journalist who broke the story linking Brexit with the Cambridge Analytica affiliate AggregateIQ, Carole Cadwalladr, remarked that Brexit took place in darkness: impermanence of news combined with black box algorithms made it near-impossible to research, and thus near-impossible to un-equivocally establish responsibility and inferred accountability.[cxciv]

Google is an exception to the rule: it designed its famous Search algorithm itself (logic), selected input constraints (information) and authorised use for commercial gains (authorisation). The rule, however, is the previously outlined great separation of algorithmic creation, control and consequences, which makes it difficult to weigh where responsibility falls, and hence difficult to legislate. To introduce accountability for algorithms, there are three parts to the solution which will be discussed in turn: *Consent*, *Recourse* and *Discourse*. Consent places legitimacy front and centre (information and authorisation). Recourse refers to what algorithms should control (logic). Discourse discusses how algorithms should evolve.

Consent Coercion

The influencer phenomenon has, by all standards, exploded over the last few years. Self-styled "beauty gurus", "gym sharks" and "lifestyle influencers" have amassed followings running into the many millions. Meanwhile, brands caught on, paying top buck for subtle product placements. There are many reasons why the influencer phenomenon emerged. Identity reinforcement, as discussed in Chapter 2, is one reason. Another is the craving for "authenticity", cited as the main reason to trust an influencer. If social media is "content over time", the strongest value being exchanged is not the content itself, which has become a commodity, but the curation behind it. I propose that the underlying reason why influencers are so popular is that they are the human embodiment of content curation algorithms. One that you, as a follower, explicitly consent to use. As general trust breaks down, the concept becomes more specific, and specific trust as a shortcut to truth becomes particularly tempting. The underlying reason why we have come to place such value on which influencers to follow is the wider consent catastrophe spanning across the internet.

Could any of the technology giants today truly claim that they have obtained "their" data fairly? *"The right to privacy ceases upon the publication of the facts by the individual, or with his consent"*, words published in 1890 in Harvard Law Review.[cxcv] One point of view is that once a user autonomously accepts the terms and conditions when signing up for a service and that this is the full extent of consent that is required. On average, reading all the terms and conditions we encounter in one year would take more than two months. In addition to time, understanding the fine print also requires legal literacy. Just how free does consent need to be to be enforceable? What is more, the choice presented does not reflect the whole picture. Accepting or rejecting cookies is not the sole consideration. Other techniques, such as browser fingerprinting (profiling browsing behaviour), third-party data selling (a prolific market), and triangulation (combining data from multiple sources), are never presented as a choice to begin with. And even if all these conditions were in place, the choice would need to be granular enough to be meaningful. For example, consenting to cookies is a one-time event. There is no continuous feedback on actual data accessed, by whom, and for what purpose.

Yet more complications arise. Data ownership is rather irrelevant when the subject is not the creator of the content, like when parents upload videos of their children. In 2019, the FTC fined YouTube $170 million in the largest penalty ever levied for violations of the Children's Online Privacy Protection Act, penalising using children's data without adequate consent.[36]

Just as one should not be too young for privacy, people should not be too poor to have a right to privacy. The choice presented cannot be a choice between using free data-mining services or losing access to work, communication and life. Mary Madden, researcher at the Data & Society Research Institute, observed that the poor experience two extremes: hypervisibility or invisibility. When it comes to online interactions it is quite simple: the poor do not have the luxury to give up a free service. They do not have the time to look for an alternative platform or the funds to consult lawyers on terms and conditions. Front and centre are the opportunity costs of not focusing on their immediate priority: getting out of poverty. On the one hand, it is truly a benefit to society that free online platforms exist and that people can enjoy their functional benefits to improve their lives. On the other hand, some business models price people out of privacy (Chapter 11). It is a choice between giving up your data to send a message to your family, or not sending a message at all. This is coerced consent in its purest form.

Can we truly say that a person has all, or even most, information available to analyse the required consent rationally? Consent is not given; consent is taken. Thinly veiled, "consent" to be the input for algorithms implies agreement with the rules used for its corresponding output.[37] This is a false choice and an insult to the

---

[36] Based on 2018 data, $170 million is equivalent to two days of revenue based on $136.2 billion annual revenue. FTC statement: "Google and YouTube Will Pay Record $170 Million for Alleged Violations of Children's Privacy Law," FTC, 4 September 2019.
[37] I call this the "False Algorithmic Contract".

original promise of the Internet. Luciano Floridi, Professor at Oxford University's Department of Philosophy and Ethics of Information worded it wonderfully: *"We never stop becoming ourselves, so protecting a person's privacy also means allowing that person the freedom to construct and change herself profoundly. The right to privacy is also the right to a renewable identity."*[cxcvi]

Recourse Rebellion

As a very first step, humans need transparency on which objectives the algorithm in question is currently optimising for (e.g. engagement), and how these objectives manifest (e.g. newsfeed). Does this mean more data for greater personalisation and ultimately more relevance, or has utility been equated with efficiency, leaving less and less room for love, downtime and sleep? What have we lost, personally, when we no longer permit ourselves to "waste" time?[cxcvii] Transparency on algorithmic objectives cannot be mistaken for accountability. Knowing something bad is happening does not make it good.

The next requirement is access to intuitive tools to set these goals on an individual level. For instance, it should be possible to configure information environments to maximise learning about a specific topic. Stuck in overzealous filter bubbles, the value of neutrality is all but forgotten. These goals could even include digital downtime, directly challenging the current "gamification" trend to maximise time online.[38] Personal customisation of information, may that be

---

[38] The application of traditional game playing elements (e.g. point scoring, rewards) to other activities as a technique to increase engagement.

search or social feeds, is one of the most intuitive applications. What if stated values instead of observed online behaviour would guide algorithmic recommendations? What if you could indicate you care about climate change, and the retail algorithm responds with sustainable fashion choices? Long overdue, humans should be able to set their own optimisation goals.

AI professor Stuart Russell points to a common fallacy: algorithms must *understand* your values, not *have* your values. The world is too diverse to find one value system that satisfies everyone. Eventually, the conversation should become not about algorithmic objectives, but how algorithms can achieve human objectives.[cxcviii]

Consider the following. There are two points of view on preferences: either individuals are their preferences or individuals are more than their preferences. If individuals are 100 percent their preferences, this depends on all those preferences being visible. But, not all preferences are expressed in behaviour and behaviour does not express all preferences. The rich internal layering of emotions and thoughts is not always explicit. Some preferences are conscious, some are unconscious. Yet, the expressed behaviour is what algorithms use as data points to build human profiles. If we believe individuals are *more* than their preferences, and that this holds across the board, it is implied that there are certain rights that should be available to all individuals. This also means those rights need to be considered when developing algorithms. Whichever we believe to be true, if we believe that individuals are working with more complete data about themselves and their goals than an external party, individuals need to be empowered to set their own algorithmic goals.

Professor Russell proposed to provide feedback to algorithms via a "switch-off" game. Once you receive a recommendation, you should be able to make the choice to switch-off or continue. This way, behaviour does not need to be consistent for the recommendation to be useful. As personality tests taught us, randomness of behaviour differs per person. As humans figure out the world, their place in it, and themselves, this could be one mechanism to take AI with us on that journey.

Control even can and should extend to visibility into results, for example a time-tracker on your favourite procrastination app or the carbon footprint of your daily commute. The quantified self is a person who has decided to gather data for a purpose: to direct future behaviour. In that sense, the quantified self goes directly against deterministic algorithms (executing the same logic again and again) and rather favours self-learning algorithms (those learning from feedback). Rather than making decisions for you, technology should empower you to become a better decision maker.

Algorithms give people what they want, or at least more of what they click on. This means that either we make a deliberative effort to think about what we want, or we agree to let our impulses dictate our lives. There is a constant need to be aware of outsourcing the responsibility to think independently. Humans need to explore and examine preferences if we do not want an external party to impose our preferences on us in the future. At the moment, we are at risk of allowing that to happen. The brain is a muscle. If we solely trust algorithms to do the work for us, we should not be surprised if we forget how to do the work. We need to demand visibility into the information environment we are already in, and the tools to change it. Pull, not push. That is control.

But contesting conclusions that have already been drawn is nearly impossible if there is no visibility on how those conclusions were reached in the first place. Should there not be an obligation to disclose reasons for rejection? Current practices normalise asymmetric decision making. Yet calculating the future should actually be a conversation, not a one-sided monologue. Trusting an AI explanation requires clear regulatory guidelines of what such an explanation should cover and entail. To arrive at a shared consensus discourse is essential.

Discourse Dilemmas

Human values evolve over time and so does our interpretation of them. Dismissing discussion on algorithmic accountability is equal to dismissing this historic truth. The implications reach even farther: hard-coding algorithmic values is a form of fundamentalism. Decision-making algorithms need to adhere to criteria which can and must evolve and progress over time, just as humanity evolves and progresses. If there is any future where AI and humanity peacefully coexist, this future must include both digital and human feedback loops on all facets of algorithmic decisions.

The future will need a new area of research: *Algorithm Archaeology*. How did the algorithm come to be? What were design choices made along the way? What do these decisions signal about values held at that point in time?

Even when healthy (machine-readable, anonymised, high-quality and high volume) data is paired with sensible objectives, bias can leak into the system if the information baseline is not representative. Representation starts at data collection. Just as police data reflects police practices and policies, this holds true for any and all systems. Biases need due process and due diligence. The kind and extent of required regulation will depend on how deeply a particular bias is embedded in society. Important algorithms will carry IDs, not only dramatically increasing their usefulness but also serving as a point for feedback. Based on these IDs, algorithms can build reputations, and be subject to independent audits based on a global governance framework. For example, evaluation on if the model adequately covers the group of people it aims to address. Because preference models are almost always incomplete, algorithms should know what they do not know.

Of course, there are reasonable technical reasons of how and why bias unintentionally creeps into a dataset. In this case, roughly two types of correlations appear: patterns that actually correlate with the meaning of the data, like the paint on a painting or the mane of a male lion, and patterns that happen to exist within the training set but not generalise to other contexts, such as the square shape of a painting, or the colour yellow for four legged mammals.[cxcix] Where do we need certainty, and where do we need probability? What is the cost we are willing to pay for each?

A technique called "inverse reinforcement learning" seems to offer a promising solution. Its counterpart, "ordinary" reinforcement learning maximises rewards and minimises punishments to optimise the total outcome. Inverse reinforcement learning however, looks at the behaviour, and tries to figure out which outcome that behaviour is trying to maximise: what is the reward function? This could not only uncover hidden value systems of humans, but equally re-introduce transparency into black box algorithms.

When black box algorithms exhibit bias, another potential solution is proposed by AI researcher Sandra Wachter. To understand the effect's input, as well as shining light on specific decisions, we have to turn our gaze towards the output, for example by checking whether changing someone's race or gender affects a decision (which would be discrimination). Then the algorithm can be retrained with "counterfactual explanations" to correct for the bias. Here, counter-factual explanations are the *"smallest change to the world that can be made to obtain a desirable outcome"*.[cc]

It follows that usability testing needs to be complemented by abusability testing. One of the most unethical things to do as a company is not making an absolute effort identifying, understanding and preventing negative unintended consequences and biases. Do not make the mistake to only focus on the harm that is obvious.

Last but not least, problem complexity is not just computation. If we step back it is actually quite irrational that we are so convinced that irrational beings can code rational logic which would be universally acceptable to the other eight billion irrational beings. *"Doubt is not a pleasant condition"* writes Voltaire *"but certainty is absurd."*[cci] If a certain degree of doubt is unavoidable, in some scenarios we are bound to judge algorithms harder than humans, and the other way around. Who is worthy of our trust? The trust delta will differ per category. Scholar, author and entrepreneur Cesar Hidalgo has researched this topic by contrasting human and machines as the main actors in over 80 different scenarios.

Consider the following two example scenarios:

"In a subway station, an **officer** *sees a person carrying a suspicious package who matches the description of a known terrorist. The ..."* (**Human**).

"In a subway station, a **computer vision system** *sees a person carrying a suspicious package who matches the description of a known terrorist. The ..."* (**Machine**).[ccii]

Study participants were asked questions such as: was the action intentional; was the action harmful? It turns out that we do not see categorisation, identification and classification of a "thing" as the same as assigning a value to it. Just as markets have moral limits, so do algorithms: there are spheres of life where they do not belong. The Swedish AI expert and University of Oxford philosophy professor Nick Bostrom makes a valid counter-argument: *"To the extent that ethics is a cognitive pursuit a super intelligence could easily surpass humans in the quality of moral thinking"*.[cciii] Continuous and critical evaluation is required if we use digital logic for problems that require human logic, or the other way around. As Picasso accused machine intelligence; *"They can only give you answers."*[cciv] Humans should not forget how to ask questions.

The bright side is that algorithms and AI can be leveraged to make us more trustworthy as humans. There is a widely carried consensus that following your gut is a poor compass for large parts of government officials, medical practitioners and police officers. People are black boxes too, but we now have the power and opportunity to build something that, in a positive and meaningful way, transcends us.

Reason & Autonomy

The last three chapters made the case for rebooting autonomy of being, knowing and reason.

Chapter 6 made the case for decentralised identity for humans and things, recapturing the identity proxies that underpin privacy taxes on the Internet. The first law declares that digital identity is a human right. Secondly, digital identity is a public good. Thirdly, governments are responsible for foundational identity. Fourth, the private and public sector provides value through contextual identity. Fifth and last, things must have an identity to be accountable. Chapter 7 explained that access to independent information of high integrity is foundational for democracies, arguing that democracies depend on freedom of thought, and the deeper relation between truth and reason. Chapter 8 made the case that preserving human autonomy in the long-term includes an awareness of algorithmic autonomy, with a meaningful dialogue between the two.

As the opening thesis of this book argued, in the 21st century data privacy precedes the capability to make up one's mind across a spectrum of alternatives, and the ability choose to act accordingly. The next two chapters will closely examine the two optimisation games which hold a stake in these human choices and actions, starting with profit optimisation games. If data privacy becomes a core driver of the future of human autonomy, how can we ensure that in the quest for privacy the many potential benefits of data are not cast aside, and ultimately lost? The next chapter examines if it is possible to have it all.

9. Liberating Data

"If you wish to make an apple pie from scratch, you must first invent the universe."
- Carl Sagan[ccv]

When the French Emperor Napoleon invaded Russia, he rallied his troops to go where no leader had gone before; to achieve the impossible. The victors would harvest the riches of the old forests, master the white tundra and revel in Russian treasures. Yet, after wading through snow for hours and hours, his soldiers found that the houses in which they had hoped to take refuge were burned or destroyed. Whenever they grew hungry and scoured the land for food, ashes lay where crops used to grow. Time and time again, the French soldiers encountered the neigh undefeatable opponent of scorched earth. The thinking behind this tactic is simple, yet effective: to stop the water from flowing, turn off the tap – to stop the enemy from advancing, burn everything of value. Today, this is also one response to the chaos we find ourselves in. Some argue that if triangulation cleverly leverages the combination of primary and secondary data, its lifeblood is the very same. No data, no triangulation. However, mercilessly and systematically destroying the feeding ground of triangulation to prevent abuse would equal the systematic destruction of all the benefits that data brings in the same stroke.

Instead, we should take inspiration from another man who has gone down in history: Leonardo da Vinci. Throughout his life, this master of many trades developed a fondness and aptitude for drawing, painting, sculpting, designing, engineering, architecture, medicine, military technology, poetry, philosophy and politics. Yet Leonardo da Vinci's burning desire was something else entirely: he dreamed of flying. In pursuit of this obsession he produced more than 35,000 words and 500 sketches on flying machines and the nature of air and bird flight. However, despite his apparent genius, he failed to grasp that humans did not need to keep refining flapping wing devices to better approximate feathers. We needed to invent the plane. This story holds the nugget needed to reimagine data privacy for the 21st century, whilst respecting, encouraging and yielding the many benefits of data, such as artificial intelligence.

To free data from the restraints of misuse, we need to liberate individual data autonomy. To liberate individual data autonomy, we need to imagine a world in which both data autonomy and data utility co-exist. This chapter proposes five streams of privacy: *Encryption*, *Impermanence*, *Distribution*, *De-identification* and *Decentralisation*. Some of these metaphorical streams will swell, some will dry out; some will mix, some will diverge. All of them will matter.

Encryption

Although the full consideration of whether encryption is always desirable is beyond the scope of this book, we will briefly look at why encryption matters, how it works, and how it could be useful. Of course, encryption, anonymity and privacy are inherently linked. While varying degrees of anonymity exist, the desirability of each is context-dependent and might imply moral judgement. This ranges from intuitive, generally shared assumptions (e.g. sharing child porn should have no expectation of anonymity) to the mundane (e.g. browsing recipes on your favourite food blogger's website should enjoy a high expectation of anonymity). Such questions are further weighed in Chapter 10.

Generally defined as a mathematical method of reversibly transforming information, the most important kinds of encryption include encryption-in-transit, end-to-end encryption and zero-knowledge proofs.

Most likely, you have already used encryption-in-transit, as this is commonly used in Internet browsers today. The web browser prefix "HTTPS" denotes encryption between the service (e.g. a website) and you, the user. Encryption-in-transit has two main benefits. The first benefit seems obvious: the content is encrypted, and thus private. The second benefit is less obvious: when encrypted, it is not possible to edit or otherwise alter the content in the data package that is being transferred. In other words, the integrity of the message is protected. Yet, although most web traffic now flows using HTTPS, the majority of email, chat and audio messages do not.

Tech pioneer Jaron Lanier observed that we cannot have a society in which, if two people wish to communicate, the only way that can happen is if it is financed by a third person who wishes to manipulate them.[ccvi] For the large majority of digital communication, there is no denying that the opportunity to do just that exists. There is something particularly unsettling about not knowing whether that opportunity has been seized.

This is what sets the second kind of encryption, end-to-end encryption, apart. Only the users that are communicating with each other can read the messages. WhatsApp, for example, uses a combination of public and private keys, reminiscent of the knight in the castle from Chapter 6.[ccvii] Some up and coming messaging applications, such as Telegram and Signal, mostly enjoy traction thanks to their privacy-first design. For example, Signal uses a new symmetric key for each message, providing a feature cryptographers call "forward secrecy": decrypting one message does not decrypt the rest. This guarantees that information remains for your eyes only.

Encryption has the potential to preserve privacy across a wide variety of digital channels of communication. This does not just include the information you share with others, but also information you would like to share about yourself (i.e. attestations). Since a scalable identity meta-system has to work on all platforms, it needs to be safe on all of them. One particularly interesting cryptographic technique is called "zero-knowledge proof", or "zk-snarks" for short.

Zk-snarks owe their name to their ability to require zero knowledge of content to reliably verify said content. This means trusting the proof, without trusting the party providing the proof. Using this type of cryptography, someone you severely dislike and most certainly do not trust could hold a blue M&M in their closed fist and prove to you it is an M&M without revealing its colour – and you would trust that this claim is true.

Summed up in one word, the idea behind zk-snarks is "minimisation". When data is disclosed, that disclosure should involve the minimum amount of data necessary to accomplish the task at hand. To be exclusively identified, all claims must be authenticated, but it does not require exclusive identification for a claim to be authenticated. Set in a different context, zk-snarks could prove that Waldo is in the book, without pointing him out. Zero-knowledge encryption is the antithesis of data leaks: it does not mean anonymisation, but selective sharing.

Mathematically, zk-snarks would most simply be expressed as $f(x)=y$, where x is private, and y is public. The private attestation ("x") is treated with a function to arrive at the public proof ("y"). Different from earlier techniques, the information is encrypted before it is uploaded, and the key is never shared. To work, zero-knowledge proofs must have at least two properties: "completeness" and "zero-knowledgeness". Firstly, let's explore completeness: if a statement is true, the verifier believes the result of the proof. Reminiscent of Chapter 6, this is why attestations always have to be both objective and verifiable. The second property is zero-knowledgeness. The verifier does not learn any other information about the person providing the proof other than what is in the proof.

The types of questions which can be answered using this method are incredibly diverse. Consider a Paris-based man, 50 years old, who graduated from Oxford University. Is this person between 18-65 years old? Yes. Does this person live in the EU? Yes. Does this person have a valid university degree? Yes. The zk-proofs did not specify his age, nationality or university, but did confirm that such proofs exist. Crucially, these answers would only be cryptographically unlocked if explicit consent is given to do so. Similarly, the unlocking of these answers is recorded, offering an accountability data trail.

Combining human trust and cryptographic trust, encryption techniques have the potential to simul-taneously minimise digital footprint, reduce data liability and increase underlying reliability. In addition to encryption, there is another privacy stream about to transform how we think about data minimisation: impermanence.

Impermanence

In the age of cloud computing (data storage) and permanent connectivity (data capture), for the first time ever, remembering is cheaper than forgetting.[ccviii] Impermanence, the counterbalance to this trend, is the second form of minimisation.

Just as WhatsApp and Telegram rose on the wings of encryption, the rise of Snapchat is largely owed to its messaging impermanence. One major drawback of today's systems is that they neither forgive nor forget. Party pictures on Facebook from ten years ago are most likely still there because keeping pictures takes less effort than deleting them. In the future, reducing permanence will become a messaging-first design feature. The messaging app Signal already allows its users to customise disappearance intervals which are shared by everyone in the conversation. One application for which this will likely become stunningly popular are dating apps such as Tinder and Bumble. As Signal puts it, the good memories will last even if the words vanish.

Tellingly, although deleting messages is not a feature for Facebook's users, different rules apply to its executives. Reportedly, early messages from its C-suite, notably its CEO, have gradually started to disappear from inboxes. The now removed thread below between a 19-year old Zuckerberg and a friend provides a clue as to why[ccix]:

> **Zuckerberg:** *Yeah so if you ever need info about anyone at Harvard*
> **Zuckerberg:** *Just ask.*
> **Zuckerberg:** *I have over 4,000 emails, pictures, addresses, SNS*
> **[Redacted Friend's Name]:** *What? How'd you manage that one?*
> **Zuckerberg:** *People just submitted it.*

Zuckerberg: *I don't know why.*
Zuckerberg: *They "trust me"*
Zuckerberg: *Dumb fucks.*

But it is not only people who would benefit from the impermanence of certain types of data. A strong business case exists as well. In fact, data will likely become the hot potato which nobody will want to hold. If there is no strategic significance, companies will want to get rid of it. Legislation has started formalising responsibility, and regulators have begun to hold companies accountable. Furthermore, hoarding data and not using it actually makes it worth less than zero. Not only is the time value of data negative, all steps in the data supply chain, from capturing to cleaning to storing it, carry a business cost. Instead, data will be literally accounted for on the balance sheets of the future. The current implied value will become explicit by law. In the future, data will either be an asset or a liability.

The new data value paradigm will be "what adds value to data is logic". If this is true, maximising the value of data means that the most valuable logic needs to be matched with the most relevant data. For that to happen, either the data or the logic needs to move. To maximise the movement of data and logic in the 21st century, there are three exciting technological developments. These take place in the computational field (distribution), in the differential privacy field (de-identification), and in the distributed ledger field (decentralisation). They target where data is processed, what it looks like, and who it is shared with.

Distribution

If encryption and impermanence are all about data minimisation, data distribution is all about location, location, location. As the computation of data is pushed to the edge, this directly affects where data is processed and stored. Instead of going to the cloud, which is the current default, the question changes if the logic was brought to the device. What would happen if personal data would not move off-device?

Just like an indoor cat that refuses to leave its sunny spot next to its bowl of cat food, you might call this "fat" data. What if fat data could stay on-device, bringing the cat food to its bowl? The data could stay in its comfortable spot, while enjoying the benefits of chasing birds outside all the same. It would be like living in paradise.

Two particular advantages of this approach stand out. Firstly, data security gets an upgrade. Less movement means less places that need to be secured. Secondly, with billions of mobile devices around the world and AI chips becoming increasingly powerful, using edge computing will open up a wealth of computing power. Ultimately, this will extend way beyond the reach of the largest data centre in the world. As data sets grow larger and models more complex, decoupling machine learning from the need to store data in the cloud becomes more attractive.

Edge computing is a great alternative to cloud computing, in more ways than one. Ultimately, it can, firstly, provide a faster, more personalised end-user experience thanks to lower latency and custom logic. Secondly, it can reduce cost via bandwidth efficiencies, and, thirdly, it can train the main model when combined with machine learning. The technical term for the latter is "federated learning".

Compared to the centralised training approach, federated learning is a distributed training method. It enables, for example, mobile phones in different geographical locations to collaboratively teach a centralised machine learning model, while keeping all personal data that may contain private information on-device. As self-sovereign identity shifts the centre of gravity towards the individual, federated learning takes this interplay between near and far processing further.

Google describes the underlying process of federated learning as follows. First the device downloads the current model, improves it locally on-device, and subsequently summarises the changes as an encrypted update. Because of the separation of data ownership and control in edge computing, the data packages must be encrypted. Once uploaded to the cloud, this update is immediately averaged with other user updates to improve the (centralised) shared model. All training data remains on-device, and no individual updates are stored in the cloud.[ccx]

Data access control is more comprehensive if data stays on-device, which is why, in the federated learning model, there is no reason why data would not be portable on the user level. In other words, you are still the product, but you are a little bit safer, a little bit more anonymous, and exploitation is a little bit more efficient. All in all, a great start.

There are even more benefits to this approach. Locally, personalisation is easier. With higher degrees of personalisation to the individual user, these models have shown better results than their centrally trained counterparts. Additionally, on-device data is dynamic and live, shielding it from the negative time value of centrally stored data. Also, personalisation and model improvements are based on training data which, in some cases, exclusively resides on-device, hinting at a potential competitive advantage.

Edge computing might soon become the only acceptable way to treat certain types of data. Think of hardware breakthroughs that make it possible to verify and encrypt fingerprints and faces securely, and exclusively, on-device. Consider other, highly sensitive personally identifiable information, such as voice and other biometrics. Ultimately, the shift to edge computing will enable personalised privacy-preserving micro-services, whilst the economic efficiency of edge solutions will slowly cut away at centralised systems. As the increased centralisation and rise of "hyperscale" centralised computing architectures dominated the past decade, the next decade may well be marked by the rise of edge computing.

De-identification

De-identification, the fourth privacy stream, is underpinned by a technique called "differential privacy". Although the term is currently less well known than some of the previously discussed techniques, its impact will be considerable. While encryption and impermanence are all about minimisation and distributed computing is all about location, differential privacy is primarily about maths.

This addresses privacy's greatest sin: being such an abstract concept. Differential privacy puts a stop to abstraction by putting a number on privacy. This privacy delta is called "epsilon" (like the Greek letter ε), or the "privacy budget", and introduces noise mathematically. The degree of noise (as represented by epsilon) is the capped maximum of privacy exposure. Because differential privacy can be expressed through maths, it elevates privacy discussions from the abstract to the tangible.

In contrast to traditional methods, which use concealment as a shield, this technique makes it clear to exactly what extent data has been transformed. Such transparency precedes accountability. In particular, differential privacy may be seen as a technical solution for analysing and sharing data, while protecting the privacy of individuals in accordance with existing legal or policy requirements, for example in compliance with de-identification or disclosure limitations.[ccxi] Not only is this relevant, even paramount, to legislative purposes, it also improves the results. As opposed to leaving data processors and users with uncertainty regarding the accuracy of an analysis, the epsilon spells out the degree of uncertainty with certainty. You know exactly what you are working with.

Using elegant mathematical models, differential privacy de-identifies the individual whilst preserving the trend. Also, the mathematical, local nature of this technique automatically provides a robust security layer, independent of the methods and resources used by a potential attacker. Excitingly, it follows that differential privacy tools can be used to provide broad public access to data while preserving privacy, opening the door to data which could not have been shared otherwise. This pertains to microdata, such as the way a foot hits the ground when running, sensitive data, such as weight gain during pregnancy, and controversial data, such as domestic abuse reports in a neighbourhood.

Most importantly, de-identified data could well lead to allowing and incentivising access to *more* data. When we reframe data as a global resource, things change dramatically. De-identifying data could turn the tide on the isolated benefits in centralised silos in favour of open data economies. In combination with other techniques, differential privacy could help spread the benefits of AI by equalising opportunity to data access.

Multiple implementations of differential privacy have already been deployed by corporations such as Google, Apple and Uber, but opportunities extend way beyond the private sector. Consider aid workers trying to eradicate Ebola. If they could bring their own logic to anonymised data sets, the insights that would be unlocked could literally make the difference between life and death.

Combining differential privacy with distributed computing – combining maths with location – is a particularly elegant solution. This could work as follows. Anonymisation can be achieved by removing device identifiers, sending the previously discussed encrypted data package. This starts the differential privacy process, eliminating personally identifiable metadata and IP addresses, and transforming the remaining data using a particular epsilon. The final step is aggregation and analysis. For example, for health applications, Apple could use a privacy budget with an epsilon of two and limit user contributions to one donation per day.[ccxii] Bringing in impermanence, Apple then chooses to limit the timeframe in which it retains the collected data to, say, a maximum of three months.

Under Apple founder Steve Jobs, the company proudly touted privacy as one of its core values. Jobs even proclaimed that, to him, *"Privacy means people know what they are signing up for, in plain language, and repeatedly."* Today, what do our societies value more? Improved privacy, and by extension, reduced cost of privacy breaches and greater sharing of data giving rise to new business models, or pure computation in silos, sacrificing individual rights in the process? These considerations lead to the final privacy stream, which addresses the final question. How far can we push data collaboration in the 21st century?

Decentralisation

There is no shadow of a doubt that artificial intelligence has far greater potential than what it is used for today. If we stick to developing AI along a centralised, profit-oriented philosophy, much of its potential will remain unexplored, and perhaps ultimately lost. If we believe AI will bring huge risks and huge benefits, we need to understand what we can do now to improve the chances of reaping the benefits and avoiding the risks.

Decentralised collaboration might hold some of the answers. In particular, there are four exciting opportunities for decentralised data, and decentralised artificial intelligence.

The first opportunity is to tackle ownerless problems. Climate change or the United Nations Sustainable Development Goals are good examples: their outcome is relevant to everyone on the planet, but the issue is owned by no one. The second opportunity is to solve niche problems. Consider crowdsourcing the labelling of asteroid data for the European Space Agency ("Hubble Asteroid Hunters") or citizen scientists searching for the Higgs boson particle for CERN ("Higgs Hunters").[39] The third opportunity is to finally address big problems. Some challenges are simply too large to solve alone. For instance, developing autonomous vehicles may require more data than any one company could possibly possess and process alone, although Tesla and Waymo (Alphabet) would likely dispute this. The fourth, and last, opportunity is to work together on shared problems. We need to collectively move away from the rationale that there are problems that only companies such as Facebook or Google can solve, with the implied reason behind it being that they control the required data. If the right infrastructure is in place, shared problems can be met head-on via decentralised collaboration. The challenge then becomes to match problems looking for data with data looking for problems, and to do so at scale.

Which tools are needed to realise these benefits, and, by extension, to democratise data? To reach any

---

[39] ESA: 300,000 classifications for 10,874 images from the ESA HST archives, recovering 1,300 asteroid trails. CERN: Over 37,000 citizen scientists, from more than 170 countries, became part of the team to search for interesting features in LHC data: higgshunters.org.

meaningful collective scale, individual autonomy is key: data needs (1) *consent* to be (2) *encrypted*, (3) *prepared*, (4) *processed*, (5) *analysed* and (6) *rewarded*. The future of decentralised AI means informed data consent for benchmarked algorithms, which will be processed in a decentralised, privacy-compliant manner. Because steps two to five all involve techniques similar to the ones previously discussed in this chapter (encryption, impermanence, distribution, de-identification), we will focus on the first and last step: consent and rewards.

As consent is given *by*, and the corresponding rewards are given *to* people, these concepts have an obvious connection: they require a strong incentive to entice people to share their data. In essence, such incentives reflect human preferences, and have thus become the latest addition to intellectual property (IP) in the 21st century. If the British philosopher John Locke was alive today, he would likely argue that the expression of preferences makes data (intellectual) property.[40] In the 21st century, there is a new opportunity to licence this particular IP, and, as outlined above, there are two reasons why humans would grant consent to do so: financial and societal rewards.

The potential financial rewards are diverse: whenever individuals control data that can be used to add value, personal data markets are born. On a technical level, this could work as follows. If Web 2.0 platforms have many participants and centralised value centres, Web 3.0 protocols have many participants and decentralised value centres. Interestingly, under this second set-up, one sale of data could have multiple beneficiaries. If you provide the raw material for a

---

[40] The English philosopher John Locke (1632-1704) is well known for his work on inalienable rights, understood as rights we cannot give up nor take from somebody else.

product, and every step of the supply chain is a new value layer added on top, this is digitally reflected in your so-called "smart contract" (i.e. codable logic).

These rewards will be fractional, because the data is fractional. Fiat currencies, therefore, might not be the best payment vehicle for digital micro-payments. Smart contracts could automatically accept compensation in the form of "tokens" (i.e. codable currencies). These types of rules are captured in protocols, or the "rule engine" of Chapter 6. For example, I pay you A to execute trusted function B, on my data which has been attested by party C. This is "tokenised federated learning".

Techniques like tokenised federated learning include individuals in the value creation process for the first time. Today, an end-to-end data supply chain consists of many steps, and it is already agreed that not all of these steps need to be executed by the same entity. In the 20th century, the American industrialist Henry Ford famously popularised the assembly line, where each worker specialised in a set of tasks. Blockchain takes this a step further: specialisation and collaboration no longer require being in the same factory; you can be based anywhere in the world, as long as the coded rules are verifiably followed. Data could be cleaned by one stakeholder and segmented by the next. Others could focus on value adding activities such as auditing and benchmarking algorithms. And so forth. Meanwhile, all contributions are logged on-chain to obtain the corresponding reward via a smart contract.

Decentralising value centres results in the opportunity to mix and match benchmarked data and algorithms, whether this happens to be open source data or an open source algorithm, bringing about new forms of value creation. This new capability to "move" data and logic, building on all techniques previously discussed in this chapter, changes the commercial lens from being mandatory to discretionary. This brings us to the second reason individuals could choose to share their data: societal rewards.

There is a certain perception, a certain feeling, that technology has happened to us, or at least to a large portion of us, rather than being driven by us. Any way out of this dilemma needs to involve a greater sense of agency. People trust systems that they helped create. Pioneered by Nobel Prize winner Elinor Ostrom, there are some communal goods for which trust is necessary; one of these is decentralised artificial intelligence.[ccxiii]

The opportunity to leverage decentralised data and decentralised AI to address the four types of problems mentioned previously (ownerless problems, niche problems big problems and shared problems) is significant. Such an opportunity is meaningful enough for a diverse set of stakeholders to further explore the techniques proposed in this chapter.

Additionally, there is some precedent for this type of thinking. The scientific community is built on massive international collaboration via open source publications. The deep learning community, for example, is taking baby steps on the path of transparent algorithms by open sourcing meaningful findings. However, there are many more societal rewards linked to people's willingness to share data, which are explored in more detail in Chapter 11.

In conclusion, if the new data utility function is to maximise the value of data by matching the most valuable logic with the most relevant data, distribution, de-identification and decentralisation lay the technical framework to do so. Distribution will personalise control, de-identification quantifies privacy, and decentralisation allows for democratic movement of data to realise individual and societal benefits. All in all, this would suggest that decentralised AI is indeed possible.

When rewards come into play, so does the opportunity for exploitation, which brings us to the final section of this chapter: profit games.

Profit Games

Consider the following thought experiment, running through the scenarios in which an individual (data subject) and a corporation (data collector) can coexist. The outcome of this experiment is the holy grail of profit games: *"The Data Equilibrium"*. This is represented by a matrix in which the currency is trust.

The Data Equilibrium Matrix	John Ltd Inclusive Strategy (B1)	John Ltd Extractive Strategy (B1)
Sarah Absolute Consent (A1)		
Sarah Coerced Consent (A2)		

On the left-hand side is the data subject, Sarah, and, on the other side, the data collector, John Ltd. Sarah is a user of John Ltd, accessing the service the company provides. As the data subject, Sarah has provided either *Absolute* (Informed; Option A1) or *Coerced* (Uninformed; Option A2) consent to share her data in return for the service. Her choice is to trust, or not trust, John Ltd. As data collector, John Ltd has the choice to decide – once Sarah has chosen – to reward her trust by using one of the aforementioned techniques or not.

John Ltd could either opt for an *Inclusive* (Good faith; Option B1) or *Extractive* (Bad faith; Option B2) strategy. In this game, there is an uncapped number of rounds.

If Sarah has not provided absolute consent, while John Ltd can nonetheless gather and use her data but chooses not to do so, John Ltd acts in good faith and nothing bad happens. Sarah did not explicitly trust John Ltd, but John Ltd all the same acts as a good actor (A2, B1; 0,0). This is the *"Benevolent God"* category. The company could, but did not, exercise its power. Like a thief with a key who does not enter the house, but keeps the key just in case. This is asymmetric consent. Even though you are happy you are not being robbed, you never consented to give away a copy of your key in the first place. Yet, even though 0,0 is not a bad outcome for Sarah, preserving her privacy, it is less attractive to result-driven companies. When faced with coerced consent, what if John Ltd would choose an extractive strategy instead?

The same situation with a different reaction would result in now familiar headlines. Think of GDPR violations, Cambridge Analytica, and the $5 billion FTC fine awarded to Facebook. By playing the combination of coerced consent and extractive strategy both sides stand to lose (A2, B2; -1,-1). John Ltd incurs reputational and financial damage and Sarah loses her privacy. The re-energised enforcement of checks and balances in this category is a reaction to the real-life result that has lent this category its name: *"Fines & Fury"*.

Rebooting the game, what would happen if Sarah did trust John Ltd, and provides absolute consent? If John replies with an extractive strategy, Sarah knowingly draws the short straw. Remember that the game has an uncapped number of rounds. Trust implies vulnerability which is why its violation hurts and feels personal. When trust deteriorates, so does loyalty. In the context of recent headlines this implies the following: had Facebook been part of a market duopoly at the time of the Cambridge Analytica fall-out, its platform would likely have been collectively abandoned. The move set would not repeat infinitely, growing more unlikely with every round. This is called the *"Trust Timebomb"* (A1, B2; -1,1).

The Data Equilibrium Matrix	John Ltd Inclusive Strategy (B1)	John Ltd Extractive Strategy (B2)
Sarah Absolute Consent (A1)	**Trust Loop** (A1, B1; 1,1)	**Trust Timebomb** (A1, B2; -1,1)
Sarah Coerced Consent (A2)	**Benevolent Gods** (A2, B1; 0,0)	**Fines & Fury** (A2, B2; -1,-1)

Note that as soon as Sarah's trust breaks, John Ltd cannot win anymore. What if John Ltd had rewarded Sarah's trust the first time around? If Sarah and John Ltd had both played A1 and B1, the outcome would be mutually beneficial (A1, B1; 1,1). The win-win characteristics of mutual trust ensures that the game will repeat, creating the *"Trust Loop"*. Because data has value over time, this game will repeat again and again. Trust begets trust.

In sum, if Sarah chooses A1 in good faith, and there is no reward, the next choice is going to be A2, after which John Ltd will never win. Therefore, the best move for the company is playing B1 immediately. Mutual trust is the only way to break the extractive loop of profit games.

The shape of this trust will depend on a case by case basis. It could take the form of personalisation or perhaps the form of a monetary reward. The crucial consideration is choice. Asking people to give up their privacy for the company's monetary gain is a decision that has to be at their absolute discretion. Legislation, such as the European GDPR, already acts as a checks and balances mechanism for bad corporate actors. To keep benefiting from the many advantages data can bring, companies must change strategy.

All in all, the combination of encryption (crypto-graphy), impermanence (time), distribution (location), differential privacy (math) and decentralisation (collaboration) offers a feasible alternative to profit optimisation games without compromising data benefits. Is it worth all this effort to create more equitable systems? Yes, it absolutely is. Privacy is not a lost cause, yet. We can achieve both great artificial intelligence and great privacy standards. We can and we must. It is not only a possibility; it is our responsibility. The next chapter will cover the last remaining aspect of the identity meta-system: power optimisation games.

10. The New Social Contract

'It is not always the same thing to be a good man and a good citizen.'
— Aristotle[41]

Power games are embedded in and emboldened by profit games. While profit games justify data collection, power games justify data surveillance. Having established that power games in the East and West have different characteristics, it is worth acknowledging that their history, and the rationale behind this history, is quite different. Risking unfair generalisation, a more accurate fault line is the differentiation between authoritarian and non-authoritarian regimes. The first describes a government that concentrates political power in an authority that does not answer to its people. The second often

---

[41] The philosopher Aristotle (c. 384–322 B.C.) in his opus defining work on Nicomachean Ethics, speculated to be based on his lectures, thought every purposeful action in this world pursues a certain desirable aim ("telos"). This led him to conclude that when pursuing the most perfect of virtues, being a good man does not necessarily equal being a good citizen.

describes a form of democracy in which citizens can punish missteps. This chapter explores how the role of data cannot be seen in isolation from the role of the government. In the first part of this chapter, we will explore how mass surveillance proliferates in the East and West alike, followed by weighing arguments for the justification of such a system by examining the social contract between citizen and state. Finally, we will discuss how political value systems will manifest, evolve and clash.

The Case for Mass Surveillance

"We cannot ensure the defence of the West if our allies grow dependent on the East," said US Vice President Mike Pence at the 2019 Munich Security Conference.[ccxiv] This is a strongly worded statement with far-reaching implications, and maybe even an admission – there is a lot to unpack here.

But first, let's take a step back: first invented in the US, the Internet has never fully shed its American character. Fast forward to 2019 and Google's market share of global search hovers consistently at the 90 percent mark. YouTube is the world's largest video platform (and the second biggest search engine in the world), Google Chrome is the world's dominant browser (the gateway to the worldwide web for many), while the cloud business of Amazon Web Services (centralised data processing) covers around 50 percent of the global market. Additionally, the Facebook portfolio counts nearly a third of the world's population among its active users (planting an immovable flag in digital communication). All three parent companies (Alphabet, Amazon, Facebook) are headquartered in the US. Further fault lines for the control of the Internet are hardware, software, routers, modems, cables, satellites and other connectivity enablers. As this list goes on, the connection between profit and power games becomes undeniable. Because individual data is already shared with a third party – any third party – that action has forfeited any future right to privacy from a governmental surveillance perspective. And, if these third parties include US companies, that includes the US government.

Not keen on being at the mercy of US internet policies, countries have strategically responded by nationalising data centres (in the case of India – Chapter 3), establishing a sovereign Internet (in the case of Russia) and setting up firewalls (the great firewall of China – Chapter 7). Out of the three, China is the most considerable thorn in America's side, as Chinese products are competitively priced and well-designed with competitive functionalities. China's market share in semiconductor chips, for instance, is growing steadily. "Made in China" sells well. Huawei comes in between Samsung and Apple for global smartphone market share. The telecom giant also intends to be competitive with Nokia and Ericsson in the battle for 5G.[ccxv] Mike Pence continued his statement as follows: *"The United States has also been very clear with our security partners on the threat posed by Huawei and other Chinese telecom companies, as Chinese law requires them to provide Beijing's vast security apparatus with access to any data that touches their network or equipment. We must protect our critical telecom infrastructure, and America is calling on all our security partners to be vigilant and to reject any enterprise that would compromise the integrity of our communications technology or our national security systems."* In other words, mandated data access to private Internet enablers by a foreign government, in this case Huawei and China, is not only considered a direct and immediate security threat to the US if its own citizen's data traffic has touched it, but also if its allies do. The outrage of the US against the Chinese company Huawei suggests the existence of a governmental mass surveillance system built on a hybrid of private and public internet infrastructure, at least somewhere in the world. This is apparently already dangerous enough to worry about. The American reading of the threat level is an educated one, as it has similar capabilities.

In 2011, a keynote speaker at a public data conference was announced as follows: *"If you do not give a big round of applause for our next speaker, he is going to find out and it is going to go on your permanent record."* The speaker in question was the CIA's chief technology officer Gus Hunt. Hunt spoke as to why the CIA is interested in data surveillance. *"So our problem is, since you cannot connect the dots you do not have, it drives us into a mode of fundamentally trying to collect everything and hang on to it forever, forever being in quotes of course."*[ccxvi] He spoke to the capabilities to achieve this interest. *"It is really very nearly within our grasp to be able to compute on all human generated information."* The word "all" was underlined by Hunt. He also spoke to the CIA philosophy behind data analysis. *"We care about people, we care about places, we care about organisations, we care about time, events, things and concepts."* Reading between the lines suggests that metadata is most definitely not benign. In fact, Hunt noted that based on the sensors in a smartphone, someone can be identified (with 100 percent accuracy) by the way they walk. He spoke to much more, before concluding with: *"Our belief: Big Data democracy wins."*

Hunt argued that the CIA's rationale for mass surveillance was as follows. If the agency does not know the future value of data, it cannot connect the dots it does not have. Believing there is no point to storing something until it becomes useful, lacking indication when that would be, implies the desire for permanent storage and global coverage. On its own PowerPoint slide from 2011, prepared for the Five Eyes, the NSA described the process as *"Sniff It All, Know It All, Collect It All, Process It All, Exploit It All, Partner It All"*.[ccxvii] For example, the NSA's XKeyscore programme is reported to function like a search engine for people, mapping all forms of online activity and relationships.[ccxviii] Because metadata analysis can be automated (Chapter 3), XKeyscore can extract and tag metadata and content from raw data for analysts to easily search it. Researching the Snowden files, the Intercept reported that as of 2009, XKeyscore servers were located at more than 100 field sites all over the world. According to a 2009 document, some field sites received over 20 terabytes of data per day. If XKeyscore has continued at a similar pace the last decade, it is likely considerably more powerful today. If such capabilities exist, considerable time, effort, expertise, resources and funds have gone into developing this capability.[ccxix] This begs the question: which benefits justify such an investment?

From the most empathetic point of view, we might appreciate how US intelligence agencies came to self-justify this radical approach. Traumatised by the terrorist attacks of 9/11, the motto was "never again". In politics, blame is often attributed based on a perceived lack of control. *How did you not know?* If the argument is that a government that ignores data is as bad as one that ignores how people should vote, generating data becomes a moral obligation. *"Denying our adversaries anonymity allows us to focus our lethality. It's like ripping the camouflage netting off the enemy ammunition dump,"* wrote Glenn Krizay, director of the Defence Forensics and Biometrics Agency, referring to the over seven million biometrically rich identities of those who have come into contact with the US military abroad.[ccxx] It is obvious that surveillance is a potent tool of law enforcement.

Yet taking this line of thinking to the extreme means ignoring the conclusion of the 9/11 Commission report:

necessary information to identify the terrorists already existed at the time, but the dots were not sufficiently connected to act on it.[42] Similarly, the UK found its own 9/11 moment in the tragic London bombings on 7/7 in 2005, when bombs in three trains on the London Underground and one bus killed 52 people and injured more than 700. Despite the available data, the attacks could not be stopped.

What makes this all the more meaningful are the conclusions reached by the journalists from The Washington Post (US) and The Guardian (UK) who were among the first to scrutinise documents shared by whistle-blower Edward Snowden when he went public in 2013. The security initiatives exposed in these documents were diverse in nature, and of varying scope. The Washington Post reviewed an estimated 22,000 surveillance reports collected by the NSA between 2009 and 2012. The 160,000 intercepted conversations originated from more than 11,400 unique accounts. 11 percent of the accounts were NSA targets. The remaining 89 percent of the accounts were bystanders, or non-targets.[ccxxi]

On the other side of the Atlantic, The Guardian reported on surveillance practices of GCHQ, the UK counterpart to the NSA.[ccxxii] Reportedly, GCHQ files from 2008 to 2010 explicitly describe a programme called Optic Nerve, responsible for capturing still images of Yahoo webcam chats in bulk every five minutes, regardless of any suspicion of wrongdoing pertaining to these individuals. Over one six-month period in 2008 alone, more than 1.8 million Yahoo accounts were affected globally, and a substantial quantity contained explicit images. The document estimates that between three

---

[42] The 9/11 Commission Report was written by five Republicans and five Democrats, on behalf of the National Commission on Terrorist Attacks Upon the United States.

and 11 percent of the Yahoo webcam imagery harvested by GCHQ contains *"undesirable nudity"*. The initiative was part of a wider effort to improve facial recognition capabilities and it seems even webcam capabilities of gaming consoles were considered.[ccxxiii]

In 2010, the Foreign Intelligence Surveillance Court (FISA) approved a list of 193 foreign governments that the NSA could conduct surveillance on to gather foreign intelligence. Each year a new certification must be approved by the court to permit such surveillance under Section 702 of the FISA Amendments Act.[ccxxiv] Notably absent were the remainder of the Five Eyes: Canada, New Zealand, Australia and the UK. But the Five Eyes is not the only global intelligence sharing programme. The so-called "Nine-Eyes programme" comprises the UK, the US, Canada, Australia, New Zealand, Denmark, France, Norway and the Netherlands (founded in 1982, in the midst of the Cold War); the "14-Eyes programme" includes those countries plus Germany, Belgium, Italy, Spain and Sweden (established after 9/11, focused on counterterrorism). [ccxxv] The Snowden documents detail deliberations in 2013 on where a permanent base should be located for the latter, citing *"pushback"* from certain European countries on grounds of *"concerns for European Human Rights"*.[ccxxvi]

In response to the Snowden NSA documents, the European Parliament published a 135-point report, acknowledging the validity of the documents and the practices described, proceeding to condemn these practices in strong terms.

Points specifically to US NSA intelligence programmes allowing for the mass surveillance of EU citizens through direct access to the central servers of leading US internet companies (PRISM programme), the analysis of content and metadata (XKeyscore programme), the circumvention of online encryption (BULLRUN), access to computer and telephone networks, and access to location data, as well as to systems of the UK intelligence agency GCHQ such as the upstream surveillance activity (Tempora programme), the decryption programme (Edgehill), the targeted 'man-in-the-middle attacks' on information systems (Quantum-theory and Foxacid programmes) and the collection and retention of 200 million text messages per day (Dishfire programme).[43]

Maybe the true danger is the normalisation of surveillance, continuously moving the needle of what is a "reasonable" expectation of privacy until there is none left. In a globalised world, connected by the Internet and worldwide markets, what do governments consider a reasonable expectation of privacy?

---

[43] Report by the European Parliament on the NSA documents containing strong language, such as: *"Condemns the vast and systemic blanket collection of the personal data of innocent people, often including intimate personal information; emphasises that the systems of indiscriminate mass surveillance by intelligence services constitute a serious interference with the fundamental rights of citizens; stresses that privacy is not a luxury right, but is the foundation stone of a free and democratic society; points out, furthermore, that mass surveillance has potentially severe effects on freedom of the press, thought and speech and on freedom of assembly and of association, as well as entailing a significant potential for abusive use of the information gathered against political adversaries; emphasises that these mass surveillance activities also entail illegal actions by intelligence services and raise questions regarding the extraterritoriality of national laws"* [Point 10]: "European Parliament resolution of 12 March 2014 on the US NSA surveillance programme, surveillance bodies in various Member States and their impact on EU citizens' fundamental rights and on transatlantic cooperation in Justice and Home Affairs," European Parliament, Strasbourg, 12 March 2014.

The New Government

At the beginning of this chapter, we established that the role of data could not be seen in isolation from the role of the government. In this section we will explore potential justifications for the new role governments have assumed in the 21st century.

The principles of the democratic societies of today owe a lot to the thinking of British philosopher John Locke, who argued that any form of political authority hinges on consent. In exchange for this consent, the government is morally obligated to protect the in-alienable rights of its citizens, while its citizens grant the government the enforcement power to do so in return. The French philosopher Jean-Jacques Rousseau referred to this exchange as the "social contract".[44] Locke's inalienable rights included liberty, life, and property – in the US Declaration of Independence, the latter was later replaced with the pursuit of happiness. According to Locke, any arbitrary infringement on these rights is strictly prohibited. Drawing on Locke, one – and only one – of the following three statements about today's social contract must be true.

1. *Government mass surveillance is justified because it protects the inalienable rights of its citizens using just enforcement power.*

2. *Government mass surveillance is not justified because of arbitrary infringement on the inalienable rights of its citizens.*

3. *Government mass surveillance is not justified because the inalienable rights as described by Locke,*

---

[44] The French philosopher Jean-Jacques Rousseau (1712-1778) roughly argues that in the ideal social contract, everyone will be free because they all forfeit the same number of rights and impose the same duties on all.

written in the 17th century, are incomplete given the
realities of the 21st century.

All three statements argue that a government mass surveillance capability exists, which is what we will address first. Secondly, to differentiate between the first and second statement is to differentiate between the protection of, or infringement on, inalienable rights of citizens. On both sides, lines can be drawn at different points, and we will briefly highlight the main arguments for each. The third statement takes a different standpoint, arguing that the inalienable rights as proposed by Locke are incomplete, which is what we will address last.

Based on the original documents leaked by Snowden, as well as the reporting of award-winning journalists, the conclusions of the European Parliament – which found *"compelling evidence"* for the collection, storage and analysis of communication data *"of all citizens around the world, on an unprecedented scale and in an indiscriminate and non-suspicion-based manner"* in its own independent report – and the public admissions of executives from the US institutional branches, the conclusion elicited by all available information goes as follows. The US government, amongst others, expanded the social contract without gaining its citizens' consent. Rather than serving as the basis for an open discussion, the initial disclosure actually discouraged further and future disclosure. Even if one believed these capabilities to be vital for the government-citizen social contract in the 21st century, debate on this decision was clearly not welcome. Authoritarian states deploy the same logic.

Setting the unilateral expansion of the social contract aside, imagine that this expansion was up for debate by both citizens and state. Working from a blank slate, which arguments could be made for and against mass surveillance? What grants a government-run mass surveillance system legitimacy to spy on its own and foreign citizens? Nuances exist regarding scope, outcome, sharing and consent.

Starting with scope means taking the "mass" out of "mass surveillance" to improve legitimacy, which is in theory enforced by checks and balances. Arguably, there is a difference between using all private citizen communication as intelligence signals and specific surveillance of persons of interest. The difference is that in the first case, everyone is a person of interest, or could become a person of interest, depending on the ideology of those in charge. It depends which checks and balances are in place to obtain warrants. This looks far from promising at the moment: in 2015, the Foreign Intelligence Surveillance Court (FISC) approved all submitted NSA surveillance requests. In 2014 Reuters reported an identical 100 percent acceptance rate.[ccxxvii]

The outcome is another consideration. Is there an obligation of citizenship to give up individual privacy in exchange for collective security? What about the collective security of a foreign country? This argument is built on mutual benefits: both citizens and government benefit from a safe society. Utilitarian-style reasoning argues along the lines of providing the greatest good for the greatest number of people. Yet if we acknowledge these mutual benefits, we must also acknowledge its one-sided cost: the cost of citizens giving up their privacy. As outlined in Chapter 3, privacy is measured by the accumulation of societal rules of the past, present and future, and the actors with an interest in enforcing those rules. For inspiration on the potential consequences, any history book will do. Helen Nissenbaum, Professor of Information Science at Cornell Tech, phrased it as follows: *"Public surveillance violates a right to privacy because it violates contextual integrity; as such, it constitutes injustice and even tyranny".*[ccxxviii] In democracy, "kratos" (power) of the "demos" (people) is bolstered by privacy. Furthermore, this line of reasoning is satisfied with tacit consent. It demands that, by being born here, and living here, you implicitly agree that giving up privacy is a citizen's obligation.

From there, maybe consent is the main consideration. Does the government protect or infringe on current inalienable rights? One could argue that, as long as citizens explicitly agree, mass surveillance is valid. However, it could also be argued that consent is conditional. The line in the sand could be drawn at various points, for example at specific surveillance, at domestic mass surveillance, at foreign mass surveillance or at international sharing. But can today's generation give consent for future generations? Is it fundamentally ethical to ask humans to give up privacy? Is privacy something that can be given away, or is it an inalienable right?

This brings the third statement to the forefront. Given the realities of the 21st century, when government mass surveillance is possible, unlike the 17th century, when the inalienable rights were outlined, could these rights simply be incomplete? The power of the government is limited to what individuals can give away, which is capped at their inalienable rights. Mass surveillance has a natural trade-off with data privacy. Human capability for reason is a form of liberty, and if we believe data privacy to precede capability for reason, as we have seen time and time again throughout this book, is data privacy not also an inalienable right?

If mass surveillance is found to be illegitimate, dissent is ethical. If found legitimate, its cross-national nature implies that using the Internet confers acceptance with these conditions, for all facets of information are controlled by some data conduit. If found legitimate, but only for some, a framework of use needs to be established. If we cannot agree on the role of the institution, evaluation of how it does its job is bound to result in conflict. The whole situation is further complicated by nation states extending their own policies to other nation states. What if world powers with differing ideologies, such as China, the US and the EU, decide on different policies?

Wars of Morality

Thus far we have established that power games are embedded in profit games, and that, pending final judgement, the scope of the social contract has been broadened unilaterally. The crux of the matter seems to be that the data that governments have access to, and what they decide to do with that information, is what matters most, as the power of information is limited by how it is put to use. Political reactions to this will vary. Of particular interest are differing choices across countries. Driven by cultural differences and political strategies, three dominant data value systems will solidify: China, the US and the EU.

If the previously raised societal questions were to be explicitly debated – individual vs. collective; free speech vs. moderation; privacy vs. security – different cultures will arrive at different conclusions. Two of the ingredients for these conclusions are institutional and societal trust.

In China, for example, societal trust is considered to be low. Scam scandals are rife. Reportedly, one local court system launched an app to track blacklisted debtholders within 500 meters, with an option to share the information via social media and a reporting function to the authorities.[ccxxix] Low interpersonal trust is one of the reasons why China's citizens did not collectively balk at the social credit system. China's residents are also aware that the relationship between Chinese companies and the Party is historically close. This is underscored by the willingness of WeChat to turn to censorship and the alleged backdoors in Huawei systems. Acceptance of these practices is indeed closely related to trust on one hand, and mistrust on the other. The application of video surveillance and algorithmically determined detention-scores to the Uighur population in Xinjiang as well as travel bans for those with low social credit scores across the mainland both provide early indications as to what this data access will ultimately be used for: encouraging uniformity to better facilitate control. Unapologetically, one of the facial recognition providers proudly used its ability for ethnic profiling as a selling point.[ccxxx] Meanwhile, Chinese facial databases expand. Recent regulation mandates a face scan before buying a smartphone. Facial recognition adoption is also driven by the commercial sector: applications include unlocking doors for short-term rentals, paying at convenience stores, smile-to-pay programmes, banking, retail, transport, schools, offices and even the prediction of KFC orders according to profile and mood. Over 100 million Chinese citizens have willingly signed up to use such systems.[ccxxxi]

The US and the EU view institutional and societal trust differently to China, and also to each other. Observing *"human rights with Chinese characteristics"* from a diplomatic distance, the EU has been more vocal on what it thinks of the US approach, the second value system. Its report on the NSA files contains phrases such as *"Emphasises that trust has been profoundly shaken: trust between the two transatlantic partners, trust between citizens and their governments, trust in the functioning of democratic institutions on both sides of the Atlantic, trust in the respect of the rule of law, and trust in the security of IT services and communication".*[ccxxxii] Again trust emerges as a core theme, but here the trust is violated via the unilateral expansion of the social contract, and the wider international consequences of one country imposing its policies on the many.

At the time of writing, the US and EU disagreed on the role of device IDs, IP addresses and cookies. The EU definition is wider than the US shorthand. GDPR states: *"Natural persons may be associated with online identifiers provided by their devices, applications, tools and protocols, such as Internet protocol addresses, cookie identifiers or other identifiers such as radio frequency identification tags. This may leave traces which, in particular when combined with unique identifiers and other information received by the servers, may be used to create profiles of the natural persons and identify them."*[ccxxxiii] Dry as it might sound, what the EU acknowledged in GDPR regulation is a significant leap in thinking: online identity matters as much as offline identity.

As the US is made up of its states, the EU is the sum of its member states. A critical difference, however, is that the countries who comprise the EU enjoy higher autonomy than their cross-Atlantic peers. One could make the educated guess that this impacts potential data sharing. And not only that, but because Europe boasts fewer prominent technology giants, fewer backdoors could be leveraged, if in place. Therefore, we can assume that, given its emphasis on privacy, cultural diversity and smaller technological footprint, the EU represents an ideology with a smaller permanent data pool, which is more infrequently accessed, and that collection follows more clearly defined reasons. These reasons are mostly security related, for now.

London, still part of the EU at the time of writing, has already started predictive policing practices, which causes reason for concern. One British citizen in Romford, a small town in East London, was part of such a trial. Tucking his baseball cap down and pulling his sweater up, he was not keen on being a guinea pig in the London Metropolitan Police experiment. The man was stopped, an argument ensued, and he was forced to scan his face with an app cross-referencing criminal charges. When nothing came up, he suggested that the police should "piss off", and was charged collected a £90 fine (around $120).[ccxxxiv] Today, London counts 420,000 CCTV cameras.[ccxxxv] Reportedly, facial recognition is already live at Kings Cross, one of London's most prominent central stations, and is about to be rolled out to Canary Wharf, London's financial centre. City-wide roll-out is expected soon. When opt-out options are removed from democracies, this should give pause.

With the Chinese insistence on uniformity in exchange for trust, the US trade-off between security and privacy, and the European emphasis on individual rights, how will this tension unfold? For instance, how will we deal with the fact that all companies need to have headquarters somewhere, given that US and Chinese companies are increasingly dominant? Do these companies only have to adhere to national law, with loyalty to national citizens? Or is accountability owed to all users, irrespective of headquarters? What about Google's other 95 percent users? Should national IDs be biometrically enhanced, effectively building a centralised database of faces and fingerprints of the issuing country, as well as all other countries processing such information, whenever somebody crosses their borders? Unavoidable future collisions include GDPR, political censorship, and, most controversially, collecting data on foreign citizens. The EU's highest court has ruled that Facebook can be ordered by member states to remove defamatory material worldwide, yet Google only needs to apply the "right to be forgotten" within EU borders, for now.[ccxxxvi] Where do value systems begin and end in a globalised world?

Considering the impending conflict between the three value systems, two things are worth pointing out. Firstly, if policy decisions were expressed in technology, codified law or code carrying value systems, this would reduce manifestations of external influence and could potentially exacerbate existing differences between nations. Ironically, an increasingly connected world could become a more sharply divided one. If the Internet is increasingly nationalised, it becomes increasingly localised. Pushing this line of thinking to its logical extreme means that algorithmic laws could lead to algorithmic enforcement, which could cement values, dramatically increasing the difference between communities and nations until it eventually ends in war. We previously saw that hard coding too many assumptions could very well cause a country to stagnate. On whatever level, any AI system we build, no matter the use case, needs to be agile enough to internalise changing norms. If not, the system and its results will quickly be rendered useless. Under the status quo, "normal behaviour" will be decided by Facebook, Google, Microsoft and Amazon in the West and Alibaba, Baidu, and Tencent in the East.

Secondly, as super-power dynamics change, predominant value systems will change in parallel – as China's companies increasingly export their products and services, its value system spreads. Pushing ethnic profiling software in the hands of other governments, normalising the values which underpin it, is acutely dangerous for democracies. When tourists cross the border into the Uighur region in Xinjiang, malware is installed on their phones. The malware downloads text messages, calendar entries, and phone logs, scanning the device for over 70,000 different files.[ccxxxvii] This precedent is plenty of cause for alarm. The more powerful China becomes, the less its suggestions are optional. Reportedly, Google is still working on (re-)entering the Chinese market, and is rumoured to accept censorship constraints this time.[ccxxxviii] After a cybersecurity law mandated user data to be stored in China, Apple confirmed it would open its first data centre in China, forming a partnership with a Chinese company to run the centre and handle data requests from the government.[ccxxxix]

If any, which of these three value systems will become dominant over the next few decades? One battlefield will be data control: with one hand governments will try to fend off data access by foreign governments, and with the other hand they will try to access data of foreign citizens themselves.

The first case in which the US Committee on Foreign Investment asserted that Chinese control of a social media app could have national security implications, was for the LGBTQ+ dating app Grindr. Grindr has a few million users, and the data captured includes self-reported HIV status and location data – by all standards rather sensitive information. Recognising a wealth of potential blackmailing material, the committee called for the acquisition to be unwound before June 2020.[ccxl] Next on the list is TikTok, the viral short video app, which has been one of the few Chinese apps to gain traction in Western countries, ranking the second downloaded app worldwide, after WhatsApp.[45] With 110 million downloads in the US alone, regulators publicly identified TikTok as a *"national security risk"* and *"counterintelligence threat we cannot ignore"* if used to spy on American citizens *"to support and cooperate with intelligence work controlled by the Chinese Communist Party"*.[ccxli] This identified conflict extends well beyond the US and China. Australia, Canada, New Zealand, South Korea and Switzerland are among those countries who insist on localisation requirements.[ccxlii] With countries retracting in fear, the success and open nature of the Internet is no longer a given.

---

[45] Q3 2019 app downloads Top 5: 1. WhatsApp; 2. TikTok; 3. Messenger; 4. Facebook; 5. Instagram.

However, keeping Chinese influence over Grindr and TikTok at bay with one hand, US companies practise "data colonisation" with the other.[ccxliii] Facebook's "Free Basics" programme offers free data access to "basic online services" without data charges, naturally including Facebook.[ccxliv] Targeting rural areas, the initiative was sorely needed and thus embraced by the regional population, yet the true terms and conditions remained hidden in the fine print. Just like ads, this version of the Internet is sponsored. The Philippines accepted. India refused. Facebook board member Marc Andreesen reacted in a since deleted tweet: *"Anti-colonialism has been economically catastrophic for the Indian people for decades. Why stop now?"*[ccxlv] Outrage ensued, and Zuckerberg's praise for the Indian people quickly followed. In the future, more initiatives to wall off foreign data access will follow, from nationalising data centres to unwinding or blocking mergers and acquisitions, even extending to blocking free services.

What will this mean for the rest of the world? Some argue we need a new Schengen agreement for the Internet – follow the rules or get out – returning its original US character. A fragmented Internet is a fundamentally bad idea because fragmented information environments will further enhance existing divides. Dividing cohesive information access, through subsets such as the "halal" net in Iran and the national intranet "Kwangmyong" in North Korea, is not going to bring the world closer together. Rather, fragmentation would only further exacerbate and enable practices such as "turning off the internet", as happened with the protest in Iran when the government decided to unplug.[ccxlvi] Walling off access to data in such manner would equally wall off access to public information as an additional casualty.

The clash between the data value systems of China, the US and the EU will send geopolitical ripples. To understand the ultimate stakes, we need to address artificial intelligence. Artificial intelligence evokes a mythical, objective omnipotence, but it is backed by real-world forces of money, power and data.[ccxlvii] According to professor Ron Deibert, governments have moved from what was initially a deliberate laissez-faire attitude towards cyberspace to one where wars are being fought and won. The US National Security Commission on Artificial Intelligence (NSCAI) reached a similar conclusion: *"AI will accelerate the already serious threat of cyber-enabled dis-information campaigns"*, *"present states with greater capabilities to monitor and track their citizens or those of other states"* and that *"at least 74 other countries are engaging in AI powered surveillance, including many liberal democracies."*[ccxlviii] In their 2018 report Freedom House confirmed that an increasing number of repressive governments employ artificial intelligence to identify perceived threats and silence undesirable expression: of the 65 countries assessed, a record 47 featured arrests of users for political, social or religious speech.[ccxlix] Next to mass surveillance and its political ends, national data pools are directly relevant to the global AI race. The ultimate question then becomes: possessing far greater data pools than most companies and profiting from each other's exploits, what happens when nation states deploy "Cambridge Analytica-like" strategies? This question cannot remain unanswered for long.

Power Games

To what extent should profit games exist, and to what extent should power games be able to leverage for-profit infrastructure? Time and time again in this book we have seen that there is a link between data privacy and human autonomy. This chapter highlighted the natural trade-off between data privacy and mass-surveillance. An argument could even be made that that data privacy is an inalienable right. Yet, as these questions are debated, geopolitical superpowers are exporting their version of answers worldwide. And, at the moment, the three dominant value systems are China, the US and the EU.

Just as competition between liberal democratic, fascist and communist social systems defined much of the 20th century, how will the struggle between digital liberal democracy and digital authoritarianism define and shape the twenty-first? "Swing states" across Africa, Asia and Latin America will have to choose which way to go. Which superpower will export its digital value systems most successfully?[ccl]

Moving beyond borders, leaving national interest behind, privacy is a fundamental right recognised in the UN Declaration of Human Rights, the International Covenant on Civil and Political Rights and many other international and regional treaties. The universal declaration of human rights reads: *"No one shall be subjected to arbitrary interference with his privacy, family, home or correspondence, nor to attacks upon his honour and reputation. Everyone has the right to the protection of the law against such interference or attacks."*[ccli]

Beyond all the theory, headlines, history and science, everything boils down to politics. A guiding question will be: who decides? When weighing the individual vs. the collective, free speech vs. moderation and security vs. privacy, it is humbling to remember that what is ultimately at stake is the future of liberal democracy. Is the "Big Data Democracy" an oxymoron? What is certain is that a social contract involves two consenting parties. Whatever shape the social contract will take in the future, it serves to remember that a contract is not a mandate. The best way for democracies to stop the rise of digital authoritarianism is to prove that there is a better model for managing the Internet.

Power games completed the identity meta-system, joining profit games and the autonomy of being, thought and reason. The third and final part of *Identity Reboot* is dedicated to the final question of change. Part One asked if we should change. The answer was a resounding yes. Part Two asked how to change, to which the last five chapters have provided an early answer. Part Three leaves the final question: can we change?

III

CHANGE

Are **profit and power** optimisation games
inevitable?

What happens if we
succeed?

What happens if we
fail?

11. Actors of Change

"When the issue is one of Truth and Justice, there can be no differentiating between small problems and great ones. For the general viewpoints on human behaviour are indivisible. People who fail to regard the truth seriously in small matters, cannot be trusted in matters that are great."
— Albert Einstein cclii

A t this moment, humanity is caught in the space between two stories. What is it going to take to make the leap to the other side? Do policy makers need to create and update laws and regulations? Yes. Is that enough? No. Do technology giants and their employees need to examine their role in today's chaos? Yes. Is that enough? No. Should people reflect on their own relationship with data? Yes. Is that enough? No. True, lasting change will require all these things, and more. This chapter explores the politics and economics of change. Is there redemption for those who have embedded and emboldened the status quo? What role should regulation play? How should we treat the economics of privacy? And, what new and exciting opportunities await us?

Politics of Change

Right now, we have the unprecedented opportunity to watch history unfold in regard to the conflicts between corporations rolling out digital business models across the globe and governments trying to control these efforts. For example, Google offered the justification that data is actually more like sunlight than oil, one day after being fined $57 million over its privacy and consent practices.[ccliii] However, recovering from the public relations nightmare that many of these companies currently find themselves in will require more than the creative use of metaphors.

In the near future, two forces will be pulling at companies: *Redemption* and *Regulation*. As we will see, the quest for redemption could be financially motivated, publicly enforced, or intrinsically driven. Those companies not interested in redemption will increasingly face regulation.

Redemption

The quest for redemption will take place over three acts: competitive advantage (financial motivation), the role of centralisation (public motivation), and finally genuine desire to change (intrinsic motivation).

The first act opens on a scramble to retain competitive advantage. As awareness grows, ethical data strategy will give companies an edge over their competitors. It seems as if Apple is taking the lead in repositioning itself as a "privacy-first" company, while Microsoft and Twitter are vying in the vanguard. Conversely, playing fast and loose with people's data will carry consequences. Convenience trumps trust, but only until another, better option becomes available. Just as the connected nature of the Internet contributed to the meteoric rise of Web 2.0 platform companies, the fall will come just as quickly. When technologies rely on the mob, businesses cannot be surprised if underlying business models are also at the mercy of the mob. Marc Andreessen, early investor in

Facebook, explains: *"I think network effects are great, but in a sense they are a little overrated. The problem with network effects is they unwound just as fast. And so they are great while they last, but when they reverse, they reverse viciously."*[ccliv] Failure to pivot will have a delayed effect – stock prices follow reputation, not the other way around – and these problems are not going to solve themselves. Companies will have to find viable solutions, or their users will do it for them. There is no point remaining rigid if the result is irrelevance.

Front and centre in the second act is centralisation. Privatised profits and socialised cost have a due date. The friction between the two will expose industry ironies, such as technology advocates passionately defending the potential of free markets while putting their own money on oligopolies and monopolies. On the macro scale, some of these companies are more powerful than countries, and the resulting power vacuum has created a responsibility vacuum. The Sherman Antitrust Act of 1890 outlawed monopolies in the US, with politician John Sherman declaring on the floors of Congress: *"If we will not endure a king as a political power, we should not endure a king over the production, transportation and sale of any of the necessities of life. If we would not submit to an emperor, we should not submit to an autocrat of trade with power to prevent competition and to fix the price of any commodity."*[cclv]

Today's equivalent of the danger Sherman saw in 19th century America is not price fixing – after all information is given away for free in many of these cases – but what we should not endure is the mass linking of data, and the inferred cost of information. In response to Facebook's desire to integrate the technical infrastructure of WhatsApp, Instagram and its main platform, the FTC was rumoured to be planning an official investigation. The market reacted immediately, yet in contrast to the earlier rewarding of the $5 billion fine which the market had treated as a fee, this time the reaction was different. At the end of the trading day Facebook stock was down almost three percent.[cclvi] Holding the private sector to account is undoubtedly connected to the debate around the larger role of centralisation.

Centralisation will likely shift to become a public liability, with increasingly louder calls to break up big tech. Accountability is not selective. Corporate insistence on centralisation will be paired with public insistence on responsibility. The debate around weighing this responsibility will touch upon an unfortunate combination of challenges: single points of failure and the new generation of companies that are too big to fail.

The tension between the two is best embodied in the loudest argument for self-regulation, which Facebook's CEO describes as follows: *"It is not the case that if you broke up Facebook into a bunch of little pieces you would not have those issues – you would still have them but you would be less equipped to deal with them."*[cclvii] Such reasoning speaks to the new generation of too big to fail. Who is more powerful: the king or the king maker? In effect, what Facebook proposes here is that it is not only best suited to regulate itself, but also to regulate all that depend on its platform to do business, work and interact.

It is a daring statement, considering the company's recent track record. All the technical, business and regulatory signs point to the fact that self-regulation is closer to a game of whack-a-mole than addressing root issues.[cclviii] Yet another failure of self-regulation was unearthed by the news outlet Vice in 2018. Before government ID became mandatory to run politically charged Facebook ads, the reporters posed as a hundred sitting senators, running ads in their names.[cclix] Facebook approved all. Self-regulation by oligopolies and monopolies reinforces the single point of failure by self-rationalising that they are best suited to address these challenges, and hence too big to fail. This reasoning circles back on itself.

Escaping this circle brings us to the third act: "first, do no harm". A Hippocratic oath for data science, if you will. The United Nations Human Rights OHCHR recommends to governments and companies that violating humans rights online should matter as much as offline violations.[cclx] Soon, we will see the rise of the role of Chief Ethics Officer, a person deeply rooted in both ethics and technology to restore some of the moral high ground that has recently been lost. If redemption is generally possible, what checks and balances need to be in place to make sure that this holds?

Regulation

What would happen if we did not regulate privacy at all? We have seen that if public servants do not weigh how moral dilemmas shape policies, corporations will. Regulation is an opportunity. Brad Smith, Microsoft's President and Chief Legal Officer, confirms: *"We need a new generation of laws to govern a new generation of tech."*[cclxi] Our society is only as good as our leaders guide us to become. Looking back at the solutions proposed in Part Two of this book, we will attempt to break down what this new suite of laws could look like: how could regulation support autonomy of being, thought and reason, and contribute to data equity and privacy?

The five laws of identity proposed in Chapter 6 suggest that digital identity is a human right (Law 1); a public good (Law 2); that governments are responsible for foundational identity (Law 3); that the private and public sector provide value through contextual identity (Law 4); and that things must have an identity to be accountable (Law 5). For governments, this means that they need to acknowledge the first and second laws, execute on the third, and to provide the foundation for the fourth and fifth. Foundational identity is a fluid term. In 2020 and beyond, this will most likely at least include the same information now captured on passports. More specifically, it will contain the information that allows you to cross borders: name, date of birth, nationality, etcetera. Once this foundational identity has been provided by the government, individuals are free to strengthen these claims with additional attestations, should the credibility of the government decrease in value, no matter why (see Chapter 5). The foundation for the fourth and fifth laws is to regulate private identity infrastructure, so non-governmental identities become feasible. For example, what are suitable criteria for an identity provider? What types of attestation should be inclusive, and where is monetisation suitable, perhaps even desired? What are design requirements? For example, is the inclusion of a revocation registry mandatory in every wallet? What forms of cryptography are allowed or even encouraged? There is a historic opportunity for governments to define guidelines on what a "good" identity encompasses. Politics needs to move at the same speed as the market; identity is only portable (and thus functional) if it carries the same legal weight locally. Reminiscent of the large overhauls of the US infrastructure system, the forest must be planted all at once.

Once the autonomy of being has been established, there is room for governments to strengthen autonomy of thought. Rampant manipulation and censorship have led some to doubt the existence of objective facts. We concluded earlier that even though the creation of disinformation cannot be prevented, it is possible to slow its advance. To mandate transparency on the funding of paid content is a start. Although political content is of immediate importance, the role of advertising as route to the consumer should also be examined on a governmental level. Google rightly weighs a usefulness factor when evaluating ads.

We can build on this: depending on the political goals, the line could be drawn at performance, usefulness, or could we perhaps even expect ads to enrich lives? Politics has the opportunity to set a new bar: advertisements should be useful, should not fall in the mis-, mal-, and dis-information categories, and should be targeted based on information for which absolute, non-coerced consent was given. More specifically, this translates to encouraging new business models, revising the rules for algorithmic amplification, and extending access to intuitive tools for people to curate their information environments.

Completing the data autonomy trifecta is autonomy of reason, split into *consent* (algorithmic legitimacy: information and authorisation), *recourse* (algorithmic control: logic) and *discourse* (algorithmic evolution). The first item on the agenda is to reimagine what consent looks like, and what the legislative minimum should be. The same applies to the second agenda item, recourse: trusting an AI explanation requires clear regulatory guidelines on what legitimate explanations should cover. Finally, for discourse, decision-making algorithms need to adhere to certain criteria, and what those criteria look like will evolve and progress over time; lawmakers need to create space in the private sector for those discussions.

As outlined earlier, regulation could recommend "how" to treat "what" in profit games. Here, regulation could mandate that certain types of data (e.g. personally identifiable information) should be en-crypted by default. Likewise, certain biometric information could be subject to processing require-ments, such as distributed computing of fingerprints, and only be stored for so long (impermanence). For example, why do we have a situation where we have automatic deletion of fingerprints and DNA while the same does not apply to facial recognition images?

Lifting privacy from the abstract, de-identification is another area which lends itself exceptionally well to profit game legislation: when privacy can be expressed mathematically and verbally, it becomes possible to express it legally.

The last privacy technique is decentralisation. Decentralisation is native to self-sovereign identity, but this is just one of many different expressions of decentralisation. Because we are used to markets with centralised value capturing mechanisms, it would be useful for governments to share clear guidelines for future decentralised solutions. Completing the set of regulatory guidelines, data should become a balance sheet liability. Executing on the above results in a set of governmental guidelines for a more equitable, privacy conform data economy: just as faulty products are recalled when in violation with consumer protection regulation, such thinking could be extended to the digital level. As suggested by GDPR, what is needed is a radically different mindset: it is not up to the individual to justify him or herself – but to the data collector.

Lastly, in power games, governments could open the conversation, make their positions explicit, and put the choice to the voters. Research shows that four in five Americans think that the potential risks of data collection by companies about them outweigh the benefits, and 66 percent say the same about governments.[cclxii] With better information becoming available about what data the government intends to capture, how this data will be used, and with whom this data will be shared, citizens can exercise their democratic rights accordingly.

This new generation of laws will need to be a combination of reactionary laws to mitigate damage already done (such as slowing dis-information) and building the foundation for something new (for example self-sovereign identity). If politics is the coordination of large bodies of people in nation states, that coordination is increasingly taking place online. Therefore, politics has a role to play in debating, proposing, and if need be, regulating these new digital norms. Differences, disputes, values and visions which could have been ignored in the silos of offline life are pushed to contrast and conflict online. And, as often is the case, the root of many conflicts is money, bringing us to the economics of change.

Economics of Change

What if we would take the commercial angle out of misbehaviour? In one month, for example, one of my ad blockers reported to have stopped around 200,000 ad requests. Although no adblocker captures everything, this is not an uncommon number. On average, one person is served around 5,000 online advertisements per day. Sadly, this figures dates from 2007.[cclxiii] It is estimated that over 47 percent of global Internet users are now using ad-blockers.[cclxiv] If advertisements cannot be served, unwarranted data collection goes unrewarded.

Continuing this line of thinking, if data cannot be resold, this is further affirmation that unwarranted data collection goes unrewarded. In a recent controversy, telecommunication providers T-Mobile, Sprint and AT&T were reportedly selling access to their customers' location data, and that data ended up in the hands of those not authorised to possess it. An investigative journalist found this out first-hand.

For a few hundred dollars he could find the current location of most phones in the US, a bounty hunter told the reporter. The next step would be to send the number to his own contact, who would track the phone.

A subsequent screenshot of Google Maps followed, containing a blue circle indicating the phone's current location, accurate to a few hundred metres. Strikingly, this location process relied on real-time location data sold to bounty hunters, ultimately originating from the telecommunications firms themselves, including T-Mobile, AT&T and Sprint. Publicly condemning this practice and hiding behind a complex supply chain when it goes wrong still raises eyebrows as to why customer data was sold in the first place. Adding incompetence to insult, why is there no visibility on where it ultimately ends up?[cclxv] DNA might now be the only thing harder to anonymise than geolocation information.[cclxvi] From identifying presidents to every-day people, where do we draw the line?

If such business models are perceived as extractive and perhaps even unethical, what is the alternative? The Internet being free has always been inseparable from the concept of the Internet itself. It is perceived to be a self-evident truth and a great source of pride. Facebook's homepage long beamed *"It's free, and it always will be."*[46]

The Internet was supposed to be the great equaliser. Free to use, for anyone, anywhere, extending equal access to information to empower everyone, every-where. And yet, is this actually what happened? Is the power of the Internet not concentrated in the hands of the few, rather than the many? Is the datafication of human behaviour not a commodity, rather than the result of free will? In the absence of traditional revenue models, companies wanted – and in fact needed – to make money elsewhere. A free Internet was the dream; capitalism was the reality. Even when marketed as free,

---

[46] In 2020, this text has disappeared from the Facebook homepage.

subsidising true cost with advertising has made the upfront cost of general knowledge high.

If advertising encourages people to want things and to satisfy desires, to what extent do we want to create space to critically reflect, restrain or elevate these desires? If people do not want to be the product, then maybe we need to dispose of the notion of "free".

The Price of Privacy

What if we were wrong and we should pay for privacy? If so, what is privacy worth?[cclxvii] To inch closer to a solution, let's consider another series of thought experiments.

If Sarah chooses to keep her data and John Ltd chooses not to infringe on this decision, data does not flow, and the company's service would slowly deteriorate due to a lack of input. The market is effectively dead. This is immediately the case of the Chapter 9 scenario "Benevolent God" (Coerced consent; Inclusive Strategy), and eventually in "Fines & Fury" (Coerced Consent; Extractive Strategy) as well as "Trust Timebomb "(Absolute Consent; Extractive Strategy). Assuming both parties want to create a mutually beneficial situation ("Data Equilibrium") and establish a "Trust Loop" (Absolute Consent; Inclusive Strategy) how can this be done?

The Trust Loop has roughly two forms. In the first scenario the company offers Sarah a deal: normally the product is listed at $20 per month, but in exchange for sharing her data, the company can apply a discount. The reverse would be if John Ltd listed the product for free and offered a paid version with more privacy functionalities. In the second scenario, Sarah markets her own data. She either determines the price herself, trusts the market do it for her, or hires a third-party broker. Depending on the deal, the conditions, such as anonymity, will vary.

Both scenarios assume privacy has a price. In the first scenario, agreeing on a premium or discount for privacy is a one-off choice; the market determines price and responsibility is pushed on the individual, in this case Sarah. Agreeing to a discount (indirect price) or premium (direct price) is already a common practice, which camouflages structural challenges when this logic is applied to privacy. If Sarah actively markets her data, as proposed in the second scenario, how should she set a price? What is fair?

The forward-looking technologist Jaron Lanier rightly professed that we currently value privacy at exactly zero cents, yet its value is definitely not zero.[cclxviii] Facebook completed its initial public offering on 18 May 2012, with a market capitalisation of $104 billion and a total of 850 million users. Facebook's market capitalisation at the end of 2019 is closer to $570 billion, counting 2.4 billion users. Doing the maths, it appears the market valued every Facebook user at around $122 and $237 respectively.[47] Doing more maths, we are thrown back to Facebook's Onavo VPN scandal, when it paid a group of young users around $20 per month for nearly limitless access to their devices (Chapter 4). This roughly works out to confirm Facebook's market value per user. However, does this price feel right? If not, why does this still feel wrong?

Setting a price for privacy is difficult. There is a natural discrepancy between the buyer and the seller. If you buy a carton of milk, there is no conscious calculation how this particular carton of milk could inform supermarket stock, or the packing industry

---

[47] Market capitalisation / Users = Market value per user. 2012: $104B/850M=$122 per user. 2019: $570B/2.4B=$237 per user.

evaluating biodegradable materials, or the farmer taking care of his cows or the purchasing significance to your healthcare provider. The same logic applies to data: most likely you would not put much consideration towards the particular data format, type, quality or volume generated. The cost to the market could be something entirely different than the cost to consumers. A weekly log detailing my location might be worth a few dollars to a data broker, but that does not guarantee I would be happy to sell for that price, if at all. As in any market, everybody will have their own price point. One guy on Kickstarter datamined his own life, with prices starting at two dollars for *"an entire day's worth of data,"* including *"around 70 websites; 500 screenshots; 500 webcam images; mouse cursor movements; GPS location; and an application log".*[cclxix]

Preferences (*I like sushi*) are a higher level of abstraction of raw data (*I buy sushi*). Not deterred by the Onavo fiasco, Facebook is back at it again by launching Facebook Viewpoints. Viewpoints is a market research application awarding points for completing surveys, which can be converted into funds.[cclxx] Preferences are less ambiguous and for that reason arguably easier to value. Yet this does nothing to address the fact that the sum of information asymmetry and contextual value makes it difficult to put one definitive price on data.

Although both models struggle with pricing privacy, there is a significant difference between asking individuals to pay (directly or indirectly) and empowering individual controls. In case of the former, yield is captured between companies, whereas in the latter individuals are among the stakeholders benefitting from the data exchange.[cclxxi] It is the difference between bearing the cost or sharing in the benefits. The effectiveness of this option remains to be seen, for redistributing Facebook's profit across its users yields only $7.50 a year per account.[48]

Both scenarios are further plagued by two particular moral dilemmas. Is it fair to price privacy? And, if yes, how can we value privacy – should privacy even be up for sale?

Addressing the first question first, is it fair to put a price on privacy? The value of money is relative. If premiums or discounts would be charged, the poor would always be coerced to pick the lower of the two. This reminds us of the consent coercion of Chapter 8 and the Facebook Free Basics programme of Chapter 10. If privacy came at a cost, it would only be accessible for the rich, fully taking data colonisation to its extremes. The privacy tax for being poor is real and, if we believe data privacy to be an inalienable human right, unfair.

This brings us to the second question: should privacy even be up for sale? Treated as a source of private gain rather than as a source of public good, the commoditisation of information has left its mark on how we value it.[cclxxii] What begins as a market mechanism becomes, more often than not, the norm. Arguably, people's lives are not objects for monetisation, and their desire to enrich themselves with knowledge should not be penalised. To what extent is the Internet a civic good and to what extent is it a business? Arguing privacy is a human right and has a price is an oxymoron. We would not accept having to pay for any other human right. [cclxxiii]

In addition to moral dilemmas, there are practical considerations. As companies do already, what happens when individuals follow their footsteps and intend to

---

[48] Facebook's revenue for the calendar year ending 30 September 2019 was $66.53B. Facebook's net profit margin as of September 30, 2019 is 27.08%.
($66.53B*27.08%)/2.4B=$7.5 per user a year.

market data about other people? For example, what happens if someone tries to sell information about another person, such as a parent selling out his child or an employer her employees?

The risk of such third-party exploitation is addressed by self-sovereign identity: by centring the point of control at the individual level, this effectively becomes impossible. Combining intelligent data treatments, such as distribution and de-identification with decentralisation, these reimagined data markets could become revocable and transparent. This could introduce the choice between personalisation and monetary compensation. What this does not solve for, however, is the privacy tax of being poor and the difficulty to value data. Moreover, considering the magnitude of the information we generate on a daily basis, managing such a system is a lot of hard work, something not everybody will be keen to sign up for.

One solution could be that, when using a broker, a minimum degree of anonymisation is provided, as well as the ability to exercise basic rights, such as the GDPR "Right To Be Forgotten". Another manifestation could be to eliminate mass quantification of lives altogether, and to only share data that you are truly proud of. Lanier proposes that such a market, built around real agency, would allow you to sell data that is "*beautiful and unique to you.*" For example, a collective of gardeners who sell data that helps programme gardening robots, or data on a rare tumour that you willingly (and anonymously) donate to science to save lives.[cclxxiv] Clearly there is a lot to be worked through, but what speaks for privacy solutions with agency is data-driven innovation *by* people, not on the back of the people.

Once the data monopolisation angle has eroded or been eliminated, then what? What if we could not only take the commercial angle out of misbehaviour, but also go a step further, and provide a commercial incentive for good behaviour?

The New Well

The business of privacy will extend far beyond paid products and services. New forms of identity come with new forms of monetising the infrastructure of that identity. There are many, and listing all would merit a book of its own, therefore this section will focus on trust brokers, cryptographic key management solutions, rented logic and data provenance business models.

The first new line of business considered here are trust brokers. *How do we know this person or entity is who they claim to be? Can we complete transactions with this person? How can we deliver the right services to them? What do they need to know about me? How do I know they will not misuse my information?* To verify the identity of a person, businesses currently need to maintain many relationships, relying more and more on large amounts of data from multiple sources to reliably and seamlessly authenticate individuals, causing fragmentation, duplication and greater security risks. What is more, innovators trying to deliver pure digital offerings are forced to use physical channels.

Self-sovereign identity provides an alternative, not only achieving operational efficiency and stronger cyber security, but also building a bridge toward greater interoperability and collaboration. Trust anchors offering identity proofing and attestations will expand from governments and banks, which traditionally played this role, to retailers, technology platforms, hospitals, mobile operators, e-commerce platforms, universities and many more. As governments will be responsible for foundational identity and the private sector for contextual identity, expect to see a split between free and premium attestations. This will form a hybrid of basic attestations for all and specialised attestations catered to different systems which require different identity assurances.

Evidently, one-size-fits-all privacy solutions will not serve all communities equally: there will never be one system, because the characteristics that would make any system ideal in one context would disqualify it in another. The meta character of the identity meta-system allows for specialisation. Decentralisation will ultimately lead to specialisation at scale. For different people, different apps will be life changing. There will not be a single "killer app". The killer app in decentralisation is interoperability. When the market brokers trust, it is important that competition for trust does not infringe on its usability. Adoption needs a unified user experience. Just like keying in a phone number allows you to make a call, a prerequisite for self-sovereign identity is for people to be techno-logically literate. As digital life crosses geographic and sector boundaries, people, organisations and things, identities will, too.

Next to trust brokers, another new line of business will be key management solutions. Imagine friends who own fragments of your cryptographic keys (semi-decentralisation), advanced key functionalities (clone, split, merge, aggregate) and more elaborate key management software, such as key owners who own agents who own agents. Imagine key stewardship for those who cannot, or do not want to, manage crypto-graphic keys themselves, such as children or the elderly. Remember that if key management is broken, everything else will be broken as well. Therefore, key management will be a critical and profitable piece of the puzzle.

Open source or rented logic is going to be another interesting niche. Perhaps counter-intuitively, self-sovereign identity empowers individuals to fully explore their quantified self. Like a magnet surrounded by millions of little steel balls, individuals could bring logic to them. This logic could be anything from health algorithms to fitness trackers and could build an entirely new market for the quantified self.

Data provenance is another exciting area. The new Chief Ethics Officer will reflect on many new questions. *Is this data ethically sourced? How many hands did it pass through? How sensitive is it? How reliable is it? Did the data subject verifiably give consent?* Nearly 95 percent of organisations see negative impact from poor data quality, resulting in wasted resources and additional cost.[cclxxv] Clear provenance profiles could reduce this number dramatically.

Recent research found that organisations believe poor data quality to be responsible for an average burden of $15 million per year.[cclxxvi] Therefore, "data trusts" will emerge: brokered data lakes with explicit, auditable terms and conditions, and mandated consent for admission. This will be the beginning of data-as-a-service. This will allow modern data demutualization to take form. In such an environment, trust brokers could even be cities: imagine city data captured in "civic data trusts", independently run by the cities themselves as a non-profit, equitably distributing benefits of the use of de-identified citizen data.

In all this, blockchain technology demands: how much should we pay to trust one another? New pricing models will emerge. Internet sovereign money will make it possible to pay per second or to pay per byte. Interestingly, introducing the identity of things and the corresponding new distribution of value-creating activities could also give rise to a new type of capital tax on the device level.

Reflecting on these new business models, placing them in contrast to today's more extractive models, we see some encouraging signs of small steps in the right direction. For example, Facebook's business model is diversifying. Recalling from Chapter 4: the less diversified the revenue, the more aggressive the data collection. With this in mind, Facebook's announcement that it will start taking a cut of subscription revenue of paid-for exclusive content on pages is a promising development.[cclxxvii] Or consider hardware. Only one handset maker sells its phones for a profit – Apple. For the majority of the industry, handset profits are non-existent. To comply with the five billion dollar antitrust fine imposed by the EU for bundling products, Google is going to charge Android manufacturers a per-device licence fee to install its apps (unbundled), rather than paying them.[cclxxviii] Meanwhile, Apple's Safari has blocked fingerprinting and third-party tracking by default.[cclxxix] Incentives shape outcomes. When Apple classifies tech giants as malware and Amnesty International calls Google and Facebook *"surveillance giants"* engaged in an *"assault on privacy"*, maybe that is a clue underlying business models should change.[cclxxx]

As the "Web 2.0" model revolved around platform plays, the "Web 3.0" model revolves around infrastructure plays. While the technology is clearly ahead of the economics, Web 3.0 shows great promise. To realise this promise we need tools that inherently work better in a decentralised system than in a centralised system. When the Internet was in its infancy, it was not uncommon to pay upwards of one million dollars for a website. Today, a handful of freelancers will get it sorted within a week. Privacy preserving technologies, such as blockchain, will follow a similar pattern. Just because something is initially difficult does not mean that it is not worth the effort.

Time To Fight

After looking more closely at the politics and economics of change we found that each comes with its own opportunities and challenges. On the one hand there is room for a new generation of laws to govern a new generation of technology, but, on the other hand, governments should not be tempted to micro-manage innovation. At the same time, many new and exciting business models exist, but, as we have seen, pricing goods is challenging when privacy is involved. This forces us to ask: is change actually viable?

We often like to see humans as shapers of the world around us. Starting with the perception that we shape ourselves, we believe that we shape technology, shape others, and shape our future. Humans manipulating humans is a tale as old as time. Only now the tools for this manipulation have arguably exacerbated to such an extent that it degrades our ability to reason, due to the commoditisation of information and the monetisation of choice architecture.

Politicians have a clear incentive to solve this problem: there is a need to protect the integrity of democracy. If we agree with the EU in chapter 10, and believe that *"privacy is not a luxury, but a foundation for a free democratic society"*, pricing people out of privacy is undemocratic.

Companies, however, are on the fence. We should not kid ourselves that companies will change gladly just to make the world a better place. As techno-sociologist Zeynep Tufekci explained, we are building a dystopia just to make people click on ads.[cclxxxi] However, the possibility of a handful of companies destroying entire industries through careless design *is* a motivator for the remainder to get serious about inclusive value creation, and to hold deviators to account.

We need to ask ourselves, even though privacy preserving business models exist, if we were to come up short when we count the dollars at the end of the day: would we still make the choice to do the right thing, or do markets always win even if democracy is at stake? If it truly is the latter, which would speak more to current civic attitudes than anything else, we need to appeal to our best and brightest to think long and hard about new business models. I think there is something profound about the idea of creating new markets with morality as the starting point.

So far, the previous eleven chapters have taught us that we should seriously consider change. The final chapter asks, what happens if we succeed? And, what happens if we do not?

12. Blue Pill, Red Pill

"The dead outnumber the living fourteen to one, and we
ignore the accumulated experience of such a huge majority
of mankind at our peril."
– Niall Ferguson[cclxxxii]

This is not the Internet we signed up for. While it is impossible to imagine profit and power optimisation games without the Internet, it is entirely possible to imagine the Internet without optimisation games.[cclxxxiii] Technology, with all its bits and bytes, is, in essence, neutral. Through the ages, technology, like any tool, has been used for good and bad purposes. There is an opportunity to frame this challenge in a different way: to consciously engineer a system that weighs humanity's challenges accordingly.

To see what is in front of one's nose needs a constant struggle. George Orwell said it first, but it still applies to technology today.[cclxxxiv] Glorifying change and its speed has led to important shifts going unnoticed, manifesting and institutionalising in ways few would have expected. As the world will never move slower than today, the most predictable part of change is that we can be sure it will happen, which makes no position also a position. What is more, delaying the necessary change will simply make the problem worse.

We are standing at the crossroads. What happens if we all decided to harden our convictions, reject the uncomfortable story this book has pointed out, and stubbornly stick to our current course? And, what happens if we all decide to change track, walking towards a different future? What happens if we succeed and what happens if we fail? This final chapter captures weak signals of the future and magnifies these signals to imagine what these futures could hold. Should we choose the blue pill, or the red pill?

The Blue Pill

Like a frog in water slowly getting heated to its boiling point, revelling in blissful ignorance feels better than waking up to the underlying realities of optimisation games. What happens if we all reject change? To answer this question, let's consider three potential futures.

The first future will be defined by the digital "haves" and "have nots". In this future, online and offline inequality will continue being captured in identity. Take, for example, Afghanistan, which currently has the largest gender gap in ID coverage, with 94 percent of men owning IDs, compared to only 48 percent of women.[cclxxxv] Ironically, in a world of hypervisibility, invisibility is still a problem for millions. The World Bank reports that, globally, close to 40 percent of the population aged over 15 in low-income countries do not have an ID. If you are not counted, you do not count.

The recent refugee crisis in Europe has further brought home just how important portable, verifiable identity has become in a globalised world. Identity systems should be an asset rather than a liability to citizens. Rebuilding attestations from the individual level up will have a tremendous impact on people everywhere.

From women in Afghanistan who want to vote, to farmers in Africa who want to prove land ownership, to recent graduates in China who want to carry their university diplomas across borders – failing to act now could mean that we will face a future in which digital identity widens the divide. The World Economic Forum advises that if we act wisely today, digital identities can help transform the future for billions of individuals, all over the world, enabling access to new economic, political and social opportunities, while enjoying digital safety, privacy and other human rights.[cclxxxvi] This is the choice between a future that is either more, or less, equal.

The second possible future is one of permanent connectivity. In a world with permanent connectivity, what happens if you do not want to share information? Fending off companies trying to figure out someone's pregnancy status or health risks, digital breadcrumbs will be so prevalent that nothing will be private enough to qualify as a secret. As the British man who told the facial recognition trial administrators to leaving him alone ("piss off") found out first hand, insisting on complete privacy would mean a life spent completely offline, cut off from all communication (messaging), information (online content), outside space (cameras), and payment functionalities (digitally logged). Even encryption alone would not suffice, as quantum computing will make it possible to break most encryption retroactively. If you decided you wanted to go down this route, you would have to become a hermit, opting out of all of interaction with the rest of the world.

The absence of privacy in a world of permanent connectivity is indiscriminate. It is harder to keep a secret for citizens, but the same applies to governments. For example, the fitness app Strava infamously, and unwittingly, gave away military secrets by auto-publishing runs of its users, among whom happened to be military personnel running their laps on bases in Iraq and Syria.[cclxxxvii]

Auctioning off attention is a pervasive, global phenomenon. British people already check their smartphones, on average, every twelve minutes. Millions look at their phones within five minutes of waking up, and five minutes before the lights go out. China alone has more Internet users than the US and Europe combined and produces the largest volume of data in the world. Africa has more internet users than North America. In this future, we will never "turn off". As the American author Neil Postman put it, we are amusing ourselves to death.[cclxxxviii]

Data completeness in permanent connectivity will not stop at something as trivial as death. If you die, your digital-self lives on. Digital remains range from online accounts to any information or value stored on those accounts. Facebook is arguably the largest virtual cemetery in the world. Just like in the "real" world, you would need to appoint a legacy contact for your digital will. On Facebook, you can already appoint a friend to manage your account after you die. To gain control over your account, your friend actually needs to prove your death. Alternatively, under "memorialisation" settings, you could opt to automatically delete your account when you pass away.

Fail to make provisions for digital life after death and you could find yourself in the heart-wrenching situation that some German parents found themselves in. After their 15 year old daughter fell in front of an underground train, Berlin court ruled that the parents, desperate to check if her suicide had been related to bullying, held no claim to access her account.[cclxxxix] Dead Facebook users may outnumber the living by 2050 but GDPR does not apply to the dead.[ccxc]

Value stored in online accounts is equally complex. If an audiobook library is in effect a non-transferable licence to information, all associated rights technically die when you do. The same applies to digital films, games or songs. Access by anyone but you would be classified as "pirating material". Altogether, one in four Brits want a data death when they die.[ccxci] Data ownership after death is maybe one of the most emotional arguments for identity decentralisation.

Taking this world of permanent connectivity a step further, even death does not mean death.[ccxcii] When developer Eugenia Kuyda's best friend died, she "revived" him with artificial intelligence. While building the digital monument for her friend Roman, a bot, she wondered: what if it did not sound like him? What if it did? She then asked the avatar: *"Who's your best friend?"* The Roman bot replied: *"Don't show your insecurities"*. Kuyda used 8,000 lines of text to model the bot. Now, consider the level of fidelity if that would result if you used all information floating about a person online. In a world of permanent connectivity, your offline death might not mean online death.

If generations of humans live and die in such a world, what will we unlearn? What future are we leaving behind for the next generation? Students across the world volunteered to participate in a study to unplug for 24 hours. The results were deeply worrying. *"I went into absolute panic"* (US). *"I felt dead"* (Argentina). *"I am an addict"* (UK). *"I didn't use my cell phone all night. It was a difficult day... a horrible day"* (Chile). "*I felt I was in kind of another world*" (Uganda). *"Something important was drawn out from my life"* (China). *"It was an unpleasant surprise to realise that I am in a state of constant distraction, as if my real life and my virtual life were coexisting in different planes, but in equal time."* (Mexico).[ccxciii]

The social media era is barely fifteen years old and yet social media platforms have already replaced a form of labour that was previously invisible: emotional labour. The hit of virtually triggered dopamine is safeguarding us from the harsh backdrop of the real world. French sociologist Jean Baudrillard elaborates on the simultaneous blend and divide of reality and fiction: *"The more exponential the marketing of images is growing the more fantastically grows the indifference towards the real world. Finally, the real world becomes a useless function, a collection of phantom shapes and ghost events. We are not far from the silhouettes on the walls of the cave of Plato."*ccxciv49 From tourists cramming to take selfies with Rodin's sculpture The Thinker to Britons spending more time watching food shows than preparing and consuming actual food, we once again need to remind ourselves that the human brain needs to be exercised just like our other muscles. If we replace emotional labour in the real world with its digital counterpart, what does this mean for the human capacity for compassion?

When worshipping permanent connectivity, it is worth stressing that connectivity does not necessarily mean harmony. We can expect to see further misunderstandings between nations and neighbours, with ever increasing stakes. It is also imperative to resist the temptation to become numb to data scandals and let the fatigue creep in. Again, the system is not optimised to support humans. Favouring simplification for easier optimisation, this implies a preference for humans as simplistic rather than complex beings. As machines optimise humans, humans are at risk of be-

---

49 The allegory of the cave, or Plato's cave, is a dialogue the Greek philosopher Plato attributed to Socrates, describing a group of people chained in a cave, watching the shadows of the outside world on the blank wall in front of them. To the prisoners, the shadow world is reality. Jean Baudrillard speculates that in today's complex society we, just like the prisoners, rely on heavy use of symbolism and second-hand (or even further removed) information to make sense of the world. For example, today's equivalent of a loving hug is a "like". "Unboxing" videos on YouTube confer the feeling of buying gifts for yourself. News coverage of elections equals the totality of the elections.

coming machines. Technology should be designed and developed to serve humankind, and not the other way around. In this future, there will be no part of human life, no layer of experience, that is not going to be used for economic value. Ultimately, this will redefine what it means to be human.

The third future we will consider is called the "mirror world", a complete representation of the world in digital form. Every person, action, tree, building, wind gust, sun ray, check-out counter and loaf of bread will be captured as a digital twin. Pierre-Simon, marquis de Laplace, imagined such a world in his 18th century work Exposition du Système du Monde.[ccxcv]

> *"We may regard the present state of the universe as the effect of its past and the cause of its future. An intellect which at any given moment knew all of the forces that animate nature and the mutual positions of the being that compose it, if this intellect were vast enough to submit the data to analysis, could condense into a single formula the movements of the greatest bodies of the universe and that of the lightest atoms for such an intellect nothing could be uncertain and the future just like the past would be present before its eyes".*

This deterministic view of the world is called "Laplace's demon". Perfect information to create a perfect world. Reality fused with a virtual shadow, forcing the chaotic world into meaningful order. Just like the life simulation game "The Sims", but with real people.

Some aspects of the mirror world are pretty incredible. The ability to search spaces (images), hyperlinking objects into networks of the physical world, just as the web hyperlinked words. If things and places become machine readable, this opens up a whole new family of algorithms. In this 4D world, it will be possible to scroll forwards and backwards in time.

To interact in the mirror world, the centre of interaction will move from the smartphone keyboard to the camera. Yet if we arrive in the mirror world and the business model on offer is still attention, exploitation will reach entirely new heights.

Natural entries for humans into the mirror world are via augmented and virtual reality ("non-invasive") or via the "transhumanist" movement ("invasive"). Augmented reality is a digital layer "overlaying" reality. Like projecting the surface of Mars into your living room, just beyond your dining table. Virtual reality invites someone into a completely new world, where everything is digital. Interacting with both will be enhanced by technologies such as haptic gloves, allowing solid human hands to manipulate the virtual. An escapist sanctuary and an addictive stimulant for the imagination, the mirror world has the power to suck people in, its awesomeness perhaps sufficient to ignore that, with every new layer, human beings are being mapped in greater detail.

Another expression of the mirror world is the "transhumanist" movement, i.e. individuals fusing themselves with technology. By inserting chip implants in their body, for example, the individual quite literally becomes the sensor, absorbing its capabilities. This will range from benign capabilities, such as swiping your arm to check in at work in the morning, to acquiring additional processing power and memory. Likewise, this will make deeper relations between humans and machines possible, like enhancing technology with human characteristics, such as uploading information into bots and robots, and, at later stages, brain-to-computer interfaces. Serial entrepreneur Elon Musk describes this as a mesh-like "neural lace" implant to facilitate lag-free interactions, allowing for two-way communication.[ccxcvi]

The infrastructure here is once again unequal. A human brain is limited by how fast it can fire neurons, theoretically capped at 10^{17} operations per second. Even the smartest human in the world is not conscious of 10^{17} interactions per second. Data speed, however, is only limited by the speed of light and unbounded in scale. Musk's long-term rationale means hedging against AI wiping the human race out by creating symbiosis between humans and machines. However, when viewed from a monetisation standpoint, the nature and volume of information exposed to exploitation will be unfathomable. From capturing purchasing decisions via direct brain access to a detailed emotional log overlaid with daily activities, such access could, for example, end up quantifying just exactly how much you really like each friend you have interacted with on any given day. Overlaying biometric, behavioural and biographic data with brainwaves for content specialisation, and granting the private sector access to our brain neurons after saturating our eyes and ears, is clearly a disaster waiting to happen.

As we magnify today's weak signals of these three futures, pondering potential outcomes and how we feel about them, the advice of this chapter's opening quote by Niall Ferguson might be of use: *"The dead outnumber the living fourteen to one, and we ignore the accumulated experience of such a huge majority of mankind at our peril."*

The themes which have come up time and time again are trust and control. Control to force trust versus trust in just control. Two giants of history warn us about the potential pitfalls. *"Why does this magnificent applied science which saves work and makes life easier bring us so little happiness?"* lectured Einstein in 1931. *"The simple answer runs: because we have not yet learnt to make sensible use of it yet"*. Decades earlier, philosopher Henry David Thoreau made a similar observation: *"Our inventions are wont to be pretty toys, which distract our attention from serious things. They are but improved means to an unimproved end.*"ccxcvii What is the goal, and what are the unintended consequences? We could end up using the wrong data, logic and authorisation with more power, confidence and consequences.

This fear is reflected by the fact that George Orwell's dystopian book "1984" has recently enjoyed somewhat of a renaissance. Since storming the Amazon best-seller list in 2017, 68 years after its publication, it has stayed on the list ever since. The novel includes a lexicon of classics that seem as relevant as never before and include the following expressions.

> **Newspeak:** *a simplified version of English to limit free thought and free speech;*
> **Telescreen:** *TV-screen with built-in camera and microphone designed to monitor every movement and capture every conversation;*
> **Thoughtcrime:** *politically unorthodox thoughts, such as unspoken beliefs and doubt, inferred by behaviour;*
> **Big Brother:** *the surveillance state run by the government;*
> **Doublethink:** *accepting two contradicting "truths".*

1984 was written as an exaggerated extrapolation of non-fiction, transformed into fiction through abstraction. Intended as a criticism of a society that could be, showing a world without morals, not despite technological progress, but because of it. The assumption was that such control would need to be imposed by a dictatorship. Yet, themes of these terms already feel uncomfortably familiar, calling into question what the rest of the 21st century will have in store for us.

What might it feel like if we woke up one day and found that the world had changed overnight? Forgoing deliberate choice, we might wonder what had happened – and, after reflecting on this new position, perhaps where to go from here. Do we want to live this way? And if not, what is the point of creating a world in which we do not want to live? These are all futures which will not necessarily come to pass but which are possible all the same. The rise of technology might be inevitable, but how we use it is not. If these futures are undesirable, we need to understand what it is that we do want, as we will never achieve technology's true potential without the full faith and confidence of the people who use it.

The Red Pill

But what happens if we all decide to change after all?

-

It is 20 January 2021, and the US presidential inauguration has just taken place. Like last time, foreign governments deployed bots and troll farms to engage in coordinated inauthentic activity. It was the first year that saw deep fakes thrown into the mix. Unlike last time, we were prepared. Google opened an online registry where deep fake images and stills could be uploaded to scan for common inauthenticity patterns. The New York Times launched its blockchain authenticity trail to prove provenance of important editorials together with the facts they contained. There now is a global, trusted index for dis-information domains, which was invaluable to take the commercial angle out of the mix. On the political front, Facebook followed Twitter's example and banned political advertisements. Acknowledging that freedom of speech does not equal freedom of reach, algorithmic amplification of organic political content was revised, encouraging long-term constructive discussion over immediate polarisation.

The health of democracy has become the highest priority. To increase voter participation, government committees have found self-sovereign identity the most secure, robust and portable means of identification, declaring digital identity a human right and a public good, provided without profit to all members of society for the well-being of all. Next to government trails, companies are also experimenting. The first university diploma attestations have been authenticated in wallets and the first banks have issued their own wallet solutions.

Dissent against privacy exploitation by both companies and governments has amplified. Enraged by news stories providing colour and detail to the extent of the optimisation games, from the sharing of detailed geolocation patterns to removing the innocence from seemingly mundane actions to better profile our deepest desires, a turning point had been reached. The frog has jumped out of the boiling water. In a world where the incentive structure is literally stacked against individual privacy, every person feels a responsibility to reclaim it.[50] In response, people have bought VPNs, installed ad blockers and downloaded encrypted messaging apps. As a result, the model of an Internet subsidised by advertisements was called into question.

On a corporate level, the danger was two-fold. Those refusing change saw their users leave en masse. Even if users stayed, the danger was equally existential, as governments had started to take notice. The European GDPR regulation is now battle-tested. The California Consumer Privacy Act (CCPA) has come into its own, which mean that the first Americans have received the right to exercise data protection measures. Countries

---

[50] To get started install: Privacy Badger, uBlock Origin, HTTPS Everywhere, and please, buy a VPN.

have issued legislation on what their own version of privacy looks like at rapid pace, making different choices, however, on the extent of governmental access to private infrastructure.

-

It is 20 January 2025, and the US presidential inauguration has just taken place again. One central theme across campaigns was to break up big tech. After years of pushback, the Facebook acquisitions of WhatsApp and Instagram have finally been unwound. Amazon split off its cloud division Amazon Web Services. Alphabet was ahead of the curve with its restructuring of Google and other subsidiaries and came out relatively unscathed, but any new mergers and acquisitions are now scrutinised under a magnifying glass. The linkability of data across subsidiaries has been penalised.

Designing equitable data solutions is a booming industry. Strategies such as encryption (cryptography), impermanence (time), distribution (location), differential privacy (math) and decentralisation (collaboration) are commonplace. Trust loops realise business results. New business models such as trust brokers, cryptographic key management solutions, rented logic and data provenance are booming. The first blockchain companies are ready to compete globally. Those not using privacy respecting techniques are under increasing scrutiny and regulatory pressure. Privacy regulation, which was narrow at first, has been expanded. Legislation such as CCPA does not just focus on individuals exercising their rights, but establishes a legal basis for data collection together with a new code of conduct.

Freshly empowered by self-sovereign identity, bringing logic to owned data has re-energised the idea of the quantified self. People have developed a new relationship with algorithms, which have been reimagined to understand people's values and goals. Both human and digital feedback loops on information, logic and authorisation of algorithms have become mandatory. Self-sovereign identity has reached the early majority of adoption. Additionally, requesting authentication of identity attestations is but the click of a button away, with banks and universities among the first to provide these services.

There are 22 billion IoT devices, capturing hundreds of zettabytes of data. A few prominent IoT product lines have been recalled because of hacks and privacy design flaws. Facial recognition has been banned in half of Europe for public use, but the commercial sector has successfully incorporated the technology in popular product lines. In response, the governments have prevented the linking of databases and have prescribed specific treatment of what is captured, such as impermanence and edge computing. In the East, facial recognition is incredibly popular in China.

Meanwhile, the last few years have seen heated public debate on the role of the social contract between governments and citizens. The differences between the value systems of the US, the EU and China have amplified. International political misalignment in data treatment has undermined international trust. Governmental intervention of mergers and acquisitions from a national security perspective has increased. Cyber warfare has become common. In the background, the global AI race is in full swing. China has launched its cryptocurrency nationwide and the EU has launched its own equivalent.

-

It is 20 January 2029, and the US presidential inauguration has just taken place yet again. It has become obligatory for entities and things to have an identity. Against this identity, reputation is stored. More than half of the top 10 companies in the world are now blockchain companies. Physical passports have started to become relics.

Acknowledging that the AI race is a race to the bottom for humanity, the UN has called on governments to collaborate on decentralised data and decentralised artificial intelligence. The EU was among the first to sign up.

-

Let's leave the world of the future and come back to the present. This book opened with the thesis that, nowadays, data privacy precedes human capability for reason, which in turn precedes the spectrum of human choices and actions. Human behaviour has been devalued to an optimisation problem and people are providing the data that will be optimised for, demonstrating an individual focus within profit games and aggregate behaviour within power games.

Three pieces of the puzzle came into focus: data autonomy (autonomy of being, thought and reason), data equity in profit games, along with data privacy in power games. From the integrity of individuals to the institutions the individuals collectively make up, such as democracies, we have seen that identity lies at the heart of the optimisation equation.

Both games need individuals accepting the terms of the game to persist. In this new world, the second story, optimisation may still take place, but it will likely look completely different, because the benefactors will be the people making up these systems. Switch the centre of focus and the outgoing ripples will change too.

Crossroads

Back in 1858, when the transatlantic telegraph cable was completed, some heralded world peace. There were fireworks on the day of the inauguration. More connectedness would lead to better understanding of each other. Technology evangelists preached the same thing. A few years ago, Facebook CEO Mark Zuckerberg was not an unlikely candidate for the Nobel prize. Technology has always been a prime candidate when we look to solve society's problems, yet, like any tool, it has intended as well as unintended consequences. We now face an opportunity to consciously decide how to wield this powerful tool.

Michael Sandel, the American moral philosophy professor, taught his Harvard class the following on moral dilemmas: *"It is true that these questions have been debated for a very long time, but the very fact they have recurred and persisted, may suggest that although they are impossible in one sense, they are unavoidable in another, and the reason that they are unavoidable, the reason they are inescapable, is that we live some answer to these questions every day."*[ccxcviii]

Although many of the variables of our own identity debate are different, the reason why this particular debate feels deeply personal is because, may we be aware of it or not, we actually live the answer to this question on a daily basis. If we accept that the state of the world produces data, which informs the models, and that the models drive actions of individuals and invite feedback, then we should not forget one more important action path: individuals can also provide feedback on the state of the world.[ccxcix]

Even if the companies in this book might no longer exist in ten or even twenty years, if left unaddressed, it is more likely than not that we will face the same problems. Arguing that technology giants such as Facebook and Google should never have been founded in the first place because we presently find fault with the current use of their infrastructure is like arguing that automotive giants should never have been created on the ground of climate change. We are here, now. The question is how we will move forward.

Data privacy is not an end goal but a process – evolving in parallel to the technology that underpins it. Changing identity will create plenty of problems, but not reinventing identity creates more problems, and these problems are even worse. Assuming that the familiar is the ideal is a comforting fallacy. How deep does trauma need to go for something new to emerge? Buying time is not a strategy. Especially because we do not have much time left to start making the right changes.

Like climate change, the consequences of gradual privacy erosion are not visible immediately, but the long-term consequences are serious and should be taken seriously. Like climate change, privacy is not an individual, but a collective harm. Like climate change, while we are not all equally impacted, we are all impacted. And like climate change, the time for intervention has to be now.

Despite all the challenges that were pointed out: this is, in essence, an optimistic book. Acknowledging that something is wrong is inherently optimistic. Starting an open dialogue means that there is still hope to create the right solution. Naivety or sticking your head in the sand, however, will lead to just the opposite. It means we have given up.

If identity is the most valuable thing that we own, democracy is the most valuable institution that we have created. Democracy allows us to institutionalise our voices, creating a world in our own image. But it stops working when we lose our voice. This book charts a path to reclaiming our voice. Identity is a fundamental asset of interaction: it is the very first step towards humanity in our data-driven society.

The future is yet to be written - and we will all have the opportunity as well as the responsibility to contribute. The time for change is now.

IV

APPENDIX

ACKNOWLEDGEMENTS

ABOUT THE AUTHOR

SELECTED RECOMMENDED READING

NOTES

Acknowledgements

I am grateful to all who generously shared their ideas and work in this sector, without whom this book would not exist.

This book is greatly in debt to friends and family, who have generously and relentlessly shared their love and support during the creation of this work. In particular I would like to thank Sandra Steingraeber for proof reading with angelic patience, Will Smit for offering historical context, and Rolf Bulk for listening to my many theories and ideas before they touched the page.

At the end of the book sits a recommended reading list, including selected works by some of the scholars and pioneers which have inspired this book, as well as detailed notes with references and comments for those who want to explore the material on a deeper level.

Lastly, I would like to thank you, the reader, for making it this far. This is not an easy topic, but I feel it is an important one, and I am proud of you for wanting to make the world a little better than you found it.

About the Author

Arwen Smit specialises in technology ethics and its intended and unintended consequences on society.

Smit is the author of Identity Reboot, a book examining how the breakdown of personal data privacy is being exploited from profit and power perspectives, arguing that human behaviour is being devalued to an optimisation game, and that we are providing the data that will be optimised for.

Smit holds a BSc in International Business Administration from the Rotterdam School of Management and a MSc in Business and Management from the Stockholm School of Economics.

Over the course of her career, Smit has worked within strategy roles for a broad range of technology companies, such as the non-profit automotive blockchain consortium Mobility Open Blockchain Initiative (MOBI), venture capitalist firms, various start-ups (of which she founded two), Google and Facebook.

Her ideas have been featured on global institutions (European Commission, European Space Agency), renowned platforms (Aspen Institute, TEDx) and leading universities (London Business School, Rotterdam School of Management).

Selected Recommended Reading

Rachel Botsman – Who Can You Trust
Nick Bostrom – Super Intelligence
Kim Cameron – Laws of Identity
Luciano Floridi – The Fourth Revolution
Yuval Noah Harari – Homo Deus
Jaron Lanier – Who Owns the Future
Kai Fu Lee – AI Superpowers
Kevin Mitnick – The Art of Invisibility
Stuart Russell – Human Compatible
Michael Sandel – The Morality of Markets
Edward Snowden – Permanent Record
Jamie Susskind – Future Politics
Shoshana Zuboff – Surveillance Capitalism

Notes

---

i Apple's CEO Tim Cook defended privacy in his speech at a conference in Brussels which was themed "Debating Ethics: Dignity and Respect in Data Driven Life". See *Keynote address from Tim Cook, CEO, Apple Inc*, 24 October 2018, youtube.com/watch?v=kVhOLkIs20A.

ii Gloria Mark, Professor in the Department of Informatics at the University of California, in conversation with Tristan Harris, Google's former Design Ethicist, for the Your Undivided Attention podcast hosted by Humane Tech: Gloria Mark (Humane Tech), *Episode 7: Pardon the Interruptions*, 2019. Typescript available at humanetech.com/podcast/.

iii Commentary by the consistently sharp a16z partner and venture capitalist Benedict Evans: Benedict Evans, "Microsoft, Facebook, trust and privacy", *Benedict Evans* [blog], 13 March 2019.

iv Dubbed the world's most famous hacker, Kevin Mitnick wrote a practical guide on personal privacy online: Kevin Mitnick, *The Art of Invisibility: The World's Most Famous Hacker Teaches You How to Be Safe in the Age of Big Brother and Big Data* (Hachette Audio, 2017).

v See the work of Shoshana Zuboff for definitions of terms such as "surveillance capitalism", "decision markets", and behavioural surplus": Shoshana Zuboff, *The Age of Surveillance Capitalism: The Fight for a Human Future at the New Frontier of Power* (PublicAffairs, 2019).

vi News article on how Facebook handled its role in the genocide question in Myanmar: Jen Kirby, "Zuckerberg: Facebook has systems to stop hate speech. Myanmar groups: No, it doesn't," *Vox*, 6 April 2018.

vii See Facebook's community guidelines for an up to date overview: en-gb.facebook.com/communitystandards.

viii News article on the meeting between Zuckerberg and Macron: Chris White, "Facebook To Help France Prosecute Hate Speech," *The Daily Caller*, 26 June 2019.

---

ix See statista.com for the latest statistics on search engines and browsers. See Gartner.com for the latest statistics on IaaS. See newsroom.fb.com/company-info for the latest statistics on Facebook users.

x Research paper from MIT: De Montjoye Y. A. et al, "Unique in the shopping mall: On the reidentifiability of credit card metadata," Science 347 (2015): 536-539.

xi I recommend both 1984 and Animal Farm: George Orwell, *1984* (Houghton Mifflin Harcourt, 4 April 2017).

xii At Microsoft, Identity Architect Kim Cameron authored one of the foundational papers for what later became known as "self-sovereign identity": Kim Cameron, "The Laws of Identity," (May 2005).

xiii A chronicle of two marathon hearings where Zuckerberg was forced to testify in front of Congress: Tom Brenner, "Mark Zuckerberg Testimony: Senators Question Facebook's Commitment to Privacy," *The New York Times*, 10 April 2018.

xiv News article quoting company attorney Orin Snyder to US District Judge Vince Chhabria: Ben Popken, "Facebook lawyer says 'there is no privacy,' hinting at the challenges of Zuckerberg's pivot," *NBC News*, 2 June 2019.

xv General Data Protection Regulation (GDPR) is applicable to all EU citizens and any business entity that transacts with them, regardless of the location of the business. One woman asked Tinder for her historical information on file: Judith Duportail, "I asked Tinder for my data. It sent me 800 pages of my deepest, darkest secrets," *The Guardian*, 26 September 2017.

xvi Ibid Zuboff.

xvii Ibid Kim Cameron.

xviii The School of Life provides accessible interpretations of philosophers and other great historical thinkers. See The School of Life, *Great Thinkers: Simple tools from sixty great thinkers to improve your life today* (The School of Life Library, 2018).

xix Sun Tzu, *The Art of War* (Pax Librorum, 2009).

xx A translation of the original and official edition of The French Civil Code, Paris, 1804 by William Benning, London, 1827.

xxi The passport was the first globally accepted identity proxy: Home Office, "Historical background information on nationality," *Home Office*, 21 July 2017.

xxii Used as an identity proxy, the Nansen passport captured the right to cross borders: the editors of Encyclopaedia Britannica, "Refugee," *Encyclopaedia Britannica*, 20 July 1998.

xxiii Juan Enriquez asks: What if Andy Warhol had it wrong, and instead of being famous for 15 minutes, we're only anonymous for that long? See Juan Enriquez, *Your online life, permanent as a tattoo* (TED 2013). Typescript available at: www.ted.com.

xxiv Interview with then Google CEO Eric Schmidt: "Google's Privacy," CNBC, 29 December 2009.

xxv Glenn Greenwald was one of the first reporters to break the Snowden files: Glenn Greenwald, "Why privacy matters" (TED Global 2014). Transcript available at: www.ted.com.

xxvi A bizarre story about trolling, 4chan and Shia Labeouf: Mack Lamoureux, "How 4Chan's Worst Trolls Pulled Off the Heist of the Century," *Vice*, 11 March 2017.

xxvii Commentary on privacy: Jameson Lopp, "A Modest Privacy Protection Proposal," *Cypherpunk Cogitations [blog]*, 29 September 2018.

xxviii Report by Pew Research: Brooke Auxier et al., "Americans and Privacy: Concerned, Confused and Feeling Lack of Control Over Their Personal Information," *Pew Research*, 15 November 2019.

xxix Survey by the internet security company AVG conducted in 2010. Commentary by the Atlantic: Taylor Lorenz, "When Kids Realize Their Whole Life Is Already Online," *The Atlantic*, 20 February 2019.

xxx See the NYT Podcast, the Daily: Hosted by Michael Barbaro, produced by Andy Mills and edited by Larissa Anderson (The Daily), *"The Business of Selling Your Location,"* 10 December 2019.

xxxi Stuart A. Thompson and Charlie Warzel , "Twelve Million Phones, One Dataset, Zero Privacy ," *The New York Times Opinion*, 19 December 2020.

xxxii Stuart A. Thompson and Charlie Warzel, "How to Track President Trump," *The New York Times Opinion*, 20 December 2019.

xxxiii A deep dive into data resellers: Natasha Singer, "Mapping and Sharing the Customer Genome," *The New York Times*, 16 June 2012.

xxxiv The scope of the Marriott data leak: Nicole Perlroth et al., "Marriott Hacking Exposes Data of Up to 500 Million Guests," *The New York Times*, 30 November 2018.

xxxv Research and investigations available at hacken.io.

xxxvi News article discussing the algorithmic mechanics behind dating apps using a game called Monster Match: Arielle Pardes, "This Dating App Exposes the Monstrous Bias of Algorithms," *Wired*, 25 May 2019.

xxxvii The Target story was first reported in the New York Times: Charles Duhigg, "How Companies Learn Your Secrets," *The New York Times*, 16 February 2012.

xxxviii Francis Fukuyama, *Identity: The Demand for Dignity and the Politics of Resentment* (Farrar, Straus and Giroux, 2018).

xxxix Yuval Noah Harari, *21 Lessons for the 21st Century* (Spiegel & Grau, 2018).

xl Chronicle of the unfolding of Pizzagate: Amanda Robb, "Pizzagate: Anatomy of a Fake News Scandal," *Rolling Stone*, 16 November 2017.

xli Source: Washington Post reporting. Reporting by Glenn Kessler, Meg Kelly, Salvador Rizzo and Michelle Ye Hee Lee. Design and development by Leslie Shapiro. Originally published 19 May 2017. Database available at: washingtonpost.com/graphics/politics/trump-claims-database.

xlii Report by the Chinese National Public Credit Information Centre on 2018 results.

xliii Sceptical take on the social credit system: Jamie Hursley, "China's Orwellian Credit Score Isn't Real," *Foreign Policy*, 16 November 2018.

xliv Open letter by Zuckerberg known as "Facebook's pivot to privacy": Mark Zuckerberg, "A Privacy-Focused Vision for Social Networking," Facebook, 6 March 2019.

xlvJulia Angwin is an award-winning investigative journalist, formerly of the independent news organisation ProPublica and the Wall Street Journal: Julia Angwin et al., "Facebook Doesn't Tell Users Everything It Really Knows About Them," ProPublica (27 December 2016).

xlvi European Commission statement on "Mergers: Commission fines Facebook €110 million for providing misleading information about WhatsApp takeover", Brussels, 18 May 2017.

[xlvii] Kai-Fu Lee, *AI Superpowers: China, Silicon Valley, and the New World Order* (Houghton Mifflin Harcourt, 2018).

[xlviii] See also the Libra whitepaper at libra.org. Current legislative unrest makes it unclear how viable the initiative is.

[xlix] Interview with British historian Niall Ferguson: Niall Ferguson, "Financial Historian Niall Ferguson: a Big Tech Digital Dollar Would Be a Nightmare," *Breakermag*, 13 February 2019.

[l] Mark Zuckerberg's testimony before the House Financial Services Committee.

[li] News item from MIT on China's cryptocurrency efforts: Mike Orcutt, "China is about to launch its own digital currency. Here's what we know so far," *MIT Technology Review*, 13 September 2019. Reaction EU: Francesco Guarascio, "Alarmed by Libra, EU to look into issuing public digital currency," *Reuters*, 5 November 2019.

[lii] See, for example: Sam Wolfson, "Amazon's Alexa recorded private conversation and sent it to random contact," *The Guardian*, 24 May 2018. Rachel Metz, "Yes, Alexa is recording mundane details of your life, and it's creepy as hell," *MIT Technology Review*, 25 May 2018.

[liii] Lente van Hee et al., "Google employees are eavesdropping, even in your living room, VRT NWS has discovered," *VRT NWS*, 10 July 2019.

[liv] See, for example, Lily Hay Newman. "Security News This Week: Facebook's Voice Transcripts Were More Invasive Than Amazon's," *Wired*, 17 August 2019. Sarah Frier, "Facebook Paid Contractors to Transcribe Users' Audio Chats," *Bloomberg*, 13 August 2019.

[lv] Sarah Perez, "Alexa skills top 80,000 after a big Alexa-powered holiday season," *TechCrunch*, 1 February 2019.

[lvi] Amy Webb, futurist and CEO of the Future Today Institute, on the podcast Land of the Giants: Amy Webb (Land of the Giants), Alexa, What's Amazon Doing Inside My Home, 2019.

[lvii] Research on attack vulnerabilities to Google Home and Alexa: Nan Zhang et al., "Understanding and Mitigating the Security Risks of Voice-Controlled Third-Party Skills on Amazon Alexa and Google Home," Indiana University, University of Virginia, Institution of Information Engineering (3 May 2018): arXiv:1805.01525.

[lviii] Benedict Evans, "Is Alexa Working," *Benedict Evans* [blog], 30 January 2019.

lix Report: Knud Lasse Lueth, "State of the IoT & Short-term outlook 2018," IOT Analytics, 2018.

lx Vinay Rao, "Extracting dark data," *IBM Developer,* 8 March 2019.

lxi Transparency reports are available at transparencyreport.google.com and at transparency.facebook.com.

lxii Annual report on online freedom from Freedom House, assessing 65 countries globally: Adrian Shahbaz, "Freedom on the Net 2018: The Rise of Digital Authoritarianism," Freedom House, 2018.

lxiii NSA statement: Remarks by Mr. Richard H. Ledgett, Jr., Deputy Director, National Security Agency, at TED Talks 2014 Conference. Release No: PA-020-18 (20 March 2014).

lxiv The Five Eyes is an intelligence coalition, comprised of Australia, New Zealand, Canada, the UK and the US See, for example, Zack Whittaker, "Five Eyes governments call on tech giants to build encryption backdoors — or else," *TechCrunch*, 3 September 2018. David E. Sanger and Sheera Frenkel, "Five Eyes Nations Quietly Demand Government Access to Encrypted Data," *The New York Times*, 4 September 2018.

lxv The Personal Data Protection Bill (Bill No. 373 of 2019).

lxvi FISA is an acronym for Foreign Intelligence Surveillance. See also documents published by the German newspaper Spiegel: "User's Guide for PRISM Skype Collection", dating August 2012, marked top SECRET//COMINT//NOFORN. See also Glenn Greenwald et al., "NSA Prism programme taps into user data of Apple, Google and others," *The Guardian*, 7 June 2013.

lxvii Direct English translation from the system's founding document, released by the State Council in 2014: Simina Mistreanu, "Life Inside China's Social Credit Laboratory," *Foreign Policy*, 3 April 2018.

lxviii For examples of algorithmic bias see, for example, Jacob Snow, "Amazon's Face Recognition Falsely Matched 28 Members of Congress With Mugshots," *ACLU*, 26 July 2018. Steve Lohr, "Facial Recognition Is Accurate, if You're a White Guy," *The New York Times*, 9 February 2019.

lxix "Letter from Shareholders to Amazon CEO Jeff Bezos regarding Rekognition", available at aclu.org. "Open Letter to Amazon against Police and Government use of Rekognition", available at icrac.net.

lxx From the China Cables. Interactive version available at: nytimes.com/interactive/2019/11/16/world/asia/china-detention-directive.html.

lxxi Paul Mozur, "One Month, 500,000 Face Scans: How China Is Using AI to Profile a Minority," *The New York Times*, 14 April 2019.

lxxii Stephanie Nebehay, "UN says it has credible reports that China holds million Uighurs in secret camps," *Reuters*, 10 August 2018.

lxxiii Detailed Human Rights Watch report on how information on the Uighur population is captured and managed: Human Rights Watch, China's Algorithms of Repression: Reverse Engineering a Xinjiang Police Mass Surveillance App, *Human Rights Watch*, 1 May 2019.

lxxiv Shibani Mahtani et al., "Hong Kong Protestors Are Using Lasers to Distract and Confuse. Police Are Pointing Them Right Back." The Washington Post, 1 August 2019.

lxxv "Collection of Biometric Data From US Citizens Upon Entry To and Departure From the United States," Department of Homeland Security (DHS), 2019

lxxvi For the US, see the report by Clare Garvie et al., "The Perpetual Line-Up: Unregulated Police Face Recognition in America" (October 18, 2016), available at: perpeptuallineup.org. For the UK, see the report by the Home Office, "Review of the Use and Retention of Custody Images" (February 2017), available at data.parliament.uk.

lxxvii Abraham Lincoln (1809-1865) in a speech in the Illinois Legislature concerning the State Bank, January 11, 1837.

lxxviii For an accessible overview of how humans could co-exist with AI, see Paul R. Daugherty and H. James Wilson, *Human + Machine: Reimagining Work in the Age of AI* (Harvard Business Review Press, 2018). For a detailed overview of "the brain" and image recognition of cat and human faces, see Quoc V. Le et al., "Building high-level features using large scale unsupervised learning," Proceedings of the 29th International Conference on Machine Learning, Edinburgh, Scotland, UK (2012): arXiv:1112.6209 [cs.LG].

lxxix "Regulating the Internet Giants: The World's Most Valuable Resource Is No Longer Oil, but Data," *Economist*, 6 May 2017.

[lxxx] Report by AI research firm Cognilytica Research: "Data Engineering Preparation, and Labelling for AI 2019," Cognilytica, 2019.

[lxxxi] Facebook Q1 2019 Earnings Presentation reported $14,921 million advertising revenue.

[lxxxii] See, for example, Josh Constine, "Facebook pays teens to install VPN that spies on them," *TechCrunch*, 29 January 2019.

[lxxxiii] Google paper on CAPTCHA accuracy: Ian Goodfellow et al., "Multi-digit Number Recognition from Street View Imagery using Deep Convolutional Neural Networks," April 14, 2014, arXiv:1312.6082 [cs.CV].

[lxxxiv] Rodney A. Brooks, "Elephants do not play chess," Robotics and Autonomous Systems Volume 6, Issues 1-2, Pages 3-15 (June 1990).

[lxxxv] Letter from Sir Jonathan Thompson to HMRC Data Protection Officer, 3 May 2019.

[lxxxvi] Abhinav Gupta et al., Revisiting the Unreasonable Effectiveness of Data, *Google AI Blog*, 11 July 2017.

[lxxxvii] Interview with whistle-blower Christopher Wylie: Carole Cadwalladr, "'I made Steve Bannon's psychological warfare tool': meet the data war whistle-blower," *The Guardian*, 18 March 2018.

[lxxxviii] Report prepared by Special Counsel Robert S. Mueller, III, "Report On The Investigation Into Russian Interference In the 2016 Presidential Election," US Department of Justice, Washington DC, March 2019.

[lxxxix] Account of the discovery of the vulnerability: Inti De Ceukelaire, "This Popular Facebook app publicly exposed your data for years," *Medium*, 28 June 2018.

[xc] Ruling of the Italian Data Protection Authority: Cambridge Analytica: il Garante privacy multa Facebook per 1 milione di euro", *Garante Per La Protezione Dei Dati Personali*, Rome, 28 June 2019.

[xci] As fines transform in fees, the absence of moral judgment allows that behaviour to become the norm rather than the exception: Michael J. Sandel, *What Money Can't Buy: The Moral Limits of Markets* (Penguin Books, 2012).

[xcii] As part of the final settlement, Aleksandr Kogan and Alexander Nix are prohibited from making false or deceptive statements regarding the extent to which they collect, use, share, or sell personal information, as well as the purposes for

which they collect, use, share, or sell such information. Statement by the Federal Trade Commission: "FTC Issues Opinion and Order Against Cambridge Analytica For Deceiving Consumers About the Collection of Facebook Data, Compliance with EU-US Privacy Shield", FTC, 6 December 2019.

[xciii] "Dis-information and 'fake news: Final Report," House of Commons, Digital, Culture, Media and Sport Committee (DCMS), 14 February 2019.

[xciv] For more examples, see Maria Lamagna, "The sad truth about how much your Facebook data is worth on the dark web," *MarketWatch*, 6 June 2018.

[xcv] Account of hacks. Gnosticplayers: Catalin Cimpanu, "127 million user records from 8 companies put up for sale on the dark web," *ZDNET*, 14 February 2019. Uber: Eric Newcomer, "Uber Paid Hackers to Delete Stolen Data on 57 Million People," *Bloomberg*, 21 November 2017. Indian PII Leak: Sergiu Gatlan, "Over 275 Million Records Exposed by Unsecured MongoDB Database," *BleepingComputer*, 8 May 2019.

[xcvi] Report by US House of Representatives Committee on Oversight and Government Reform: "The Equifax Data Breach," Majority Staff Report 115th Congress, December 2018.

[xcvii] Account of hacks. Adult FriendFinder: Zack Whittaker, "AdultFriendFinder network hack exposes 412 million accounts," *ZDNET*, 13 November 2016. US Government Avengers hack: Brendan I. Koerner, "Inside the Cyberattack That Shocked the US Government," 23 *Wired* October 2016.

[xcviii] Ellen Nakashima and Adam Goldman, CIA pulled officers from Beijing after breach of federal personnel records, *The Washington Post*, 29 September 2015.

[xcix] Survey on crime worries: Jeff Jones, Lydia Saad, Gallup Poll Social Series: Crime, Gallup News Service, 1-10 October 2018.

[c] FBI report: "Eighteen People Charged in International $200 Million Credit Card Fraud Scam," US Attorney's Office, District of New Jersey, 5 February 2013.

[ci] Jamie Susskind, *Future Politics: Living Together in a World Transformed by Tech* (Oxford University Press, 2018).

[cii] Fireside chat on the short and long term dilemmas of AI: computer scientist Fei-Fei Li & Historian Yuval Noah Harari in Conversation with Wired Editor in-Chief Nicholas Thompson, "Will AI Enhance or Hack Humanity?," Stanford Humanities Centre, California, 2019.

ciii The Bundeskartellamt is an independent competition authority whose task is to protect competition in Germany: "Bundeskartellamt prohibits Facebook from combining user data from different sources," Bundeskartellamt, 7 February 2019.

civ Analysis of the 7,000 Facebook documents leak by the EFF: Ernesto Falcon and Gennie Gebhart, "What Reporters Should Look For in Latest Facebook Document Leak," *Electronic Frontier Foundation*, 11 November 2019.

cv Putin also advised a monopoly on AI would thus be strongly undesirable: Radina Gigova, "Who Vladimir Putin thinks will rule the world," *CNN*, 2 September 2017.

cvi Background on how the "wir schaffen das" policy became a national debate: Matthew Karnitschnig, "Germany's identity crisis," *Politico*, 20 October 2015.

cvii News article on how two men—a dead suicide bomber and a man in a Serbian migrant centre—carried the same Syrian passport with the same details: Krishnadev Calamur, "The Flourishing Black Market in Syrian Passports," *The Atlantic*, 18 November 2015.

cviii Report by the ID4D World Bank task force: "Identification for Development: 2018 Annual Report," World Bank ID4D, 2018.

cix Christopher Allen, "The Path to Self-Sovereign Identity," *Life With Alacrity* [blog], 25 April 2016.

cx See, for example, "Latin American states to accept Venezuela expired papers," *BBC*, 5 September 2018. Nicholas Casey and Jenny Carolina Gonzalez, "A Staggering Exodus: Millions of Venezuelans Are Leaving the Country, on Foot," *The New York Times*, 20 February 2019.

cxi See, for example, "Discrimination in Arakan," Human Rights Watch, 2000. Julia Wallace, "Myanmar casts minorities to the margins as citizenship law denies legal identity," *The Guardian*, 3 November 2016. "12 million stateless people globally, warns UNHCR chief in call to States for decisive action," *UN NEWS*, 12 November 2018.

cxii Procedures are described at maltaimmigration.com and uscis.gov.

cxiii Available at visa.com

cxiv 2018: Arjun Kharpal, "Alibaba sets new Singles Day record with more than $30.8 billion in sales in 24 hours," *CNBC*, 11 November 2018. 2019: Arjun Kharpal, "Alibaba breaks Singles

Day record with more than $38 billion in sales," *CNBC*, 11 November 2019.

cxv Mastercard and University of Oxford study: Giulio Lovisotto et al, "Mobile Biometrics in Financial Services: A Five Factor Framework", Mastercard, University of Oxford (2017).

cxvi Ibid Kevin Mitnick.

cxvii Statement LinkedIn: "Protecting Our Members," LinkedIn Official Blog, 18 May 2016. Statement Tumblr: "we-recently-learned-that-a-third-party-had", Tumblr, 12 May 2016.

cxviii Technical explanations available at developers.facebook.com; developers.google.com; developer.apple.com and Ed D. Hardt, "The OAuth 2.0 Authorization Framework", Internet Engineering Task Force (IETF) (October 2012): 2070-1721.

cxix Commentary on the relationship between Libra and identity: Joel John, "The Libra Hustle," *Decentralised* [blog], 18 June 2019.

cxx Commentary on Sign-in With Apple: Ben Thompson, "The First Post-iPhone Keynote," *Stratechery* [blog], 4 June 2019.

cxxi Rachel Botsman, *Who Can You Trust?: How Technology Brought Us Together and Why It Might Drive Us Apart* (PublicAffairs, 2017).

cxxii "Uber's US Safety Report" covering 2017-2018. Available at uber.com.

cxxiii News article on Uber's second ban from London: Gwyn Topham, "Uber loses London licence after TfL finds drivers faked identity," *The Guardian*, 25 November 2019.

cxxiv Ibid Rachel Botsman.

cxxv Javier C. Hernandez, "Chinezen verplicht te gamen op app die Xi verheerlijkt", *Het Financieele Dagblad*, 12 April 2019.

cxxvi Jackson Cunningham, "Digital Exile: How I Got Banned for Life from AirBnB," *Medium*, 13 July 2018.

cxxvii Keith Hart, *The Memory Bank: Money In An Unequal World* (Texere, 2001).

cxxviii Account of the aftermath of the hurricane that hit St. Maarten: Natalie Meade, "St. Maarten Is Still Striving to Recover from Its Worst Hurricane in a Century," *The New Yorker*, 2 March 2018.

cxxix David Birch is considered to have pioneered the "authorisation", "authentication", "identification" model. Non-technical introduction: David Birch, *How to use Identity & the*

Blockchain, Keynote presented at the Dutch Blockchain Conference (21 June 2016).

cxxx The World Wide Web Consortium (W3C) is an international community that develops open standards to ensure the long-term growth of the Web. Technical explanation of distributed identifiers (DID): Drummond Reed et al., "Decentralised Identifiers (DIDs): v1.0Core Data Model and Syntaxes," W3C First Public Working Draft (27 November 2019).

cxxxi Context on "inherent", "assigned" and "accumulated" attestations: "A Blueprint for Digital Identity: The Role of Financial Institutions in Building Digital Identity", World Economic Forum (August 2016).

cxxxii Gertrude Stein (1874–1946) was an American author who lived most of her life in Paris.

cxxxiii Statement from N.Y.C. Comptroller Scott M. Stringer: "Amid Widespread Reports Of Voter Disenfranchisement And Polling Problems, Comptroller Stringer Announces Audit Of Board Of Elections," New York (NY), 19 April 2016.

cxxxiv Martin Gibson, "HMS Carmania Sinks SMS Cap Trafalgar 14 September 1914," *War and Security* [blog], 14 September 2014.

cxxxv Ibid Pew Research.

cxxxvi For additional statistics see, for example: Benchmark report based on a survey of >1,000 people across four countries: "2019 Global Data Management Research," Experian, 2019. "2018 Employment Screening Benchmark Report," HireRight, 2018.

cxxxvii Allen Ezell and John Bear, Review of Degree Mills: The Billion-Dollar Industry That Has Sold Over a Million Fake Diplomas, The Review of Higher Education, vol. 37 no. 2, p. 282-284 (2014): DOI:10.1353/rhe.2014.0002.

cxxxviii More information about the Known Traveller Programme is available at: ktdi.org.

cxxxix Ibid George Orwell, 1984.

cxl Propaganda is as old as the written word. Historical background: Judith Starkston, "Propaganda and Reality: Hittites v.s. Pharaoh Ramesses," *Judith Starkston* [blog], 1 March 2016.

cxli On YouTube over 500 hours of content are uploaded to YouTube every minute. Susan Wojcicki, YouTube's chief executive, talks to the Economist: Susan Wojcicki (The Economist), *Everything in moderation: YouTube*, The

Economist, 6 May 2019. Full segment available at soundcloud.com

[cxlii] Distinction between mis-information, dis-information and mal-information, originally prepared for the Council of Europe and now widely used: Claire Wardle & Hossein Derakhshan, "Information Disorder: Toward and Interdisciplinary Framework for Research and Policymaking", Council of Europe (27 September 2017).

[cxliii] Zuckerberg in conversation with Yuval Noah Harari on 26 April 2019. Video available at facebook.com. Typescript available at techcrunch.com.

[cxliv] Patrick Stokes, "False Media Balance," *New Philosopher Volume 24*, 21 May 2019.

[cxlv] Typescript of President Obama's Farewell speech: "Barack Obama's farewell speech in full," *The Telegraph*, 11 January 2017.

[cxlvi] Background readings: Hilary Hudd, "Fake News and the Looming "State Action" Problem," Harvard J.L. & Technology Digest (2019).

[cxlvii] Statement by Facebook: Nathaniel Gleicher, "Removing Coordinated Inauthentic Behaviour From Georgia, Vietnam and the US," Facebook, 20 December 2019.

[cxlviii] Ben Nimmo, et al, A Joint Report by Graphika & the Atlantic Council's Digital Forensics Research Lab: #OperationFFS: Fake Face Swarm, Graphika and DFRLab (2019).

[cxlix] Survey by Pew Research: "News Use Across Social Media Platforms 2018", Pew Research Centre, 2018.

[cl] Database "Buzzfeed News: Election content engagement", available on buzzfeednews.com.

[cli] Statement Twitter: "Information operations directed at Hong Kong," Twitter Safety, 19 August 2019. Statement Facebook: "Removing Coordinated Inauthentic Behaviour From China," Facebook, 19 August 2019. Statement Google: Shane Huntley, "Maintaining the integrity of our platforms," Google, 22 August 2019. Background on what types of post were banned: Daniel Wood et al, "China Used Twitter To Disrupt Hong Kong Protests, But Efforts Began Years Earlier," *NPR*, 17 September 2019.

[clii] The online initiative reportedly first emerged on popular local forum LIHKG and hit its initial HK$7.8 million target in about 1½ hours: Alvin Lum, "Hong Kong protesters raise US$1.97

million for international ad campaign as they accuse police of 'war crimes' and using 'chemical weapons'," *South China Morning Post*, 12 August 2019.

[cliii] Akil N. Awan, "The Virtual Jihad," Combatting Terrorism Centre at West Point, Volume 3, Issue 5 (May 2010).

[cliv] News article on how ISIS got its anthem: Alex Marshall, "How Isis got its anthem," *The Guardian*, 9 November 2014.

[clv] The Philippines tops the world internet usage index with an average of 10 hours a day. For further statistics on disinformation campaigns, including Filipino keyboard armies and Mexican Peñabots, see: "Freedom on the Net 2017: Manipulating Social Media to Undermine Democracy," Freedom House, 2017.

[clvi] "Facebook's Civil Rights Audit – Progress Report," Facebook, 30 June 2019. Available at about.fb.com.

[clvii] See, for example: "June 4th Sensitive Words – China Digital Times", *China Digital Times*, 2016. Database available at: chinadigitaltimes.net. Jeffrey Knockel and Ruohan Xiong, "(Can't) Picture This 2: An Analysis of WeChat's Real Time Image Filtering in Chats," *Citizen Lab*, 15 July 2019. Lotus Ryan et al., " One App, Two Systems How WeChat uses one censorship policy in China and another internationally," *Citizen Lab*, 20 November 2016.

[clviii] Ibid Freedom on the Net 2018.

[clix] Ibid Freedom on the Net 2017.

[clx] Universal Declaration of Human Rights, available at un.org. The Declaration was proclaimed by the United Nations General Assembly in Paris on 10 December 1948.

[clxi] Brandolini's law tweet: "The bullshit asymmetry: the amount of energy needed to refute bullshit is an order of magnitude bigger than to produce it.," Alberto Brandolini (@ziobrando), 10 January 2013.

[clxii] News article on how Defence Advanced Research Projects Agency (DARPA) funds a deep fake identification contest: Will Knight, "The US military is funding an effort to catch deep fakes and other AI trickery," *MIT Technology Review*, 23 May 2018.

[clxiii] Work on how highly realistic human head images can be obtained by training convolutional neural networks: Egor Zakharov et al., "Few-Shot Adversarial Learning of Realistic Neural Talking Head Models," (25 September 2019), arXiv:1905.08233.

clxiv See, for example, John Shaffer, "President Nixon Never Actually Gave This Apollo 11 Disaster Speech. MIT Brought It To Life To Illustrate Power Of Deepfakes," *WBUR*, 22 November 2019.

clxv Commentary by Radley Balko, "80 percent of Chicago PD dash cam videos are missing audio due to officer error or intentional destruction," *The Washington Post*, 29 January 2016.

clxvi Samantha Bradshaw & Philip N. Howard, "The Global Disinformation Order: 2019 Global Inventory of Organised Social Media Manipulation," Oxford, UK 23 pp. (2019): comprop.oii.ox.ac.uk.

clxvii Naja Bentzen, "How to spot when news is fake," European Parliament Think Tank, 19 February 2019.

clxviii Based on a dataset of rumour cascades on Twitter from 2006 to 2017 (about 126,000 rumours were spread by ~3 million people): Soroush Vosoughi et al., "The spread of true and false news online," Science, Vol. 359, Issue 6380, pp. 1146-1151 (9 May 2018): DOI: 10.1126/science.aap9559.

clxix BuzzFeed News identified more than 100 pro-Trump websites being run from a single town in the Balkans: Craig Silverman, "How Teens In The Balkans Are Duping Trump Supporters With Fake News," *BuzzFeed News*, 3 November 2016.

clxx Reports available at disinformationindex.org.

clxxi Argument why Facebook keeps political ads: Speech by Mark Zuckerberg, "Standing for Voice and Free Expression," Georgetown, 17 October 2019. Typescript available at facebook.com. Argument Twitter against political ads: Twitter CEO Jack Dorsey on Twitter, 30 October 2019.

clxxii Michael McFaul (editor), "Securing American Elections: Prescriptions for Enhancing the Integrity and Independence of the 2020 US Presidential Election and Beyond," Stanford Cyber Policy Centre (June 2019).

clxxiii See algotransparency.org for an engine to research the YouTube recommendation engine. Methodology: "*Step 1: We start from a list of 1,000+ US channels (these channels are listed below). Step 2: We gather all recommended videos from the last video uploaded by these channels. Step 3: We compute which channel was recommended the most from those videos. Step 4: We repeat steps 2 and 3 until we have gathered recommendations from 2000 channels. Step 5: For each video that was observed, we count and display from how many channels it was recommended."*

clxxiv Google paper on how the YouTube recommendation works: Paul Covington et al., Deep Neural Networks for YouTube Recommendations, Google (2016).

clxxv News item on the black market behind influencers: Nicholas Confessore et al., "The Follower Factory," *The New York Times*, 27 January 2018.

clxxvi Analysis for the United States Senate Select Committee on Intelligence (SSCI) by New Knowledge, reviewing datasets provided to SSCI by Facebook, Twitter, and Alphabet for an investigation into the Internet Research Agency (IRA) influence operations.. Renee DiResta et al., "The Tactics & Tropes of the Internet Research Agency," (2017).

clxxvii Yochai Benkler et al., Network Propaganda: Manipulation, dis-information, and radicalisation in American Politics (Oxford University Press, 2018).

clxxviii Meltem Demirors, "I'm Not an International Drug Dealer, So Why Do I Need Privacy?," *Medium* [blog], 15 April 2019.

clxxix German political theorist Hannah Arendt (1906–1975) during an interview with the French writer Roger Errera. The New York Review of Books, 26 October 1978.

clxxx Immanuel Kant (1724-1806) was a German philosopher. Major work: *Groundwork of the Metaphysic of Morals: On a Supposed Right to Lie Because of Philanthropic Concerns* (1785).

clxxxi Ibid Immanuel Kant.

clxxxii William James (1842 – 1910) was an American philosopher. Major work: William James, *The principles of psychology* (1950).

clxxxiii Socrates (c. 470-399 BC) quoted by his student Plato in The Republic. (c. 427-347 BC).

clxxxiv Microsoft Celeb Dataset (MegaPixels) available at megapixels.cc/datasets/msceleb.

clxxxv Federal Trade Commision, "In the Matter of Genesis Toys and Nuance Communications," Washtington, DC, 6 December 2016.

clxxxvi Ibid Jamie Susskind.

clxxxvii Interview with software engineer and AI researcher François Chollet: Adrian Rosebrock, "An interview with Francois Chollet," *PyImageSearch*, 2 July 2018.

clxxxviii Podcast Crazy/Genius by The Atlantic discussing algorithmic bias in the criminal justice system: Derek Thompson (Crazy/Genius), "Should We Be Afraid of AI in the Criminal-Justice System," The Atlantic, produced by Patricia Yacob and Jesse Brenneman, 20 June 2019. Available at theatlantic.com.

clxxxix From the researchers: "*We used deep neural networks to extract features from 35,326 facial images. These features were entered into a logistic regression aimed at classifying sexual orientation. Given a single facial image, a classifier could correctly distinguish between gay and heterosexual men in 81% of cases, and in 74% of cases for women. Human judges achieved much lower accuracy: 61% for men and 54% for women. The accuracy of the algorithm increased to 91% and 83%, respectively, given five facial images per person.*" See Yilun Wang & Michal Kosinski, "Deep neural networks are more accurate than humans at detecting sexual orientation from facial images," Journal of Personality and Social Psychology (February 2017).

cxc Ibid Kai-Fu Lee.

cxci Jamie Bartlett, *The People vs. Tech* (Penguin Random House, 2018).

cxcii Far ahead of its time commentary on friction: Benjamin Thompson, "Friction," *Stratechery* [blog], 8 July 2013.

cxciii Video of DeepMind's programme AlphaGo battling the legendary Lee Sedol (9-dan pro), the top Go player of the past decade: youtube.com/watch?v=l-GsfyVCBu0.

cxciv "Aggregate IQ Data Services Ltd, Enforcement Notice: The Data Protection Act 2018, Part 6, Section 149," Information Commissioner's Office, 24 October 2018.

cxcv Privacy was already linked to technology in the 19th century: Samuel D. Warren and Louis D. Brandeis, "The Right To Privacy," Harvard Law Review, Vol. 4, No. 5, pp. 193-220 (15 December 1890).

cxcvi Luciano Floridi, *The Fourth Revolution: How the Infosphere is Reshaping Human Reality* (Oxford University Press, 2014).

cxcvii A question pondered by physicist Alan Lightman: Alan Lightman, *In Praise of Wasting Time* (Simon & Schuster, 2018).

cxcviii Stuart Russell, *Human Compatible: Artificial Intelligence and the Problem of Control* (Viking, 2019).

cxcix Paper on adversarial examples: Andrew Ilyas et al., "Adversarial Examples Are Not Bugs, They Are Features," MIT (2019): arXiv:1905.02175

cc Sandra Wachter, "Counterfactual Explanations Without Opening the Black Box: Automated Decisions and the GDPR," Harvard Journal of Law & Technology, 31 (2) (2018).

cci The French philosopher Voltaire (1694-1778): "*Le doute n'est pas une état bien agréable, mais l'assurance est un état ridicule*". From the Complete Works of Voltaire, Volume 12, Part 1.

ccii Paper under review at time of writing: Cesar Hidalgo et al, How Humans Judge Machines, 2020.

cciii Nick Bostrom, *Superintelligence* (Oxford University Press, 2016).

cciv The Spanish artist Pablo Picasso (1881-1973) in an interview with William Fifield in The Paris Review 32 of Summer-Fall 1964.

ccv Astronomer Carl Sagan (1934-1996) is famous for his 13-part science documentary *Cosmos* (1980) where he travelled on the "spaceship of the imagination" through time and space.

ccvi Jaron Lanier is a known Silicon Valley outsider insider: Jaron Lanier, "How we need to remake the Internet" (TED 2018). Transcript available at: www.ted.com.

ccvii See security white papers on whatsapp.com and signal.org.

ccviii Opinion piece the permanence of data: Viktor Mayer-Schönberger, "Remembering the Importance of Forgetting," Project Syndicate, 28 April 2010.

ccix Unfortunate quotes confirmed by Zuckerberg in the New Yorker: Jose Antonio Vargas, "The Face of Facebook," *The New Yorker*, 13 September 2010.

ccx Google papers on federated learning: Jakub Konecny et al., "Federated Learning: Strategies for Improving Communication Efficiency," Google (2016). Brendan McMahan and Daniel Ramage, "Federated Learning: Collaborative Machine Learning without Centralized Training Data," Google (2017).

ccxi Semi-technical paper: Alexandra Wood et al., "Differential Privacy: A Primer for a Non-Technical Audience," Vanderbilt Journal of Entertainment & Technology Law 21 (1), 209 (2018).

ccxii Non-technical overview on differential privacy at apple.com under "Differential Privacy Overview".

ccxiii Economist Elinor Ostrom (1933-2012) was awarded a Nobel Prize for her work on the Commons: Elinor Ostrom, *Governing the Commons: The Evolution of Institutions for Collective Action* (Cambridge University Press, 1991).

ccxiv Statement by the White House: "Remarks by Vice President Pence at the 2019 Munich Security Conference | Munich, Germany," White House, Hotel Bayerischer Hof, Munich, Germany, 16 February 2019.

ccxv See Statista.com for the latest statistics on global semiconductor market share. See strategyanalytics.com for Huawei's share of global smartphone market and 5G market.

ccxvi Keynote by former CIA CTO Ira Gus Hunt at a security conference. See Ira Gus Hunt, *The CIA's Grand Challenges With Big Data, 2013*. Typescript available at: gigaom.com.

ccxvii Glenn Greenwald, *No Place to Hide: Edward Snowden, the NSA, and the US Surveillance State* (Picador, 2015).

ccxviii Documents by the Intercept detailing how the XKeyscore works: Morgan Marquis-Boire et al., "Xkeyscore: The NSA's Google for the World's Private Communications," *The Intercept*, July 1, 2015. Micah Lee et al., "A Look at the Inner Workings of NSA's XKEYSCORE," *The Intercept*, 2 July 2015.

ccxix For NSA procedures on privacy see Rebecca J. Richards, "NSA Director of Civil Liberties and Privacy Office Report: NSA's Civil Liberties and Privacy Protections for Targeted SIGINT Activities Under Executive Order 12333," 7 October 2014.

ccxx OneZero's coverage of the US Defence Forensics and Biometric Agency memo by its director Glenn Krizay: Dave Gershgorn, "EXCLUSIVE: This Is How the US Military's Massive Facial Recognition System Works," *OneZero*, 6 November 2019. Slides: DFBA: "Leveraging Biometrics Within The National Defence Strategy – Draft," Mr. Glenn Kirzay, Defence Forensics and Biometrics Agency, 18 June 2019. Available at: scribd.com/document/433613191.

ccxxi Context on the Snowden revelations: Rick Noack, "Edward Snowden revelations," *The Washington Post*, 6 October 2016.

ccxxii See, for example, the publications of NSA & GCHQ documents by the German newspaper Spiegel on how to bypass encryption in general and Transport Layer Security in specific: "Top Secret: Crypt Discovery Joint Collaboration Activity, 20 January 2011.

ccxxiii Description of Optic Nerve: Spencer Ackerman and James Ball, "Optic Nerve: millions of Yahoo webcam images intercepted by GCHQ," *The Guardian*, 28 February 2014.

ccxxiv "List of foreign governments and organisations authorized for surveillance," *The Washington Post*, 30 June 2014.

ccxxv Danish news site on how Denmark is one of the 9 eyes: "Denmark is one of the NSA 9-Eyes", *CPH Post Online*, 4 November 2013.

ccxxvi Discussion memo: "SECRET//SI//REL TO USA, GBR: Global Collaboration Environment (GCE)," 10 April 2013. Available at assets.documentcloud.org/documents/4390395/Topic3docx-v1-0.

ccxxvii Reuters reports on the 2014 and 2015 FISA figures: Dustin Volz, "US spy court rejected zero surveillance orders in 2015: memo," *Reuters*, 30 April 2016. See also the US Department of Justice Report by the Office of Legislative Affairs, available at: justice.gov/nsd/nsd-foia-library/2015fisa.

ccxxviii Helen Nissenbaum, "Privacy as contextual integrity," Washington Law Review (2004).

ccxxix See, for example: Zhang Yu, "Hebei court unveils programme to expose deadbeat debtors," *China Daily*, 16 January 2019.

ccxxx Technical deep dive into how facial recognition software and hardware targets Uighurs: Charles Rollet, "Hikvision Markets Uyghur Ethnicity Analytics, Now Covers Up," *IPVM*, 11 November 2019.

ccxxxi Takashi Kawakwami and Yusuke Hinata, "Pay with your face: 100m Chinese switch from smartphones," *Nikkei*, 26 October 2019.

ccxxxii Statement European Union External Action: "2018 Human Rights and Democracy country update – People's Republic of China," European Union External, European Union External Action, Beijing, 15 May 2019.

ccxxxiii Full legislation available at: gdpr-info.eu.

ccxxxiv See, for example, Madhumita Murgia, "How London became a test case for using facial recognition in democracies," *Financial Times*, 1 August 2019. Madhumita Murgia, "London's King's Cross uses facial recognition in security cameras," *Financial Times*, 12 August 2019.

ccxxxv Research assessing public safety innovation using 24 different indicators, among which CCTV: Darrell M. West and

Dan Bernstein, "Benefits and Best Practices of Safe City Innovation," Centre for Technology Innovation at Brookings, 2017.

ccxxxvi Statement ECJ on Facebook content moderation: "EU law does not preclude a host provider such as Facebook from being ordered to remove identical and, in certain circumstances, equivalent comments previously declared to be illegal," Court of Justice of the European Union, Press Release No 128/19, Luxembourg, 3 October 2019. Statement ECJ on Google's responsibilities applying the Right to be Forgotten: "The operator of a search engine is not required to carry out a de-referencing on all versions of its search engine", Court of Justice of the European Union, Press Release No 112/19, Luxembourg, 24 September 2019.

ccxxxvii Screenshot of a mandatory app tourists need to install if they wish to enter Xinjiang: Joseph Cox, "China Is Forcing Tourists to Install Text-Stealing Malware at its Border," *Motherboard*, 2 July 2019.

ccxxxviii Leaked documents on Google's plans to launch a censored search engine in China: Ryan Gallagher, "Google Plans to Launch Censored Search Engine in China, Leaked Documents Reveal," *The Intercept*, 1 August 2018. Open Letter by Human Rights Watch: Ronald Deibert et al., "Open Letter to Google on Reported Plans to Launch a Censored Search Engine in China," *Human Rights Watch*, 28 August 2018.

ccxxxix Paul Mozur et al., "Apple Opening Data Centre in China to Comply With Cybersecurity Law," *The New York Times,* 13 July 2017.

ccxl See, for example: Robert Kim, "ANALYSIS: CFIUS Scrutiny Forces Chinese Sale of Grindr," *Bloomberg*, 16 April 2019.

ccxli Letter by Charles E. Schumer and Tom Cotton to the Office of the Director of National Intelligence on TikTok: United State Senate, Washington DC, 23 October 2019. Available at democrats.senate.gov.

ccxlii Opinion piece on digital nationalism: Akash Kapur, "The Rising Threat of Digital Nationalism," *The Wall Street Journal*, 1 November 2019.

ccxliii Nick Couldry & Ulises A. Mejias. "Making data colonialism liveable: how might data's social order be regulated?," *Internet Policy Review*, 8(2) (2019), DOI: 10.14763/2019.2.1411.

ccxliv Explore the full programme at connectivity.fb.com/free-basics.

ccxlv For a Tweet log see, for example: "Facebook director sorry for India colonialism remarks," *New York Post*, 10 February 2016.

ccxlvi Statistics on the Iran internet shut-down: "Internet disrupted in Iran amid fuel protests in multiple cities," *NetBlocks*, 15 November 2019.

ccxlvii Julia Powles and Helen Nissenbaum, "The Seductive Diversion of 'Solving' Bias in Artificial Intelligence," *OneZero*, 7 December 2019.

ccxlviii AI committee chaired by Google chairman Eric Schmidt: "Strength Through Innovation: The Future of AI and National Security," National Security Commission on Artificial Intelligence (NSCAI), Washington D.C., 4 November 2019.

ccxlix Ibid Freedom on the Net 2017.

ccl Valentin Weber, "AI, China, Russia, and the Global Order: Technological, Political, Global, and Creative Perspectives", University of Oxford, 31 January 2019.

ccli Ibid Universal Declaration of Human Rights.

cclii The Nobel Prize winner Albert Einstein (14 March 1879 – 18 April 1955) was a German-born theoretical physicist who developed the theory of relativity. 1957 July, New Outlook: Middle East Monthly, Volume 1, Number 1, Albert Einstein On Israeli-Arab Relations, Quote Page 5, Published by Tazpioth, Tel Aviv, Israel: "*Wenn es sich um Wahrheit und Gerechtigkeit handelt, gibt es nicht die Unterscheidung zwischen kleinen und großen Problemen. Denn die allgemeinen Gesichtspunkte, die das Handeln der Menschen betreffen, sind unteilbar. Wer es in kleinen Dingen mit der Wahrheit nicht ernst nimmt, dem kann man auch in großen Dingen nicht vertrauen.*"

ccliii Statement from the French information protection agency Commission Nationale de l'Informatique et des Libertés on its 50 million euro fine to Google: "La formation restreinte de la CNIL prononce une sanction de 50 millions d'euros à l'encontre de la société GOOGLE LLC," CNIL, 21 January 2019.

ccliv Quote by Marc Andreessen in a book on high growth startups: Elad Gil, *High Growth Handbook* (Stripe Press, 2018).

cclv John Sherman (1823-1900) addressing 51st Congress on March 21, 1890: "Fiftieth Congress To Fifty-Seventh Congress, First Session, Inclusive: Prepared By Direction Of The Attorney-

General", Washington Government Printing Office, 1902 Congressional Record, Vol 21. Senate.

cclvi See, for example, "News Of Possible FTC Injunction Against Combining Apps," *Nasdaq*, 13 December 2019.

cclvii Mark Zuckerberg and Cass Sunstein during the "Afternoon of Conversation": Mark Zuckerberg, Aspen Ideas Festival, 26 June 2019. Video available at: aspenideas.org.

cclviii European Parliament report defining self-regulation as fact-checking: Divina Frau-Meigs, "Societal cost of "fake news" in the Digital Single Market," European Parliament, IMCO Committee, December 2018.

cclix News article on manipulating Facebook's "paid for by" disclosure: William Turton, "We posed as 100 senators to run ads on Facebook. Facebook approved all of them," *Vice*, 30 October 2018.

cclx David Kaye, UN Special Rapporteur on freedom of opinion and expression, recommends to use the international framework for human rights as a baseline when thinking about content moderation: "Governments and Internet companies fail to meet the challenges of online hate," United Nations Human Rights Office of the High Commissioner, New York, 21 October 2019.

cclxi Quote by Microsoft's Brad Smith: Mark Scott, "The internet is broken. Can this group fix it?," *Politico*, 25 February 2018.

cclxii Ibid Pew Research, 2019.

cclxiii Contrasting the average number of ads of 2,000 around 1977 with 5,000 in 2007: Louise Story, "Anywhere the Eye Can See, It's Likely to See an Ad," *The New York Times*, 15 January 2007.

cclxiv "Ad-blocking behaviours around the world," Global Web Index. Infographic available at: globalwebindex.com

cclxv Investigative reporting on how geolocation data flowed from T-Mobile, to Zumigo, to Microbilt, to a Bail Bond Company, to a Bail Industry source, to Motherboard.: Joseph Cox, "I Gave a Bounty Hunter $300. Then He Located Our Phone," *Motherboard*, 8 January 2019.

cclxvi Paul Ohm, a law professor and privacy researcher at the Georgetown University Law Centre to the New York Times.

cclxvii Research paper on the relative value of privacy: Alessandro Acquisti et al, "What is Privacy Worth?," The Journal of Legal Studies, Vol. 42, No. 2, pp. 249-274 (June 2013).

---

cclxviii Ibid Jaron Lanier.

cclxix See "A Bite Of Me" on kickstarter.com.

cclxx See viewpoints.fb.com.

cclxxi Research on "paying for privacy" and "personal data markets": Stacy-Ann Elvy, "Paying for Privacy and the personal data economy," Columbia Law Review, Vol. 117, No 6 (2019).

cclxxii Ibid Michael Sandel.

cclxxiii EFF opposes "pay for privacy" schemes. Hayley Tsukayama, "Knowing the "Value" of Our Data Won't Fix Our Privacy Problems," *EFF*, 15 July 2019.

cclxxiv Opinion piece on data markets: Garrett Hazelwood, "Sell Your Data. Earn Passive Income. What Could Go Wrong?," *Slate*, 28 May 2019.

cclxxv Benchmark report: 2019 Global data management research: Taking control in the digital age, Experian (2019).

cclxxvi Gartner research: Susan Moore, "How to Stop Data Quality Undermining Your Business," Gartner, 18 January 2018.

cclxxvii See, for example, Anthony Ha, "Facebook will start taking a cut of fan subscriptions in 2020," *TechCrunch*, 9 July 2019.

cclxxviii News article on the EU ruling: Sam Schechner, "Google Will Charge Phone Makers to Pre-Install Apps in Europe," *The Wall Street Journal*, 16 October 2018.

cclxxix WebKit is the web browser engine used by Safari, Mail and App Store among others. Policy available at: webkit.org.

cclxxx Research paper by Amnesty International: "Surveillance giants: How the business model of Google and Facebook threatens human rights," Amnesty International, Index number: POL 30/1404/2019, 21 November 2019.

cclxxxi Zeynep Tufekci, *We are building a dystopia just to make people click on ads*, TED Global>NYC, September 2017.

cclxxxii Niall Ferguson, *Civilization: The West and the Rest* (Penguin Books: 2012).

cclxxxiii Ibid Zuboff.

cclxxxiv George Orwell, "In Front of Your Nose," First published: Tribune, 22 March 1946.

cclxxxv Ibid World Bank, ID4D.

cclxxxvi Background reading: "Identity in a Digital World: A new chapter in the social contract," World Economic Forum, September 2018.

cclxxxvii News article on Strava: Richard Pérez-Peña and Matthew Rosenberg, "Strava Fitness App Can Reveal Military Sites, Analysts Say," *The New York Times,* 29 January 2018.

cclxxxviii Neil Postman, *Amusing Ourselves to Death: Public Discourse in the Age of Show Business* (Penguin Books, 2005).

cclxxxix News article on the timeline of the ruling: Kate Connolly, "Parents lose appeal over access to dead girl's Facebook account", *The Guardian,* 31 May 2017.

ccxc Research paper by Oxford: Carl J Ohman and David Watson, "Are the dead taking over Facebook? A Big Data approach to the future of death online," Big Data & Society January–June 2019: 1–13 (2019).

ccxci Survey by LifeSearch: "Let's Start Talking – Digital Death", LifeSearch, 13 July 2019.

ccxcii Casey Newton, "Speak, Memory: When her best friend died, she rebuilt him using artificial intelligence," *The Verge*.

ccxciii A global study of university students by the International Centre for Media & the Public Agenda (ICMPA) in partnership with the Salzburg Academy on Media & Global Change.

ccxciv French sociologist Jean Baudrillard (1929-2007).

ccxcv Pierre-Simon Laplace (1749-1827) was a French mathematician, astronomer and author of Exposition du système du monde.

ccxcvi Elon Musk at Code Conference: Elon Musk, "We are already cyborgs", at Code Conference 2016.

ccxcvii Works of philosopher Henry David Thoreau (1817-1862) include "Walden" and "Civil Disobedience". "Einstein Sees Lack In Applying Science; Man Has "Not Yet Learnt to Make Sensible Use of It," *The New York Times,* 17 February 1931.

ccxcviii Michael Sandel, "What's the right thing to do," at Justice with Michael Sandel, September 2005.

ccxcix Evolving online textbook: Solon Barocas et al, Fairness and machine learning: Limitations and Opportunities.

Made in the USA
Middletown, DE
06 March 2020

85714674R00172